HOUND OF THE SEA

HOUND OF THE SEA

WILD MAN. WILD WAVES. WILD WISDOM.

GARRETT McNAMARA

WITH KAREN KARBO

HARPER WAVE

An Imprint of HarperCollinsPublishers

HOUND OF THE SEA. Copyright © 2016 by Garrett McNamara. All rights reserved. Printed in the United States of America. No part of this book may be used or reproduced in any manner whatsoever without written permission except in the case of brief quotations embodied in critical articles and reviews. For information, address HarperCollins Publishers, 195 Broadway, New York, NY 10007.

HarperCollins books may be purchased for educational, business, or sales promotional use. For information, please email the Special Markets Department at SPsales@harpercollins.com.

FIRST EDITION

Designed by Bonni Leon-Berman

Library of Congress Cataloging-in-Publication Data
Names: McNamara, Garrett, 1967- author. | Karbo, Karen, author.
Title: Hound of the sea: wild man, wild waves, wild wisdom / Garrett McNamara with Karen Karbo.
Description: First edition. | New York, NY: HarperCollins Publishers, [2016]
Identifiers: LCCN 2016013921 (print) | LCCN 2016026264 (ebook) | ISBN 9780062343598 (hardcover) | ISBN 9780062343611 (eBook)
Subjects: LCSH: McNamara, Garrett, 1967-| Surfers—United States—Biography.
Classification: LCC GV838.M378 A3 2016 (print) | LCC GV838.M378 (ebook) | DDC
797.3/2092—dc23
LC record available at https://lccn.loc.gov/2016013921

---

16 17 18 19 20   RRD   10 9 8 7 6 5 4 3 2 1

I am not what has happened to me. I am what I choose to become.

—*Carl Jung*

CONTENTS

PART II

PART III

HOUND OF THE SEA

PROLOGUE
THE WIPEOUT

EVERYONE WONDERS WHERE YOU go when you die. I had a preview. I was standing in the living room of my mom's house in Pūpū-kea, on the North Shore of Oʻahu, talking on the phone to my doctor when suddenly the lights went out. I apparently dropped to the floor. There was no going toward the light, no reaching for a bright spot at the end of life's long tunnel. This new place was velvet black, calm, and pain-free. The lack of pain was everything. I lay there, at peace.

Then I woke up to my brother Liam crying my name.

TWO WEEKS earlier a buddy had tracked me down to tell me he'd had a dream. "The Bay was macking, bro. You paddled out past all of us and caught the biggest wave we'd ever seen. It made the cover of all the magazines," he'd said. I was crashing at my mom's place between surf contests in Japan. I'd made a name for myself there. I had sponsors and my face on a billboard in Tokyo and a bright future, something I'd never dreamed possible.

Wai-mea, a sheltered bay on the North Shore, is the birthplace of big-wave surfing, the proving ground for surfers from all over the world. It takes a huge Pacific storm to create the giant waves the place is known for. I'd driven down the hill from Pūpū-kea to check it out.

The aquamarine water was a lake, so flat you could hold a swim class for toddlers. No dream coming true that day.

Two weeks later it's a different story. In the morning the waves were nonexistent but around noon the swells started rolling in, one after another. Two feet, six feet, ten. I grab my board and head over to perform my Wai-mea ritual, which involves smoking a big fatty behind a thick clump of bushes by the paddle-out spot. Usually I would do this alone, but was always happy to share with any other surfers who happened past. Then I would walk across the sand with my board, stand before the waves, and cross myself in a modified Catholic altar-boy way. It's a ritual I maintain to this day, minus the joint.

On my way out I got stoked thinking how cool it would be to fulfill my friend's prophecy. The sets were coming in fast. Ride-of-a-lifetime waves, twenty-thirty-forty-foot faces.

I catch a ride on the current out to the lineup and there's my friend. We give each other a nod. When I paddle out past him, past everyone, here comes the dream wave. Except this is no dream.

I turn around and paddle as fast as I can, until my triceps burn. Before big-wave spots like Pe'ahi (nicknamed "Jaws") and Mavericks and Teahupo'o and Cloudbreak and Cortes Bank were on everyone's radar, Wai-mea was the world's best-loved big wave, a straightforward drop from top to bottom.

The monster rears up behind me and I take off, crouch low, solid and focused. I'm making this wave without much effort. It feels good and I stand up tall, all casual and cool. I'm on my 9'6" Willis Brothers board, big, thick, single fin. Just as I start thinking I've got this, a big boil pops up in front of me, ten, maybe fifteen yards down the wave, a white-fringed circle of unstable water created when the wave passes over an irregularity on the bottom, usually a rock, coral head, or cave. The boil can turn a great ride into your worst nightmare in a split second. At Wai-mea you never take off outside the boil unless the waves are huge.

Just as the nose of my board hits the boil some backwash grabs the rail. Suddenly I'm staring up at the sun. My board and feet have disconnected, and the board is falling beneath me. The leash tugs at my ankle. I spin around in midair. Now I'm watching my board land in the trough, fin faceup, and I land on the fin, between two ribs. Pain slingshots around my torso. I look up and see a huge, glassy barrel— the biggest I've ever seen—gathering itself up, and in a second it engulfs me. I don't remember being scared. I just go with it. Let myself get pummeled.

I know this: the wave will pass.

I come up for a gulp of air. That monster wave was the first of the set. After it rolls over me, I resurface and take a giant breath, then settle in for two more beatings. Finally, I pop up. My board is still in one piece, my leash still connected to my ankle. I pull my board back, slide on, and start paddling back out. Stoked and fired up, ready for another one. I get out to the lineup, sit up, and cough blood into my fingers.

My friend Kolohe Blomfield is standing on the point, watching. Kolohe is a respected North Shore regular, now a longtime lifeguard, and one of the guys I looked up to. When I come in, still coughing, having trouble breathing, he dashes over to me. "Man, that was the heaviest wipeout I've ever seen."

I take it to mean I'm invincible, that I can handle anything the ocean has to dish out. I'm twenty-two years old, 147 pounds soaking wet.

I don't bother with going to the doctor, much less get any X-rays, but I'm pretty sure I've fractured a rib. I self-prescribe a two-week rest. But after only a week Wai-mea is breaking again, and I decide that if I wear two wet suits, for the extra padding and compression, I'll be fine. I think about the barrel that pounded me. It was at least a twenty-footer and my goal at that time in my life was to get barreled in just such a wave. Getting barreled is perhaps the most common surfer fantasy, speeding along inside a wave's perfect tube, completely hidden from view in your own private glassy green room, where time seems to stand still. It rarely happened at Wai-mea because the waves tend to stand up, hollow out a bit, then close quickly, like a clam shell snapping shut. Rather than peel perfectly, the way they do down the road at Pipeline, the waves hit the boil, pitch up, and slam closed. Boom.

I drop my board in the water and paddle out. Today's board is magic, or so I thought at the time, a white 10'0" Willis Brothers single fin. It's a typical North Shore winter day, partly cloudy with a strong offshore wind. I've put all my faith in my own invincibility, and in that extra wet suit holding my busted rib in place. I fail to see this for what it is: idiocy and a fundamental lack of respect for the power of the ocean.

When I arrive at the Bay, the conditions are perfect, the waves clean and glassy. I watch them for a moment, cross myself, and then start paddling out. It's maybe eighteen feet on the set waves, big, not too big. I take off. The wave starts doubling up. This is what happens when the waves are generated from a powerful storm; the swells come so quickly the second one piles on the first, creating twice the energy and a greater likelihood it will hollow out: perfect conditions for getting barreled. But as the waves meet, the water gets heavier, its movement less predictable. I'm rocketing down the face of the first wave when it doubles. I air-drop ten feet and reconnect with the wave. Seconds later, another air-drop, reconnect again, and now I'm on the bottom of the wave and I look up and the lip is above me, hollow and starting to barrel.

Part of the art of getting barreled involves knowing how much to stall, so the lip can catch up to you and cover you up. When you are twenty-two, invincible, slightly stoned, and injured, your timing isn't the best. I'm a little manic now, a little too eager to pull inside the barrel. So I don't wait, or I don't wait long enough. I set my edge and, summoning all my strength, turn myself back into the wave. Suddenly, my board goes straight and I fall flat on my face. Water moving at this speed is as hard as concrete, so I skip down the surface of the wave like a stone.

As I fall my board shoots out from under me. The lip of the wave explodes square on my shoulders and head. The muffled sound of the surf roars. Underwater, I feel something hit me on the back of the head. At first I think I've hit a rock, but below me is nothing but sandy bottom. The realization that I've kicked myself in the head with my own heels brings with it a surge of nausea.

I'm underwater getting pounded, wind knocked out of me, searing back pain. The ocean pops me back up and out of habit I take a gulp of air. Black and white stars in my peripheral vision, no feeling in my legs. Then another wave, and another wave. I think I'm probably stuck in the shore break, the impact zone where you can't swim out and you can't swim in. I'm just floating, my board long gone.

Alec Cooke happens to be paddling by. He's no stranger to being pummeled to near death, is famous for being dropped into the huge swells on the outer reef by helicopter. Many years later, in 2015, he will go missing after a surfing session at this very spot, never to be found. "You okay?" he asks.

I can't speak. I make a noise that must have sounded like the most wounded animal in God's creation, because without giving it a thought Alec gives me his board and helps me get to the beach.

Something bad has happened, about that there is no doubt. Jeff, who was renting a room in my mom's house at the time, is waiting on the beach. He takes my arm, helps lie me down. A crowd forms. People asking was I okay. Asking what happened out there. Saying they couldn't believe I didn't drown.

I yell at them to get away, leave me alone. I'm in so much pain I can't deal with everyone rushing toward me, the chorus of "Are you okay?"s. To Jeff I say, "My back, it's my back." He holds my arm as I stagger across the beach, lightning crack of pain down my body, down both legs, black and white stars, the pull of nausea.

I had an old VW Rabbit with a sunroof. It needed a new transmission. The shift was dodgy and I was the only human alive who knew how to baby it through the gears. Jeff tries to drive it but can't. Somehow I manage to drive us the mile uphill to my mom's place in Pūpū-kea.

My mom must have been around, but I have no memory of her there. Inside the house I shuffle to the bathroom. I fill the bathtub to the top, grab a snorkel and mask, get in, and curl into the fetal position. This was my idea of pain management. I stay there for hours. Eventually the water is stone cold and I drag myself out of the tub and crawl out to the living room, where I collapse on the futon.

I wake up early the next morning. I've had nothing to eat or drink in close to twenty-four hours. I'd hoped the pain would go away after a night's sleep, but it's worse than ever, deep and knifelike. I know without a doubt that this is bad, that I'm going to need a doctor. It's while I'm on the phone telling the medical assistant what has happened that I pass out, collapsing onto the floor.

Luckily, Jeff is there to catch me. I'm flat on the floor, lying there a minute or an hour, coddled by the blackness, blessedly out of pain. It was the most peaceful place I've ever been. I had no desire to come back. Suddenly, I hear my brother Liam crying and saying my name. His voice rouses me, but as I climb back to consciousness the pain comes with me, and I think, *Ah no, not this place, not this pain.*

Slowly it dawns on me that I might not surf again.

PART I

A family portrait, taken soon after moving to Hawai'i in 1978.
The author (bottom right) with his mother, Malia (top left); his then-stepfather,
Darryl (top right); and his brother, Liam (bottom left).
(Courtesy of the author)

ESCAPE ARTIST

IT'S 1969 AND ALREADY I'm racing, running, going, charging down a dirt path in a diaper. Heels hit the hard ground. Wind all around me. Leaves clapping overhead. Free. While no one was looking I crawled out of my stroller and I ran out of the campus dining room, out the front door, and across the school grounds. A little dog catches up with me and trots alongside.

My mom, Malia, then calling herself Debbie, assures me now that there was never any little dog, but in my memory there was one, around then. Jenny. We reached the highway, turned, and started walking along the sandy berm. I was maybe eighteen months old. It's family lore, this story. I have no memory of it, other than a general sense that even as a diapered baby I had the urge to fling myself into the wider world.

I was born at Stockbridge, the famous progressive boarding school a mile down the road from the Tanglewood music festival in western Massachusetts. It was international, interracial, and coeducational, based on the ideals of the UN Charter. My dad, Laurence, taught English and Latin and was also the basketball coach. My mom was the housemother in the boys' dorm.

I was a Summer of Love baby, delivered August 10, 1967. It was a few months before the release of the epic counterculture ballad "Alice's Restaurant," written by Stockbridge's most famous alum, Arlo Guthrie, about the time he got arrested there for littering on Thanksgiving Day. Alice was the librarian at Stockbridge before she opened her restaurant.

Among her various duties Malia also supervised the dining room. The students, wealthy and scholarship alike, had chores, among them setting and clearing the tables after meals, doing the dishes, and cleaning the kitchen.

I was the only baby on the premises. Throughout the day students and staff stopped and peered at me, captive in my stroller. They liked to shake my feet, tickle my belly, say "Hey little baby, what's up?" As far as I was concerned the world was a fine and friendly place.

The day I hit the road Malia had parked me near the door to the dining hall so that she, or anyone else who happened past, could keep an eye on me. Malia's parenting style was on the far side of casual. She left the room or became involved in a conversation with a student or in some other way stopped paying attention. I saw my chance and was on my way.

I stumbled along until a cop car pulled up beside me. In all likelihood it was the same officer who busted Arlo only a few years back. He scooped me up by my armpits. Captured. They sat me on a hard chair at the station. Cop called around, finally reaching someone at Stockbridge. Anyone missing a baby girl?

They'd taken my blond curls at face value.

The woman who answered the phone in the front office tracked down Malia. She checked my stroller, saw I'd gone AWOL.

"Tell them to check the diaper," she said. "It's got to be Garrett."

The police drove me back, dropped me in my mom's arms. She was more amused than anything. It was the times, and she was that kind of parent.

LUTHER BURBANK

WE MOVED TO BERKELEY, California, later the same year, rolling into town on the day of a student protest. The streets were crowded with hippies carrying placards, and cops in riot gear. At a stoplight we watched students with wire cutters snipping through a chain link fence surrounding the People's Park.

The Berkeley campus was a haven for communist sympathizers, protesters, and sexual deviants, or so said the governor, Ronald Reagan. Even though my mom and dad weren't students, they fit right in. And my mom had come into a small inheritance, money that allowed them to pick up everything and move west. There, my brother Liam was born.

Did I know I'd just been granted an ally, a partner in crime? I was only a toddler myself, just two years old. Still, looking at infant Liam was like looking at myself in the mirror, and I absorbed the fact that I was now no longer the baby of the family.

We moved into a big square-shingled house with a tall redwood tree in the backyard and with a bunch of other people. There was a couple sleeping in a VW van in the driveway, and another couple sleeping in the toolshed, and another couple sleeping in the pantry. I had a little room in the eaves.

They were all just back from the Peace Corps in India. They smoked pot in a chillum, a carved stone pipe that I liked to carry around the house. The place smelled like incense and pizza, which was what my babysitters fed me when my dad was at work as a waiter and my mom was somewhere out hatching one of her plans. Our babysitters were the other women in the house, all with long, center-parted hair. When no one was looking, which was most of the time, I would go outside to our weedy yard and catch bees with my bare hands. There were huge, overgrown rosebushes and jasmine vines and plenty of bees. From the front porch I could hear them buzzing. I was stung repeatedly, but it was part of the joy of catching them, the feeling of their wings beating between my palms.

Down the street there was a woman named Geraldine True who'd come to Berkeley from Greece, where she owned a weaving factory. She was a big-deal weaver. My mom bragged about her to the others. Geraldine's weavings hung in a museum in New York. She was a single mother, her husband an atomic engineer who'd committed suicide at the thought of the bombs he'd had a hand in creating. One day she moved into one of our closets. She and my mother spent hours poring through the Whole Earth Access catalogue, a handbook for people who wanted to get back to the land. They found a forty-acre parcel near a little town called Cazadero in Sonoma County, seven hills east of the Pacific, part of an old sheep ranch. Geraldine knew some other people interested in communal living, including two professors from Stanford named Barbara and Richard, who were eager to invest in the property so that they could study this new trend.

I knew all this because the adults always talked in front of me, as if I weren't there.

• • •

AT FIRST, Liam and I were the only little kids in the commune. We lived in a ranch house on top of a hill. Every downstairs bedroom had a couple in it, and the attic, divided into three or four bedrooms, was stuffed with couples too. One guy lived in an old mail truck in the driveway: Doug McMillian, a civil engineer who practiced yoga and stood on his head for ten minutes a day, and taught my dad how to stand on his head for ten minutes a day, and who eventually changed his name to Battso Gornu. We had electricity and running water, but for heat it was a fireplace and a wood stove. My dad did a lot of the cooking, training without realizing it for the day he would leave the commune and move back to Berkeley, where he would open his own restaurant.

The commune people didn't believe in toys, but I had a little banana-seat bike my dad taught me to ride when I was four, and a Tonka truck, my prized possession. The bike was propped up against the side of the shed. One day I grabbed the handlebars and climbed aboard. He showed me how the pedals worked, then started to push me, running along beside me, holding the seat. When he saw that I had no trouble balancing, he gave me a little push for good measure and I was off.

I loved being outside. The bright yellow grass, the pond where everyone swam naked, the river running through our parcel, dry in the summer, raging in the winter. Everyone in the commune kept an eye on me, which is to say no one kept an eye on me. There was a garden where they grew vegetables and marijuana. We had a cow named Luna. My dad milked her every morning and he showed me how, and also how to throw the feed out for the chickens, how to hold my hand just right so the feed was broadcast over the sandy ground of their pen.

I learned so much about making plants grow and tending the livestock that they started calling me Luther Burbank, after the world-famous botanist and horticulturalist who developed over eight hundred new strains of flowers, fruits, grasses, and grains.

The other thing this new Luther Burbank liked to do, which I'm sure was not a hobby of the famous botanist, was to kill little animals and dissect them. I ran around the property all day long looking for snakes and scorpions, and waded into the sheep watering pond hoping to find some fish. My feet sank into the muddy bottom, rooting me in place, perhaps saving me from drowning.

I murdered Geraldine's goldfish in cold blood, and for a few days the talk of the commune became how my mom could prevent me from becoming the next Charles Manson. I was only three and didn't have the words to say that I was upset at no longer being the baby, that I missed being the sole focus of my mom's attention. It was incidental that I also liked cutting animals open to look at the organs, those small pulsing gems. My mom decided to love it out of me, and rather than putting any negative energy toward my behavior, the next time she found me on the back patio trying to cut a lizard open with a butter knife, she drew me to her and hugged me so fiercely I thought I might get smothered.

I was further saved from my grisly enthusiasm by the Head Start school run by the Kashia Band of Pomo Indians, who lived in a nearby town called Stewarts Point. After they got word that there were some kids running wild nearby, they sent a driver to pick us up. I loved Head Start. No one was worried about me or much of anything there. One day we were driving down the hill and one of the other kids in the backseat opened the door and fell out and rolled down the highway. The driver just drove to where he had stopped and scooped him up. They also allowed me to collect scorpions. I preserved each one in a glass jar filled with alcohol.

My mom and the Head Start Indians may have succeeded in turning me away from a life as a serial killer, but I still like to hang geckos from my ears, their tiny jaws gripped to my lobes like clip-on earrings, hanging on for dear life. If I'm in the mood to watch someone's eyes pop out of their head, I'm still not above allowing a centipede to crawl up my tongue and into my mouth.

WATERMELON SEED ON MY DING DONG

I WAS FOUR WHEN I took my first hit of marijuana. At night the adults smoked pot for recreation and someone would usually sing and play the guitar. It was part of the household routine, what they did after the dinner dishes were done and put away. They sat in a circle on the living room floor and passed around the chillum. There were some other kids in the mix by then: Sevin, whose parents lived down the hill in a geodesic dome; and a girl named Luba I've managed to stay in touch with.

Pinballing around the circle, probably buck naked, I looked over and saw the pipe resting between the fingers of someone's hand. But the next person wasn't taking it, so I lurched over, reached in, and grabbed it and sucked on the end. Someone leaned over and took it back from me, some stoned-out-of-his-mind commune person, and I ran out of the house over the bright yellow grass. It must have been summer. It was hot, the sun low and glinting between the pine trees. I was super thirsty, running around on the lookout for something to drink.

I saw some milk jugs lined up by the shed; usually we filled them with water there. One was only half full and I could lift it up to my mouth. I held it with both hands and took a few gulps. Something wasn't right. My face felt scorched, nose burning, insides stinging. I, who rarely cried, yowled like the losing cat in a fight. Grown-ups appeared. I still held the jug of what was, obviously except to me, kerosene or gasoline. One of the commune moms scooped me up and took me into the kitchen and forced real milk into me. It was cold and chalky. I was dozy and nauseated. Where were my mom and dad? I don't know. I wasn't scared, and neither were the women holding me and forcing me to drink the milk. They were surely too stoned to emit a sensation of fear, even if they were feeling it. I'm a father myself now, and had my son swallowed kerosene I would have raced him to the hospital. Instead, they pressed more milk down me. I could hear someone playing the guitar in the other room.

Around the same time there was a big sweat-lodge party. Our sweat lodge was low-domed, a pole frame covered with burlap bags, a fire pit dug deep in the center. It was run by a Native American guy who lived in one of the rental units. Down by the sheep pond my dad built a fire to heat the rocks. When they were red hot, he brought them inside the lodge, arranged them at the bottom of the pit, and poured water on them to make steam. So many people came to these sweat parties they had to take turns in the lodge. They showed up from all over: hippies strolled over from the adjoining parcels of land; emerged from the vans and trucks parked around the property; car-pooled from as far away as Oakland, Berkeley, and San Francisco. The Stanford psychiatrists showed up, and also a muckety-muck from Ghirardelli who brought chocolate.

That day started no different than any other day for me. I run around naked and unsupervised. It's watermelon season, and I swoop by the table where one of the women is cutting up slabs. I eat my way through one piece after another, down to the rind. I move on to a bag of milk chocolate buttons. They fit right in my sticky palm.

At nightfall someone breaks out the peyote. That was how you knew it was a happening and not just a regular get-together. Pot was the everyday drug of choice, but peyote was for special occasions. Like the milk chocolate, the button fits snug in my palm.

Down the hatch.

It doesn't taste any different than a lot of the other stuff I pick up off the ground and eat, bitter and earthy. But suddenly everything that had been on the inside of me was on the outside. A geyser of pink and brown spews out of me. Watermelon and chocolate and peyote. Someone rubs my back. I remember looking up and seeing birds with colored wings flying overhead, and the leaves of a nearby eucalyptus tree shaking like chimes. Then I look at my penis and see a watermelon seed stuck there. I can't stop laughing.

MAD BOB

ONE DAY WHEN I was four, my mom was hanging laundry and I was running around beneath the wet skirts and flowered shirts. A tall man with glasses and curly hair walked up and introduced himself as Mad Bob. A dead raccoon hung from one hand. He explained that he hit the raccoon while driving up from Cazadero, but instead of leaving it by the side of the windy road, he thought it might make a mighty fine barbecue. Perhaps because she was used to my habit of catching creatures and dissecting them for amusement, my mom didn't bat an eye, just directed him to the fire pit.

Mad Bob arrived with a woman named Carol, who may or may not have been his old lady. She set up a teepee on the property, where she lived with her baby, Joaquin. My mom, the original free spirit, found Carol to be even more so. She had once been married to a guy who manufactured PCP and with the profits bought a Bentley, but now they were divorced. Despite my parents' casual infidelities, my mom thought marriage was forever and was interested to meet a woman who'd gone her own way. My mom never supposed she would divorce my dad, but it was the free love era, so there was also no expectation that they would remain faithful and true.

Mad Bob was more adventuresome than my dad, indulging my mom in a way my dad never would. Together they traveled around the county stealing fruit from orchard trees and picking up hitchhikers to bring home to help with the canning. She wanted horses. One day Mad Bob showed up with a pair of brown geldings.

My mom was happy enough, but she was growing tired of the rainy winters in Sonoma County. She craved a warm climate. Winter days could be gray for weeks on end, and the land around the house got so muddy you could easily lose your shoes if they weren't tied on. Then her mother died, she received another inheritance, and Mad Bob said they should go to Mexico for the winter. My mom wanted my dad to come along, but he wasn't having any of it. He was a guy who liked to stay put. He said, "You took me from New York to Massachusetts, Massachusetts to Berkeley, Berkeley to Cazadero, and now I'm happy and I want to stay here."

They decided to divvy up their children. I went with my mom and Liam stayed with my dad. My mom had discovered LSD, but my dad thought that I was old enough to fend for myself; whereas Liam, who was still a toddler, needed more reliable care and attention. He built a tiny house for the two of them on the side of a hill on the far side of the property, with a wood stove and a spring-fed shower. The second floor had a vinyl window through which you could see the ocean on clear days.

My mom and I lit out with Mad Bob and his two daughters. Christina and Cathy were a little older than me, grade schoolers. The three of us sat in the back, girl-boy-girl. The VW van broke down on the first day, and pretty much every day after that. Mad Bob would pull over to the side of the road, get out, open the rear engine hood, and stand there with his arms folded staring at it, and I would do the same. Then someone would pull over, or we'd get a tow to some gas station, and I would watch someone fix it. The bottoms of my feet developed calluses from standing on the hot asphalt day after day, and I also began to understand how engines work, knowledge I still use.

We made our way across the border at Mexicali and cruised/broke down/cruised/broke down along the Mexican mainland, camping on the beach. I slept between Christina and Cathy on a bed Mad Bob built for us on the roof of the VW van. Those girls taught me my numbers to one hundred, counting all the stars. We stayed for a while at Guaymas. Mad Bob was a film nut and he said this was the place where a movie called *Catch-22* was filmed. One night the grunions were running, tiny silver fish that squiggle themselves up on the sand as part of an elaborate mating ritual. We caught them with our hands and Mad Bob fried them up on the beach. Thinking about this now I appreciate the simplicity, and my mouth waters remembering those crunchy, salty little fish.

Mad Bob and I were wading in the shallows one afternoon, looking for a fish to spear for dinner, and I saw something big and silvery flash by, with an ugly gaping mouth and a fin that looked like a hand with long skinny black fingers. It looked like a prehistoric monster, hairy and mean, and it scared the hell out of me. I leaped back onto shore and resolved never to go back in the ocean again.

"That's just a roosterfish," said Mad Bob.

We kept driving south, every day the sun beating down harder, the sand like yellow sugar and the water a warm electric blue. I played in the surf with Christina and Cathy. We held hands and spent hours jumping waves. I told them to look out for the roosterfish. I was sure they were up there with sharks on the list of sea creatures to be feared. I was sure if we went too deep one was going to lunge for me and bite my ding dong.

One day, in a tiny outlaw town near the Guatemalan border, some locals rapped on the side of the van and told us that it wasn't safe parking on the beach. Would we like to park in their driveway? My mom and Mad Bob weren't shy about taking people up on their charity. This family, probably looking at us three kids, coffee-bean brown with washboard ribs, thought we could use a good meal or three. They fed us big dinners every night: rice, beans, and iguana tamales. Or that's what they said they were. One evening my mom discovered they were selling chickens from their little coop to buy enough food to feed us. We moved on down the road so their charity wouldn't bankrupt them.

Every morning Mad Bob and my mom bought fresh rolls for breakfast from the local *panadería*. There was always a neat stack of tarnished peso coins on the dashboard of the van, set aside for just this purpose. One morning, awake before anyone else, I swiped the coins and hid them in the back pocket of my raggedy shorts. There was a dingy shop in town I'd spied a few days earlier that sold cheap souvenirs and fireworks. I had just enough for a *polumna*, a triangle-shaped firecracker with a thick red fuse. I paid for the *polumna* and the old man behind the counter included a book of matches. Across the street there was a little park with a few iron benches and an empty concrete fountain in the center. I lit the fuse, pulled my arm back major league pitching style, paused for a minute as I tried to figure out whether I wanted to throw the firecracker down the street or try to hit the empty fountain, and in that moment it exploded in my hand. I smelled the sizzle of skin. It felt like someone had socked me in the jaw. I went down on one knee. After feeling my ear I expected to see blood but there was nothing, only a high-pitched whine that wouldn't go away.

I ran back to the van. My mom popped out of the door, her hands on her hips, and I showed her my hand. She said it served me right for stealing the breakfast money. It was the first time I'd heard about karma, and how what we do comes back to us. My hand healed, but I lost some hearing in that one ear, which I suffer from to this day.

IN GOD'S HANDS,
MORE OR LESS

MAD BOB DROVE SOUTH. Our days were ordered around finding a fresh tortilla shop. Kilos of fresh corn tortillas; no GMO worries then. We ate them with cheese and beans for days on end. No one consulted a map that I could see. The only thing that dictated our direction was the location of the next bank, where my mom would receive her monthly inheritance check.

Somewhere along the way we picked up a guy named Luis. He was from a well-off family in Mexico City that made its riches manufacturing wood paneling. He was on a mission, scouring tropical jungles for cedar and ceiba to take back to the factory. My mom was the kind of woman who hit it off with people, and she and Luis stayed up all night talking. Whereas Mad Bob was all about adventure, Luis liked to talk and talk in English so heavily accented I couldn't understand him. He decided he liked the sound of our journey, and also my mom, so he joined us in the van.

Mexico turned into Guatemala. The people there were the most helpful we'd come across. The starter in the van wouldn't turn over anymore, and when people saw Mad Bob and Luis pushing it down the road to jump-start it, my mom behind the wheel steering, they would stop what they were doing and silently join in. Once the van sputtered to life, they would just as silently return to their business.

One day we stopped to get groceries and other supplies in a village near the border with a river running through it. A guy named Jose Pepe approached us as we stood outside a little shop that sold everything from sweet bread to motor oil. What he saw: two men, one a tall hippie with curly hair and wire-rimmed glasses, the other a short, broad-chested Mexican who kept his arm clamped around the shoulder of my mom; she, slender and deeply tanned with sun-streaked blond hair; two grade-school girls with scabby knees in faded sundresses; and me, blond curly hair, now deaf in one ear, trotting a circle around our assembled group, searching for a lizard or some small creature to torment.

"Excuse me," Jose Pepe said, "I couldn't help but hear your plans to camp by the river. I'm afraid that is a little dangerous. There is no doubt you will be robbed. I have a ranch not far from here. You can stay there."

Mad Bob and my mom and Luis thought that was a fine idea. Jose Pepe helped them push-start the van, and we followed him in his pickup truck down a rutted road through the jungle. We eventually came to a clearing, and there was a long low ranch house and a pasture with a herd of long-eared white cows standing in the middle staring at us.

They cooked us up a big steak dinner and had spare rooms for us to sleep in, with actual beds made with actual sheets that tucked in around the edges. The next morning Jose Pepe took us horseback riding, and took his time choosing the right horses for us three kids. Mine was big and yellow and swaybacked, and had a thick pale-yellow mane that fell in his eyes. He was the kind of horse who would take care of you, instead of waiting for you to tell him what to do. Jose Pepe's wife gave me some long pants that belonged to a slightly larger child, to protect my legs when I rode.

Two days later my mom and Luis and Mad Bob and his two daughters, who were afraid of the horses and were anxious to get back to the ocean anyway, push-started the van and chugged off. They were headed to the next bank to pick up my mom's check, and would be back soon. I was happy to be left behind. My fear of roosterfish was starting to get exhausting, and there was no threat of roosterfish at Jose Pepe's cattle ranch in the jungle.

I was five years old. Until my mom left me with Jose Pepe and his family, my parenting, such as it was, consisted of interacting with a revolving cast of mostly strung-out grown-ups coming and going and coming and going. No one paid much attention to me. No one told me what to do or what not to do. No one had ever said I should use a fork, or that it was impolite to play with your ding dong in public. I never heard, "Be careful, you'll burn yourself," or "fall and hurt yourself," or "lose an eye." Everything I knew I had learned on my own. Still, there always seemed to be arms to hold me or a lap to sit on, and if people were eating they made sure I ate, too.

My mom is a great-grandniece of Mary Baker Eddy, the founder of Christian Science, and has a powerful and eccentric belief in God. Regarding Liam and me, she dumped us in God's hands, more or less. When I was older and had become a father myself and asked about my running-wild childhood, she said she wanted my brother and me to figure things out for ourselves.

Her time at Stockbridge—she was a student there before she worked there—convinced her that nothing good came of rules, regulations, guidance, and instruction. All that created automatons and yes-men who had no ability to think for themselves, no deep sense of right or wrong, and whose instincts were programmed out of them.

She felt God was alive in us and believed He would watch over us and protect us, allowing us just enough terrible experiences to build our character and teach us about the reality of life on earth.

I lived with Jose Pepe and his family for a few weeks. It goes without saying that his household was a lot more structured than what I was used to. Sit-down meals, nightly baths, regular bedtimes. I loved it. Every day Jose Pepe hoisted me up on the back of the same drowsy yellow horse. I forgot all about the roosterfish, until one day we were headed toward the barn after our daily ride and I saw the dusty red-and-white VW van trundling up the driveway.

"If it isn't Gitana," he said. That was Jose Pepe's name for my mother. Her real name was Mary but she went by Debbie, and now Jose Pepe christened her Gitana, "gypsy" in Spanish. There was never any doubt in my mind that my mom would come back for me, but Jose sounded surprised. We got off our horses and watched as Luis parked the van and my mom stepped down from the passenger side. They were all alone.

Jose Pepe invited them in for lunch. While I sat eating my stewed chicken and tortillas I listened to my mom spin one of her stories. It's one of her gifts, making everything that happens to her sound both incredible and completely normal.

After they'd left me at Jose Pepe's ranch they picked up some hitchhikers, hippies from Guatemala City who'd been in the medical supply business but had dropped out to join a traveling circus. Mad Bob drove them all the way to the circus, and as usually happened, once the producer of the circus met my mom, he invited them all to dinner, and afterward she, Luis, Mad Bob, and his two daughters wound up staying there, sleeping under the big top with the performers. The tent had been hand-sewn out of burlap sugar sacks.

The circus charged ten cents a ticket, and they held performances every night until they made enough money to move on. The circus producer was frantic because he'd just found out there was another circus on its way to the same village. They charged twenty-five cents a ticket, but they also had a lion. The closest he came to a lion was a pair of depressed llamas who could spit on command.

Mad Bob, inspired, rigged up a loudspeaker on top of the van and spent the rest of the day driving around the village announcing the wonders of the smaller, poorer, lion-less circus. At the end of the day they offered him a job as the strongman, so he and his daughters decided to stay.

There were more stories. With my mom there are always more stories. Something about meeting someone else and going somewhere else and spending a few days discovering the wonders of Guatemalan cotton yarn dyeing and weaving. But Jose Pepe seemed to have lost interest. He was looking at me. I remember him putting his hand on the top of my head as I ate.

He waited until my mom stopped talking, then asked her whether he and his family might adopt me.

GITANA

I CAN HOLD MY breath for four and a half minutes. Still, I've wiped out and thrashed around in the wash cycle for so long my peripheral vision disappears and all I see before my eyes are black stars. Don't know which way is up. Don't even know where I am. Then the ocean gods pop me up like a cork, gifting me with a second to open my mouth and grab a breath before the next sixty-foot wave brings the next pounding. I've been rescued by friends in the lineup and by partners on jet-skis, blue-lipped and gasping and not sure I could say my last name. All of which is to say I've suffered a lot of brain hypoxia—oxygen deprivation—over the years. As a result my memory feels as if it's been rag-dolled through time, leaving me unsure of the who what when where why and how of a lot of incidents. I can reliably recall specific events and especially the names of a lot of the guys in the lineup on a certain day when I was killing it, or nearly being killed, but timelines and dates are, much of the time, a messed-up jumble.

The waters of my early grade-school memories are further muddied by my parents' freewheeling habit of swapping sons on a whim. It feels like Liam and I were always coming and going, two ships passing in the night. My dad stayed in his little house built into the hill near the commune in Cazadero, then moved back to Berkeley. My mom was in full Gitana mode, always on the move, always headed somewhere, inevitably waylaid by some hitchhiker or stoned visionary who appeared out of the jungle with pertinent advice or a life-changing premonition. Then she would switch course in midstream, head out in the opposite direction. Most of the time my dad never knew where she was, and neither did she.

MY MOM declined Jose Pepe's offer to adopt me. Together with Luis we drove north, back through northern Guatemala and the little villages where we'd camped along the coast of southern Mexico, turning inland to stop in Mexico City and visit Luis's family. I missed Mad Bob's low-key energy and even his daughters, who used to complain about my farting up the back of the van. Turns out Luis was the jealous type, and all the hippies and locals and shopkeepers and dope peddlers my mom charmed along the way were starting to get under his skin. He didn't say anything—or anything in my presence, anyway—until after we stopped in Mexico City and he accused her of flirting with his father. Then all his passionate talk and high spirits went south, and he settled into a sour mood for the rest of the drive north.

Luis was no stranger to real-deal communal living. Before he wandered into our lives he'd lived in Cuernavaca, at a commune comprising Mexican doctors and lawyers and other professional people. This convinced my mom he would fit right in to life in our commune in Sonoma County, but the vibe was all wrong. From the moment we arrived it was clear he didn't want to be there with the people she'd known before, especially my dad.

One of my mom's favorite hippie friends, Lillian, had been through a few things in our absence, had gone off to India where she'd been arrested for possession of hash, and she wound up giving birth to a baby in jail. Now she and the baby lived in a geodesic dome up in the mountains somewhere. She was anything but scared straight by this experience, and upon our return to the commune she gave my mom a sheet of mint windowpane acid, a welcome-home present. My mom threw a party for the assembled commune people and the local farmers and dissolved some of the acid in the punch. They sat in lawn chairs all night staring at the eastern horizon waiting for the sun to come up, and when it did, one farmer's wife, perched in the lap of her husband, wept and said she'd never seen a sunrise like that before in her life.

Yep, we were home.

It was all too much for Luis. Not long afterward my mom scooped up Liam and the three of them took off.

WEEKS OR months later my dad put me on an airplane in Oakland, headed to Belize. Then it was called British Honduras. I recall several stops, takeoffs, and landings, and largely empty planes. I was shown the cockpit. The stewardesses fed me grapes. On my lap I carried my mom's autoharp. She'd forgotten it at the commune during her hasty departure and now missed it.

Mom and Luis's new scheme involved making marijuana bowls by harvesting scrap hardwood and carving them to somehow de-seed your pot. I never understood how it worked, and I'm not sure they did either, because once they'd purchased a few acres of property border-ing a mosquito-infested lagoon in the jungle, they bought a cow they named Bossy and a horse they named Bitch and a bunch of chickens. My favorite chicken was named Hole-head, so called because she had a hole in her head from where the other chickens had pecked her skull clear to her little chicken brain. You could see the shiny insides in the right light.

After a while Mom and Luis set about building us a Swiss Family Robinson–style tree house in a stand of balata trees. The construction was all-consuming and they pretty much forgot all about the wood and the bowls and proceeded to get into terrible fights that startled the wildlife, and also our gentle Mennonite neighbors.

The Mennonites had emigrated from Pennsylvania. On their small farms they raised dairy cows, grew vegetables, and kept honeybees. They didn't believe in electricity—convenient, because there was none to be had—and operated a small sawmill with a team of patient-looking draft horses. I played with the little Mennonite children. The boys wore light blue cotton shirts, dark pants, and suspenders, and the little girls wore long cotton dresses. Somehow I knew to put on some clothes when I would meet them for games of hide-and-seek and tag in the sugarcane fields.

My toys were a machete for hacking through the cane fields, and the iguanas I'd capture and "walk" around the property with strings around their necks. I pretended they were my pet dogs and gave them names like Spot and Rover.

Our kitchen sat in a clearing not far from the ladder that led up to the living quarters. It had a wood-burning stove, and a thatched roof with a hole in the middle so the smoke from the stove could escape. A neighbor taught my mom how to make bread. Most days she made red beans and rice and split a coconut for dessert. Every morning I'd climb to the top of a coconut tree, cut some off, and throw them down for her.

I loved climbing trees, but my all-time favorite pastime was riding them. Long before I'd heard of riding waves I rode trees. All I needed was one of the more daring Mennonite boys to help out. I'd climb to the top of one of the young jungle trees near a clearing. Bullet trees with their lush leaves were the best and provided the softest landing. I'd climb to the topmost branch, give the word, and my playmate would chop down the tree with my machete. I'd ride it all the way to the ground.

JUNGLE LIVING did nothing to quiet Luis's inner psycho demon. He didn't like how my mom cooked the red beans and rice and made the bread and chopped up the coconuts. To get to the only store in the district my mom had to take a rowboat. He didn't like how she chatted with anyone she met on the lagoon, rowing to the store. A favorite form of abuse was kicking her in the head while wearing the muddy combat boots he wore to work in the cane fields. He wouldn't stop until she was a bloody mess.

The one great advantage to being completely unsupervised was that when the shouting started I could flee, scampering down the ladder or bolting out of the kitchen. I was there for all of the escalating abuse, and yet I wasn't. I learned the value of separating myself from a bad situation, or finding a way to amuse myself while the domestic ground shook and buckled beneath my feet. I learned to survive. I'm sure I've also just blocked a lot of it out, and there's something to be said for that as well.

Mom loved Luis—she would leave him and go back to him several times over the coming years—but she was not about to sit around and get whupped without putting up a fight. She was Gitana; she could always pack up and leave. She sold Bossy the cow and Bitch the horse to our Mennonite neighbors, and one day while Luis was out somewhere we fled in our rowboat, across the lagoon.

I sat on the wooden bench as my mom rowed, a bundle with my clothes tied in it on my lap. Once we emerged from under the jungle canopy the sun beat down on our heads. I watched the sweat slide down the bridge of her nose. I looked away, stared at the *café con leche*–colored water. What looked like a log was moving against the sluggish current.

"Mom, there's a crocodile," I said.

"We are not stopping," she said.

That cracked me up. As if.

On the other side of the lagoon there was a rutted dirt road. We walked along in silence. I was thirsty. I had shoes on for the first time in however long and felt the blisters rising on my heels. We reached the highway headed north, stopped by the side of the road, and my mom stuck out her thumb. I toed off my shoes and my mom told me to put them back on again. I remember looking up at her with pure disbelief before tossing them into the brush. I remember seeing the bruises on her arms and one on her jaw and thinking that Luis was a pure psycho freak. Would I have had those words then? We didn't have any TV, no radio; surely my Mennonite playmates would never know a descriptor like that. It could have come from Liam, who was quicker than me when it came to words, an excellent mimic, and could easily have heard one of the commune people say such a thing. He had been down to visit for a few weeks. Then one morning he was gone, shipped back to California.

The highway looked brand-new. Glitter in the asphalt. Wide blue sky overhead, the sun a milky ball, cotton-puff clouds. A few cars passed, then one pulled over. A couple of longhairs headed conveniently to a town just over the border in Mexico, Chetumal.

The longhairs knew of some Americans there, archaeologists investigating the Mayans. We camped with them until my mom was able to collect her next check, then took the train to Mexico City and flew to California. My mom would go back to Luis a few more times. She would return to British Honduras, to the house in the trees, and she would flee again, but for now we were safe in Berkeley, where my dad had opened his restaurant.

TORTILLA AND BUTTER, PLEASE

MY DAD'S RESTAURANT WAS called Ma Goodness, named after a book he used to read to Liam and me about a couple named Pop Corn and Ma Goodness, who lived atop neighboring hills. One day during a rainstorm they slid down into the valley in between, conked heads, and fell in love. Ma Goodness sat on the corner of Shattuck and Ashby Avenues, maybe a dozen blocks away from the university and a couple of miles away from another little hippie place called Chez Panisse. The other cook was Sheri, his new girlfriend, who was gentle and smelled like a mixture of incense and freshly baked bread and didn't seem to have a gitana bone in her body. Even though my dad tended to like women who weren't very maternal, Sheri was kind and I liked her a lot. On the day before the place opened my dad took about a hundred peyote buttons and put them in a pot of water and kept them on the stove all day, and to anybody who came in he'd say, "Would you care for a cup of peyote tea?" I already knew about the peyote. One day I was snooping around the new house and found a screen of buttons drying in the back of my closet.

The neighborhood was a mix of commercial and residential and we lived in a guesthouse, a little cedar-shingled three-room place behind the home of a doctor and his wife. It had an upstairs and a downstairs and for the first time Liam and I each had our own bedroom. In the morning I could look down in the yard and watch my dad doing yoga. It was summer, all the windows open, the fresh smell of eucalyptus trees and the tangy smell of salt and fish coming off the bay, the smell of pot, and also, depending on the day, my dad's vegetarian lasagna.

He was a good cook. He didn't have a lot of experience but enough to make it work. When he was in college at NYU he tended bar and cooked at a few Manhattan restaurants. After my parents first moved to Berkeley he was a waiter at some fancy place in Marin. Every day I watched him get in his van dressed in black pants, a white dress shirt, and fancy red vest. Away he would go to carve chateaubriand and assemble Caesar salads tableside. At Ma Goodness he ditched the steak. Vegetarianism was big in Berkeley. Avocados and sprouts dominated every lunch menu. My dad knew a couple, regular patrons of the restaurant—he a rail-thin black dude, she a buxom white-girl hippie chick—who subsisted entirely on wheatgrass.

The only thing I missed about living in British Honduras was chopping down bullet trees and riding them to the ground. I was developing a knack for adapting and making do, for figuring out in the moment how to have the maximum amount of fun. In our neighborhood, the next best thing to riding bullet trees was jumping off the roof.

Greg Serber, my best friend from Malcolm X Elementary School, where I was failing second grade, lived nearby in a house with a detached garage set back on the property, shielded from street view by a row of plum trees. We would climb one of the trees to get to the roof, then do our best pro-baseball pitcher imitation and hurl plums down the driveway as hard as we could. When we got bored of that, we'd jump off the roof into a sandy barbecue pit on the other side. When we got bored of that, we'd pick more plums, the really ripe ones, find Liam, and tackle him to the ground. One of us would sit on him while the other stuck the plums down his pants, then smash them in with the heels of our hands.

One of the things I noticed as I stood on Greg Serber's garage was all the kids riding their bikes and skateboards up and down the sidewalk, weaving between the strolling hippie student pedestrians and stoner panhandlers, bunny-hopping off the curb and doing wheelies. Now that I was older and lived in a regular urban neighborhood I saw all the other things boys our age were given without a thought—the skateboards, the baseball bats and gloves, the basketball hoop in the driveway.

Liam and I had never wanted for anything because I hadn't known there was anything to want. There were always enough adults around to see that we were fed and watered. When it was warm we ran around naked, and when it got cold some adult made sure we were dressed. If these basics weren't provided, if we wanted a snack and one wasn't forthcoming, we foraged for ourselves. We never had to ask to go outside, be excused, or watch another half hour of cartoons. We did pretty much whatever we wanted, and slept where we collapsed at the end of the day.

But now, watching the neighborhood kids on their bikes, I recalled the little banana seat bike we'd had at the commune, and I wanted one. Now. I jumped off the roof into the barbecue pit and set off to find my dad, to make my request known.

I can still feel my fierce determination, but how Liam and I came in possession of our own BMX bikes has escaped me. I told my dad and sometime later—a few weeks, maybe?—the bikes appeared.

One of the first things we did after we had wheels was tool on over to Ma Goodness, hopping off curbs and perfecting our wheelies. There was a small window over the stove on the side of the building. We rolled up and demanded warm flour tortillas with butter, hands down our favorite thing on the menu. My dad was cooking that day. He dropped a pair of tortillas on the grill, slathered them with butter, tossed each one onto a square of wax paper, and passed them through the window.

SKYLINE

ONE DAY SOMETHING INCREDIBLE happened. Our dad came into some money and he gave Liam and me $100 each. It was maybe 1974. Skateboarding was it. Dogtown and Z Boys down south in Venice Beach was ground zero for skateboard culture, which was evolving from the moves surfers made on the waves in Santa Monica, but we had no clue about that. We had no clue about any of it, just that our dad gave us a hundred dollars apiece—we had never seen anything close to that amount of money in our lives—and we went to the skate shop near the university and bought Banzai metal decks and Road Rider 4 wheels and Tracker trucks and we were set.

Now we had our BMX bikes and our skateboards. Looking back, I think it was only by the grace of God that we didn't wind up grammar-school dropouts.

We threw ourselves into making jumps and ramps. Jumps were easy. Any angled surface was a jump. We'd steal plastic milk crates from behind the grocery store and tie them together with twine, socks, belts, anything we could find, then lean a piece of wood on it. A couple of two-by-fours nailed together side by side worked. But sometimes, if we were on our bikes, the front tire would knock the board off and instead of going up the jump we'd crash into the now obstructing board and egg crates. Plywood was better, but weak in the middle, so it'd bow and eventually crack without reinforcement.

We scouted the city for new construction, where the ground would have to be leveled and graded. There might be several tiers of smoothed earth separated by a slope of dirt that made for great bike jumps, especially if there was a hill or slope leading down to the site. Then we'd pack the gutter with dirt to create a little ramp from the street over the curb. We'd ride up to the top of the hill and come zooming down over the curb, into the construction site, and right up the dirt tier. The tiers were three or maybe four feet tall, so with a big enough run-up, you could jump your bike six feet or more. More than a few times we'd jump too high, come down, and break a pedal. Also, if you landed too heavy on the front wheel, you'd taco the rim and end up face-first in the dirt.

Making ramps was more work. Building a halfway decent ramp could be an all-day affair, and building a good one could take an entire weekend. The size of the ramp would be determined by how much plywood we could steal. With a couple of sheets, as long as they were the same thickness, we could build a ramp that was about six feet tall and eight feet wide. We'd build a frame with whatever lumber we could find. Two-by-fours were best, but usually they'd just be scrap ends that needed to be nailed together to make longer boards. The back rectangle would be about six feet high, and the base about four feet deep. Cross braces—at least three of them—were then nailed from the back to the base. Then we'd nail plywood sheets on the frame. Even though they'd work their way out so fast and catch our tires, wheels, or skin, we were proud of ourselves. We had never been so industrious in our lives. And maybe even since.

Sometimes, our dad would drive us up to Codornices Park where there was a long steep hill. Whether on bike or board, coming down felt like straight-up flying, going so fast your cheeks wobbled and eyes watered. Then our dad would take us up to Skyline Boulevard, the ridge road that runs behind Berkeley. Skyline was even longer, and I couldn't bring myself to stand on my skateboard and ride that windy and steep road down into town. It was too scary. So I sat on my butt and raced on down. We called it butt hauling. The road wound through the forest, between stands of eucalyptus, pine, and bay oak. Sometimes between the trunks I glimpsed the sun on the Pacific, shiny like a gold coin.

WOLF

MOM CAME AND WENT. Some mornings Liam and I ran outside to grab our bikes to go to school and we would find her wrapped in a green woolen army blanket, sound asleep in a hammock she'd strung between two trees. If our landlords, the doctor and his wife who lived in the main house, disapproved of a woman camping out in their backyard, I never knew about it. Meanwhile, my dad's girlfriend, Sheri, had moved in with us. We may have moved on from the commune, but it was still the days of love the one you're with, and Mom hugged her when they met and shared a joint with her now and then. Still, Mom refused to eat at Ma Goodness. Instead, she ate at one of the local soup kitchens or homeless shelters along with the rest of the local hippies in need of a free meal. When it started getting cold at night, and the army blanket she traveled with wasn't enough to keep her warm, she moved to a neighbor's house, where she crashed on the couch.

Not long after that we saw her walking down Shattuck with a guy so tall his head floated above the crowd of freaks and flower children drifting along. She wore the army blanket around her shoulders like a shawl, her blond hair in braids. He reminded me of a Viking from a picture book, with long curly blond hair and a big nose and jaw. They turned into the occult bookstore on Ashby. Liam and I sometimes stopped on our bikes to look in the window. Crystals dangled on thin threads, throwing out beams of rainbow when the sun hit them just right, and there was also a crystal ball on a black wooden stand.

That was the last we saw of our mom for a while. We didn't think much of it.

Jackson Liquor Mini Mart was where we bought our baseball cards. The store was down the street from Ma Goodness. We thought that was also the name of the owner, who sometimes hired me to watch the register so he could run outside and shoo away the panhandlers in front, or to make deliveries on my bike. In those days, you could call up Jackson Liquor and tell him you needed a pint of rye and I might show up at your doorstep with the bottle swaddled in a brown paper bag, and he would put it on your tab.

Jackson Liquor sponsored the local Little League teams, including ours. Behind the counter black-framed team pictures marched up the wall, two by two. In the front of the counter among the gum and Life Savers, Jackson Liquor sold Topps baseball cards. My dad left change around the house on the kitchen counter and on his dresser, and Liam and I would help ourselves to it and combine it with my income to buy out Jackson Liquor's entire stock. Handfuls of packs, every day. Then one day Jackson Liquor called me back into the storage room for some reason or another and I saw the shelf where boxes of candy bars were stacked. I saw there were also boxes of Topps baseball cards. From that day on Liam and I started buying our cards in bulk.

Rookies Dave Winfield; Ken Griffey, Sr.; and Bucky Dent. Veterans Pete Rose, Nolan Ryan. There was a crown on Hank Aaron's card because he was the "New All-Time Home Run King." Our jaws ached from chewing all those hard slabs of pink gum that came in every pack. We kept our cards in shoe boxes under our beds.

We quickly figured out that Topps rigged it so that you would have fifty of some outfielder no one had ever heard of, but maybe only one of Hank Aaron with his crown. We figured out how to make strategic trades, and I tricked Liam once or twice into giving me one rare card for, say, six cards that showed up again and again. Because he was five he was swayed by the sheer number I was offering—six for one!—but he quickly learned. Our solution was to whip up baseball card mania in other kids in the neighborhood, then make our sneaky trades before they, too, wised up.

Liam and I felt like the junior mayors of our neighborhood. We were resourceful. When we were low on cash we went door to door collecting glass bottles that we'd then take to Jackson Liquor for a refund. We also baked brownies and made lemonade and put them in our Radio Flyer and cruised around the neighborhood—an early mobile food cart.

We were busy expanding our empire—moving on from baseball cards to football cards and comic books—when Mom reappeared early one sunny morning. She stood in the living room with the tall Viking, whose name was Wolf.

"Get your brother and your stuff," she said.

My dad was at the restaurant. Sheri hung in the doorway of the kitchen. She'd been baking bread. Had she talked to my dad about this already? Was it okay with him if she just grabbed us and went? I never knew.

Liam didn't want to go. He hid under his bed and I had to pull him out by the ankles. Wolf had a car, and we climbed in the backseat. We sped out of town and headed east, through the scrubby hills of

Vacaville, which I'd heard from one of the kids in the neighborhood had a couple of prisons, and I started staring at the hitchhikers we passed by the side of the road, imagining they were escaped convicts. I felt a shiver of anticipation. What if Wolf picked one up? Would he sit in the backseat with Liam and me and tell us tales of his life of crime?

Liam wasn't quite so adaptable. He was emotional, even as a kindergartener. He liked things the way he liked them, and one of the things he wasn't so hot on was change. He stared out the window. Not happy.

In the front seat Wolf and our mom talked. Or rather Wolf lectured and our mom listened, like a teacher and a pupil. He talked about the lost continent of Lemuria under the Pacific Ocean, and how the earliest and most holy races of humanity once lived there, but now that their continent had sunk, they lived in Mount Shasta in a series of tunnels and caves.

We were also headed to Mount Shasta, it turned out, but not to join up with the Lemurians. Our mom turned around and said she and Wolf had seen all the billboards around Berkeley advertising a messenger of God named Clare Prophet speaking at Mount Shasta. She was the leader of a religion called the Summit Lighthouse and preached about having a one-on-one relationship with God, who you could talk to all the time, and he would hear you and answer you.

The road began to snake around a big lake and up into the mountains. The air was cold and piney, and I occupied myself watching for Mount Shasta with its crown of dirty white snow that would catch you by surprise, rising up, as you rounded the next corner. Just as it was getting dark we stopped at a campground crowded with RVs and mobile homes from all over the country. Wolf said they were pilgrims, just like him and our mom, there to hear Clare Prophet talk to God.

Wolf and Mom got out of the car. I climbed out, too. Liam lay down on the backseat. Wolf began to set up camp, which was our sleeping bags rolled out on the dirt beside the car, when a little hippie no taller than our mom trotted over waving his hands. He wore a denim shirt with a leather vest and wire-rimmed glasses. He said that before we got settled in we should know that if we were here to see Clare Prophet, the tickets were sixty bucks.

"More like Clare Profit!" said Mom.

She and Wolf didn't have the money for such a thing. Instead, we piled back in the car and followed the little hippie to a neighboring campground where his group, called the Rainbow Family, a bunch of gypsies and leather and jewelry makers, were having some sort of reunion. They had an extra teepee we could stay in—in my memory it was white with buffaloes painted around the bottom, but I suspect I am imagining that—and Liam smiled and allowed Mom to give him a kiss and a hug. Everything was good.

CHRIST FAMILY

WE SETTLED IN WITH the Rainbow Family. They were all about the stuff my mom was drawn to—peace, love, and mind-altering substances. I found some sweet cherry trees to climb and jump out of, and I tried to talk some of the other kids in the camp into chopping down one of them so I could ride it to the ground. But they had never heard of such a thing, and there were no handy machetes lying around anyway. Liam and I would try to catch minnows in a creek that ran behind the campground. They winked in the sun and darted away from us every time we plunged in our hands, the water so cold it made our bones ache. I managed to catch one once and popped it into my mouth, swallowing it whole. The minnow squirmed and tickled all the way to my stomach. Liam said I was a show-off.

Sometimes Mom and I made tortillas over the campfire and passed them out to the assembled gypsies and hippies, the self-styled fortune-tellers and spiritualists, and they ate them right up, even without the butter. At night, Liam and I sat cross-legged in the teepee with a flashlight and looked at our baseball cards, or played tag with some of the other kids in the camp. I was learning that as long as I had something to occupy myself, I could be happy and it didn't much matter where I was.

One day I realized that Wolf had left. The little hippie with the denim shirt had also gone off somewhere. My experience of grown-ups was that they appeared and disappeared at will. The concept of obligation, duty, or responsibility was foreign; I had no idea that your job or family might keep you tethered to one spot. Even when the Rainbow Family began to disperse and the gathering was over I wasn't too worried.

Then one day Mom took us aside and told us we were leaving with another Family, this one called the Christ Family. She explained that we were now to think of her as Jesus's sister. If God was her father, she said, and Jesus was his son, that meant she was his sister. Liam and I were too young to take this argument to its logical conclusion— that God was also our father, which meant we were Jesus's brothers and thus her brothers and not her sons.

She presented us each with a white robe that she'd hand-sewn from sheets. There was a hole in the top for our heads and it tied around our waist with a piece of rope.

We were supposed to wear these robes without shorts or pants or shoes, just as Christ did. I was no stranger to walking around in broad daylight with no clothes on—I'd toddled around the commune buck naked, and played in the waves on the beaches in Mexico scared the roosterfish was going to bite off my ding dong buck naked, and ran around buck naked in the jungles of Belize until the Mennonite children befriended me and then I had to put on pants—but the idea of wearing a white robe like an angel on Halloween with my skinny legs sticking out the bottom filled me with shame.

She put on her own robe, draped her army blanket around her

shoulders and built a fire. It was late morning, a strange time for a campfire. Liam and I watched as she threw in her blouses and skirts. Before she tossed in her fringed leather shoulder bag she pulled out a little change purse, withdrew some folded bills, and threw those on the fire. When the fire was roaring she tossed on our clothes, our sneakers. We watched the plastic parts melt. I grabbed Liam's hand and we stood there, not moving an inch.

"Christ wandered the world like the wind. He didn't need anything and neither do we. No killing, no sex, no materialism," she said.

She smiled and gave a little nod, then turned and started walking away from the fire, away from the teepee that had been our home, down the dirt path that led to the highway.

We followed.

OUR MOM believed she had found the truth about how to live. Walking. Owning no possessions. Traveling south as the weather got colder. Telling everyone we met that we were followers of Christ, and believed in no killing (peace between nations, vegetarianism), no sex (there were already enough humans on the planet, we were all brothers and sisters in the eyes of the Lord, and sex caused the separation of brothers), and no materialism. This last part needed no explanation. We were barefoot, and wore our blankets around our shoulders and carried our bedrolls.

We walked twenty, twenty-five miles a day, chanting "No sex, no killing, no materialism. No sex, no killing, no materialism. No sex, no killing, no materialism. No sex, no killing, no materialism."

Funny, one time I remember walking down the road and someone called out to us, "Then where did the kids come from?"

My mom didn't insist that Liam and I chant, but we had to keep up. At first, Liam and I would goof off, grab the other's rope belt and swing him around. Liam liked to pick up cigarette butts, and tried to smoke them. I thought it was nasty and could never bring myself to do it. After days and weeks of walking, we stopped messing around. We grew weary and sullen.

We slept under trees and freeway overpasses and in churches, if they let us. U-Haul trailers parked in rental lots were almost always unlocked. We would slide the door open and unroll our sleeping bags in there.

We foraged, subsisting on fruit and vegetables we found along the road in orchards and fields. My mom had dried some apples when we were living with the Rainbow Family—a trick she'd learned from Mad Bob—and she would dole these out from a pocket in her robe on days when there were no orchards or fields, no apples rotting on the ground or tomatoes hanging off an abandoned vine.

When our group reached a town or a city, first thing in the morning we'd go in search of a cup of coffee at a McDonald's or Denny's. We would get in line at the drive-through and one of the women would make the request at the window. She might say we were there to give the counter help a "heart check," as in, could they find it in their heart to give some traveling Christians a cup of coffee. Normally they said yes.

We'd wander into grocery stores and ask if we might have any produce they were about to throw out. Sometimes, we'd just go around back and search through the Dumpsters. Sometimes, if we really hit the jackpot, we would take our haul to a local church and beg to use their kitchen and make a big pot of stew and take it to the park, where we would dish it out in plastic bowls to the hobos, drunks, and hippies looking for a handout.

One day someone at one of the churches we stopped at offered to let us sleep at her house. We were somewhere in the Northwest. I remember thick forests of what appeared to be Christmas trees and heavy, pine-scented air. The woman lived in a big square house, with a wraparound porch and tall windows, and a grassy backyard where we were told we could sleep. She asked Liam and me whether we wanted to meet her sons. While the adults were setting up camp, she led us inside to where two boys about our age were sitting cross-legged in front of the living room TV watching a football game. They glanced up at us but didn't gawp—apparently they were used to their mother's generous ways—and we sat down and watched the rest of the game with them. Then their mother gave us a snack of potato chips and RC Cola. We went outside and they showed us their bikes before hopping on and riding off down Main Street, leaving Liam and me behind.

IN THE WIND

THE FOUNDER OF THE Christ Family was named Lightning Amen. I never laid eyes on him all the time we were in the wind, drifting from place to place. But from what I understood we were on our way to meet up with him. He was either Jesus's mouthpiece here on earth, or else Jesus himself. It was unclear which, and in any case I'd stopped paying attention. But every time someone we met along the way offered to take us home, I prayed to Lightning Amen that there would be some kids there watching a game on TV. But that never happened again.

Months passed. Walking the streets. Walking the highways. No sex, no killing, no materialism. Only taking a ride when somebody offered a ride. Only accepting food when somebody offered food. Otherwise, the Dumpsters behind Safeway, eating garbage.

We kept thinking something would change and Mom would go all Gitana on us and take off and we could find our way back to Berkeley. Once, in a town in Washington not far from the Canadian border, she made a call from a phone booth. Liam and I sat on the curb pulling the blistered skin from the bottoms of our feet. We had been told by one of the other women to leave the blisters alone, that if we tore them open our feet would get infected and then we would have to go to the doctor, where we would be given a shot. Privately, I had no fear of shots. But I imagined a kindly nurse who might give me a Tootsie Pop for enduring one.

Mom called the restaurant to assure our dad that we were okay. He told her that Luis had shown up looking for her, and was now in Vancouver, Canada, waiting for her. After she hung up the phone she cried a little bit.

"How did he know to come up here? Is it the Lord's will that I reconcile with Luis?" she asked us, as if we had any idea. "And stop picking your feet."

The phone booth was at the corner of a service station near the freeway on-ramp. Liam and I stood up and followed her as she crossed the street toward the northbound lane. Then she abruptly turned and headed toward southbound. She crossed the street again toward northbound. Liam and I stood on a weedy patch waiting for her to make up her mind. We looked around to see whether there were any cigarette butts. We despised Luis, but less than whatever it was we were doing now, marching all over the country in our dirty white robes. I figured if Mom and Luis hooked up again, we would at least be able to ride in a car somewhere.

Then she disappeared for a week. Did she meet up with Luis? We never knew. In my memory she left Liam and me sitting on the curb, in the care of a fellow Family member named Ed. He was a stranger to us; the only thing we knew about him was that he also walked at the back of the group because he had a clubfoot. He wore a torn T-shirt around his head like a turban, and even though he was one of the slowest members on account of his foot, he would yell at us all day long to keep up. Unlike our mom, he didn't mind Liam smoking the cigarette butts he found along the road. After we stopped for the night he calmed down a little and showed us how to whittle little pot pipes from scrap wood.

One night I saw an opportunity. I told Ed that my brother and I wanted to go home. "We miss our dad, we miss our friends." Liam figured out immediately that the goal was to lay it on thick and started to say we missed our bikes and skateboards. We were supposed to be against materialism, so I elbowed him to shut up. I asked Ed to call our dad for us, and he agreed, but I didn't know the phone number or even our address.

Sometime later our mom showed up at a church where we'd spent the night. We were somewhere desert-y then. Arizona maybe. Where the nights were black with stars and cold, but the heat of the day made you oh so thirsty, and the sun beat down on the top of your head.

"Look at the two of you. You need some new robes." She consulted with the group leader about stopping by a Laundromat so she could check to see whether there were any sheets left behind, or perhaps someone washing their clothes would donate one. I said no, that I didn't want a new robe, and neither did Liam. I remembered once, back at the commune, when my dad spanked me for something or other, and I asked him whether that felt good, spanking me like that, and he looked surprised that I'd spoken up, but also that he'd never spanked me again.

"We want to go home," I said. "We miss our friends. We miss school."

Maybe she prayed about it, maybe she consulted Lightning Amen, but a few days later she and my brother and I hopped a freight train headed home.

•   •   •

THE TRAIN station was a good four or five miles from Shattuck Avenue and our neighborhood. We arrived in late morning, and started walking. We passed through a neighborhood of big warehouses and car dealerships, and then we were near the university and there were bookstores and little clothing shops and cafés, and clusters of hippies sitting on the sidewalks strumming their guitars. Then we passed Ma Goodness, which wasn't open because it only opened for dinner; and Jackson Liquor; and I saw a few kids we knew riding their bikes. I grabbed Liam by his rope belt and pulled him into an alley behind a row of trash cans. I was not about to walk past kids I knew wearing that stupid white robe. But the alley was a dead end. There was no way to get home without walking down our street, past Jackson Liquor, past Greg Serber and a few other kids on their bikes, circled up and watching as we passed by in our white robes, up the front walk to our dad's house, our walk of shame.

FIVE BROTHERS

FIRST DAY HOME OUR dad called up LeConte Elementary School
and enrolled us there. Fresh start, he said. New life. Sheri had left,
gone off with another guy. He got up in the morning and stood on his
head for ten minutes in his bedroom, or out in the yard if the weather
was warm. Sometimes I would stand on my head with him. Then he
drove us to school, made sure we had lunch money. I was in fourth
grade, Liam in second. The school entrance had three sets of double
doors. We stood in front and waved until he drove off. We walked
through the middle door, down the long hallway, and out the back.

We must have gone to class, must have had spelling tests and math
homework. I must have made a California mission out of sugar cubes
for social studies, as all fourth graders were required to do, but I have
no memory of it. Dad insists, now, that he has fond memories of us
coming to the restaurant after school, before it opened for evening
service, to do our homework and have a snack, but that man did a lot
of drugs.

We had a pair of old skateboards hidden in some bushes nearby.
Not the sweet Banzai metal decks with Road Rider 4s our dad had
given us money for before we left, but a pair of used boards he'd

scrounged up for us. We'd roll up Telegraph Avenue, straight to the university, and that's where we got our education.

Once in a blue moon we'd run into him around town. Once, we rolled by a coffee shop and there he was, sitting in the window with his new girlfriend. Nabia was more voluptuous than his usual type. She had a mass of curly dark hair and a big white smile and the biggest boobs we'd ever seen. She wore Indian print skirts and lots of bracelets that jangled when she walked. We heard our dad call her voluptuous. One day when we were sitting around the house we saw him walking up holding hands with Nabia. We knew they'd head straight to the bedroom because that's what our dad always did with his girlfriends. We sped into the bedroom and belly crawled under his bed. We held our breaths and watched as ankles appeared and our dad's cotton pants collapsed around his feet. It took all the discipline we could muster not to giggle like maniacs when they started going at it.

Later that day, in the kitchen, I saw him and he saw me and our eyes locked and I never thought he could move so fast. His wooden chair fell back as he leaped to his feet. He was on us before we had a chance to escape, grabbed us by our collars, threw us in the back of his car, and sped back to school. Where he walked us right up to the front door.

"Get in there!"

We went inside. We still had our boards under our arms. We watched through the window as he marched back to his car, climbed in, and sped away. Then we went straight out the back.

On Berkeley's campus we patrolled the commons and dining halls, where students left food on their trays. We also found a vending machine that, if you kicked it right, would drop a bag of Fritos.

After we'd eaten, we cruised over to a popular snack shop with a wooden deck where students stopped between classes. There were gaps between the boards, so after the students cleared out, Liam and I would crawl under the deck and collect all the spare change. That would fund our activities for the day. If the pickings were slim, we would find an unoccupied corner on University Avenue and beg for money for a little bit. We played up our big dark eyes and sad T-shirts and frayed pant legs.

Then we went to Silver Ball Gardens, the pinball place. Having hammered pennies until they were roughly the size of quarters, we'd throw them into the machine and get a credit. Or we'd take a quarter, balance the rim on a piece of dental floss, feed it into the slot, wait a second, then pull it back out. We could play a video game for hours on one quarter. On a regular basis the manager caught us and kicked us out. We'd wait a week or two, then come back. We did this over and over again.

We found our way onto the roof of some building where we discovered a tidy little pot-growing operation going, maybe a dozen plants in white plastic buckets. We pulled off enough buds to fill our pockets. We'd take the pot home and dry it and roll up the fattest joints you've ever seen. The bigger the better, we thought. One day we'd had a huge haul and decided we wanted to roll the Biggest Joint in the World. It took six rolling papers and was a foot long, easy. We had a secret spot in the back side yard where we routinely did our sneaky things. We were standing there trying to figure out how to actually smoke it when our mom suddenly came around the corner. I tried to hide it behind my back.

"What do you have there?" she said.

"Well, it's grass," I said.

"From the yard?" she said.

"No, like weed."

"Let me see that."

I stood up and handed it to her with both hands. She lit it and took a hit.

"Hey, that isn't bad," she said.

Our dad signed us up for Little League, and baseball became our number one sport. We rode our bikes to practice after school. We discovered soccer, we discovered hockey. From sunup to sunset we were skating or bike riding or swiping pot or playing some team sport. I got my job back at Jackson Liquor and began rebuilding my baseball card collection. We were full-blown urban kids and we were happy.

Dad also paid me to do chores around the restaurant. He paid us a quarter to break down boxes. One time Liam put a box on his head. I tried to kung-fu kick it off and wound up giving him a black eye. He came back at me, determined to throw a punch, but I hugged him to me hard, said I was sorry sorry sorry, and he gave up.

That's how it was now between us. The days of treating him like an irritating tag-along baby were done. All those weeks of being in the wind with the Christ Family, trailing behind our mom barefoot in our white robes, had taught us to rely on each other. Liam was still sweet and sensitive. Even though he was almost as big as I was, I still protected him on the playground and on the baseball field.

One Saturday morning there was a moving truck on the next street over, and rumor was there were some new kids moving in, boys our age. That afternoon we saw them hanging around in the alley behind our house. They were bigger than Liam and me, with dark hair and pale skin. They looked more clean-cut, more put-together, like someone cared that their clothes matched and their T-shirts were clean. Liam and I were street monkeys, always in need of a haircut.

I cruised too close to the one who would turn out to be Alan, brushing his shoulder. He threw his arm out and it was on. I spun around and gave him a good shove. He staggered back but didn't fall down. I expected him to shove me back. That's how it usually went. Instead he came back with a closed fist and punched me in the nose.

Blood gushed from both nostrils, thick and salty. Liam dragged me off by my sleeve and we went home. Dad gave me a bag of frozen peas to put on my nose. In the way of these things, we all wound up becoming fast friends. Alan was eight months older than me, Bill was a year older than Liam. We played on the same baseball team and when I went to school, Alan was in my class.

I rushed to show them every cool thing, like how you could climb up onto Greg Serber's garage roof and jump into the barbecue pit and strip the plum tree and throw the fruit at cars. Alan was taller than all of us and skinny. We started calling him Sir Lankelot, conflating *lanky* with *Lancelot*. Entrepreneurial even then, he thought that instead of wasting the fruit we should find some boxes and take it to the weekend flea market down on Ashby Avenue. Liam was a big supporter of this scheme because it meant we also stopped mashing fruit in his pants.

Everything was more dangerous and more fun with Alan and Bill. From the first day we showed them the cutting-school trick—waving with an eager-to-get-to-class grin as we were dropped off, then going straight down the main hallway and out the back—they were in. Their parents weren't together either, so their mom, Nancy, dropped them off in the mornings. She had long thick brown hair and looked like a model from a magazine. She was from New York and used to hang out at a place called Andy Warhol's Factory, which meant nothing to us.

The next time we went to the university to steal some weed it was a full-on heist. Liam and I had confined our pot stealing to easy rooftops and whatever we could stuff in our pockets. Alan found a tall, six-story residence hall where we could climb a ladder from the street. He and Bill brought a Hefty garbage bag for each of us, and once we made it to the roof they started pulling up entire plants by the roots and tossing them in their bag. The bags were so heavy! We heaved them onto our shoulders like Santa, climbed back down holding on with one hand, and rode home with the bags on our handlebars.

Anyone reading this with children probably can't imagine how all this was allowed to go on. Didn't our parents say anything when we showed up with giant black garbage bags full of weed? Didn't they wonder where all the crap we stole came from? Or why we never seemed to have any homework?

You would think. But they didn't. Bill was more introspective than the rest of us. One time he said, "I think we're as free as the grown-ups, except they can drive cars." And that was the truth.

Alan and Bill and Liam and I spent every waking hour together. Alan usually came up with the complicated schemes and I was the one who always wanted to climb up something and jump off of it. Bill was the thoughtful one and Liam was the softhearted one. We skateboarded in the parking lot at the new Berkeley BART station but rode our BMX bikes everywhere else. Berkeley was a city of parks and we combed every inch to see what kind of mischief we could get into. If there was a hidden tunnel or a little known hill we found it. We raced our BMX bikes past dreamy hippies strolling along the footpaths, hooting ai yai yai yai! as we passed within inches of their elbows, competing to see who could cause the biggest freak-out.

Everything was a competition. In 1976 we were racing down a

steep street near Codornices Park. I was ahead and I was so stoked and I kept turning around and looking back to make sure they weren't gaining on me and suddenly there was a crunching sound and I flew off my bike and into the driver-side window of a car door someone had opened right into me. I wrecked the tire, bent the forks, but was otherwise unhurt. Alan and Bill screamed past me, laughing their heads off.

We found a rope one day and strung it across Shattuck Avenue, the busy main street with office buildings and shops that bisects the city. Cars would stop, and when the drivers got out to see what the hell was going on, we would drop the rope and run and hide in the bushes. When the rope disappeared one day we stood on a corner pretending to beat one another up, to see if we could con someone into stopping and break it up.

The four of us started hanging around with a guy named Kevin, who taught us how to steal. We were fascinated by him. He came from a "nice family" (a happily married mom and dad, a real house) and still he was the gnarliest thief we'd ever met. A day spent with Kevin was a day spent stealing whatever you could get your hands on. We had more stuff than we'd ever had in our lives, and we wanted for nothing, but we loved the rush of pulling it off. We started with grocery stores. We knew better than to walk in and walk out without buying something, so we always stood in the checkout line with something small, a candy bar or bottle of soda, while meanwhile one of us would have a paper kite stuck down our pant leg. We'd discovered baseball and were big fans of the Giants and the Oakland A's, and helped ourselves to batting gloves and fielder's mitts at the local sporting goods store.

A chain link fence surrounded the back of Safeway, but there was a six-inch gap at the bottom. We'd wait until dark, then creep over.

Alan and I would climb the fence, then pass cases of Dr Pepper, our favorite, through the gap at the bottom to Liam and Bill while Kevin went in search of a lone shopping cart. We filled up the cart. Then, worried that someone might think it odd that five boys were trundling down the street with a cart filled with cases of Dr Pepper, we stripped down to our shorts and hid our haul with our T-shirts. We divvied up the cases, tore them open, shook up the cans, and used them to hose each other down in an epic, hours-long soda pop fight.

One time, after we stole some walkie-talkies from a sporting goods store, either Alan or I came up with the idea of nestling one beneath the tomatoes in the little produce section at our neighborhood health food store. We hid, and when a shopper picked up a tomato to check for ripeness one of us would say, "Don't squeeze me!"

I always thought that of all of us Kevin would be the one to wind up in prison, but he grew up to become a pretty successful small business owner.

Our dad was the alpha dog of our little section of Berkeley, and Alan and Bill's mom was, without a doubt, the prettiest mom. I decided she should meet my dad so I invited her to come to the restaurant and try our dad's good vegetarian lasagna. I didn't think she would show up, but she did. Dad knew how to work what he called the McNamara charm. That same night I was in the kitchen at the restaurant doing the dishes, another job for which we could earn a quarter, I saw Nancy sitting on my dad's lap, whispering something in his ear. He was smiling. I had a pretty good idea what that meant.

Dad and Nancy moved in together. Then suddenly—or it seemed sudden to us, since my brother and I never really thought about marriage, or whether our parents were still married or divorced, or whether it mattered, since they both had so many other girlfriends, boyfriends, old ladies, main squeezes, and fellow travelers over the years—the most amazing thing happened: Dad married Nancy, and now Alan and Bill were our stepbrothers, and Nancy gave birth to another boy, Michael. This was the best thing that had ever happened to us.

UNCOOPERATIVE AND UNRULY

I WISH I COULD remember where our mom was all this time, but she came and went so often I lost track. This time when she reappeared we didn't raise an eyebrow. She moved into a little house two blocks away from us on Emerson Street and got a job cooking part-time at an Irish pub. We spent half the time at her house and half with Dad and Nancy and our brothers. She was unhappy with our dad's relationship with Nancy. She disapproved of their drug use. Secretly, I didn't like it much either. They had started fighting. However fierce their attraction was, they were bad for each other. For here's the thing about the McNamara men—we follow the lead of our women. If our ladies have the capacity to bring out our best selves, we are all for it. And if they hook into something chaotic and destructive in us, we're willing to go down that road too. Of course, I only learned this much later.

Anyway, we paid no attention to our mom's displeasure.

Alan was eleven and I was still ten. Bill was nine and Liam eight. One day we climbed up on the roof of Greg Serber's garage. From the back side of the garage there was a view into the backyard of Benet's house. He was a big, gap-toothed Jamaican we called Rastaman, for his waist-length dreadlocks. In the middle of his tiny yard there was a canopy bed like something you'd see in a girl's room, with white ruffles around the bottom and more ruffles around the canopy and gauzy white curtains. On the bed, in the middle of the afternoon, was Benet pumping away atop some girl; they were moaning and groaning.

One of us lifted himself up on his elbows to get a better view. Benet must have seen the movement out of the corner of his eye, because he stopped midstroke, pulled himself out of the girl and onto his feet, and shouted in his Jamaican accent, "You boys!"

We flattened ourselves on the roof. We were so busted. I remember feeling the gravel cutting into my cheeks. I wondered what our dad would do. Once, when we got caught stealing and the mini-mart called him, he came and got us but didn't say a word. Maybe this would be like that.

But I needn't have worried, because Benet said, "You boys, you want to see this? Then come on down and take a look. But make it quick."

We threw ourselves off the roof and into the sand barbecue pit, then rushed to the Serbers' back fence, scrambled over, and walked cautiously toward the foot of the canopy bed.

Who should be inside but Nabia, our dad's old girlfriend. She had her hippie skirt hitched to her waist. She smiled and said, "Do you want to have a look?" and then spread her legs.

Probably our jaws dropped.

I crept closer and . . . pointed.

Alan and Bill and Liam will never let me forget it.

Our world was rocked by this event. And between cutting school and stealing weed from the university rooftops and playing baseball and riding our bikes and skateboards, our lives were busy and full and just about perfect.

Then one day our mom said that we were moving to Florida. She had suddenly decided she didn't like the way our dad was raising us. She told us that living with him had made us uncooperative and unruly. We shook our heads solemnly, having no idea what she was talking about. It seemed that at our last baseball game, she'd heard two moms sitting behind her in the bleachers gossiping. When Liam was at bat, one of the moms said, "Oh that poor boy. His mother just ran off, and their father doesn't take care of them—there's a brother, too—and they just run wild."

Alan and Bill were frantic—how dare this lady they didn't even know come and break up the brothers!—but Liam and I had been down that road enough times to have a wait-and-see attitude. Greg Serber threw us a big party, and gave us each a brown lunch sack full of candy—Marathon bars and Now & Laters. Our mom had found a guy who was driving to Florida, maybe through the want ads. He showed up the next day and we loaded up the van. Alan and Bill stood on the curb. Maybe they cried a little. Nancy gave us both a big hug.

We drove off. The next day our mom decided she didn't trust him. When he stopped for gas, we grabbed our suitcases and ran. We went back to Berkeley and everything went back to normal.

She stayed in Berkeley. She worked various jobs. She went on and off welfare. We spent half the week at her house and half with our dad. There was something wrong with our brother Michael. They said he had a thing called yellow jaundice, and Nancy wouldn't let us hold him or touch him. She started losing her temper at us and not just at our dad.

Our mom started dating a musician named Darryl. We only met

him after they were married. He was a little black guy with a monster Afro and a love of fine clothes; Liam and I called him Mickey Mouse behind his back. Darryl was a nightclub singer and, according to our mom, interested in moving all of us to Hawai'i. And also, not coincidentally, paying for all of our airline tickets.

What I knew about Hawai'i I knew from watching *Wide World of Sports* at my friend Jesse Cortez's house. I looked up to Jesse. He had the perfect family, or so it seemed to me, and was a good skater. We would skate up in Codornices Park, then climb up to a spot where blackberries grew. We would bring them home to his mom and she would bake a blackberry pie. One time while we were waiting for the pie to cool, because the pie always had to cool, you could never cut right into it, there was a surfing contest called Pipeline Masters, held on the North Shore of O'ahu, and we sat and watched guys get barreled in these monstrous glistening waves, these moving mountains of turquoise water, fringe of white water decorating the top, and I'd never seen anything like it. Just watching it took my breath away, and I don't think Jesse and I ever did eat any pie that day.

Still, I was not interested in Hawai'i. Liam was not interested. We were urban California kids. We had our brothers Alan, Bill, and baby Michael; and our neighborhood friends; our roofs we liked to jump off of; our bikes and boards; our ramps and routes; our little jobs at Jackson Liquor and our dad's restaurant; our baseball teams. And now I'd also discovered hockey and soccer and there was not a moment in the day when we weren't running, riding, climbing, or kicking, and I didn't know what was in Hawai'i other than grass shacks and girls in hula skirts and a lot of water, and when I thought of water I thought of the ocean, the memory of the big silvery roosterfish with its ugly gaping mouth and evil black-spined fin. Our mom told us about surfing. She said we could try it once we were there, but the promise of that wasn't enough to change our minds.

I said I didn't want to go, wouldn't go. She couldn't make us, we said. We'd finally found a place we liked, a place we felt we belonged. Our dad wasn't for it. Nor were our friends or even some of the parents who found our antics amusing.

But she was still making plans. Now that she had someone to pay for the move I knew we would go. Greg Serber threw us another good-bye party and gave us each another bag of candy.

Our mom, giddy with the idea of starting a new life with a new family, got out her sewing machine. The last time she got the sewing bug it was white robes made from bedsheets, so I made myself scarce.

The morning of the day we left Berkeley, Liam and I found our new traveling clothes laid out on our beds. Matching orange bell-bottoms and big-collared white shirts, to be worn beneath matching orange velvet vests. It may have been 1978, but wearing this outfit felt almost as traumatizing as the white robes, especially since Mom and Darryl were dressed the same way.

Off we went to the airport. People stared at us as if we were famous, the Partridge Family traveling with some lesser-known member of the Jackson 5. Winging their way to Honolulu.

OUR SECOND or third summer in Hawai'i we went back to Berkeley for a visit. Our dad must have come up with the money for the airfare, but when we got there he didn't look like a man who could spring for a good meal, much less two round-trip tickets from Honolulu. He had sold the restaurant and grown a bushy beard and spent his days listening to mariachi music on a transistor radio he held close to his ear. He and Nancy were barely speaking. Alan and Bill said the high point of their lives was squabbling over who would get to clean their mom's marijuana, which they did using an album cover and the long side of the Zig-Zag rolling papers wrapper.

We brothers fell right back into our old routine as if no time had passed. We were all a little bit taller, and Liam's and my hair was lighter from living in the tropical sun. Our little brother Michael had recovered from his yellow jaundice with no ill effects. He was happy to allow us to coerce him to stand at the window of the apartment and yell down to the women passing by that he wanted to bone them.

A year after that one of our uncles, who was an insurance bigwig in New York, paid to fly Liam and me east for a family reunion. We spent two days with Alan and Bill, throwing crab apples at passing cars and putting Liam's hand in warm water while he was asleep to see if he would wet his pants (he did). Then we flew home to Hawai'i where we stayed for many years without going anywhere. Alan and Bill and Michael, our brothers, fell out of our lives.

CEMENT CITY

WE MOVED INTO A first-floor apartment in Cement City, so-called armpit of the North Shore. This side of Oʻahu is country. The south shore is town. Was in 1978, still is. Dole pineapple plantation and vast sugarcane fields on one side of Kamehameha Highway, postcard-perfect yellow-sand beaches on the other. Homes were little wooden ramshackle bungalows surrounded by plumeria and mango trees, probably with a few chickens pecking around. Maybe a little white picket fence. But Cement City was a clutch of decrepit stucco apartments considered low income, low rent. Military and plantation workers and their families lived there. It could have been a neighborhood in Florida or California.

Our apartment looked out onto the parking-lot Dumpsters. Liam and I shared a room. Mom and Darryl got to arguing before the boxes were unpacked. The walls were thin so we could hear them going at it in the living room. Mom wanted to keep moving, on to Kauaʻi where, she'd told us, one of those times she'd taken off, she'd lived in a cave in Ka-lalau near the Nā-pali coast. She hollered that Kauaʻi is paradise; Darryl hollered back, so is this. Darryl needed to be able to work. He needed to be close to town, as the locals called Honolulu, an hour's drive across the island, where he might find work as a singer. Darryl paid for our tickets and paid for our apartment and paid for our blue-box macaroni and cheese, our frozen peas and creamed corn and Frosted Flakes. So we stayed in Cement City.

MOM DIDN'T know she was sealing the fate of Liam and me when she dropped us in the red-hot center of world-class surfing. She may have mentioned it when she was trying to convince us to leave Berkeley, but we were basically clueless city boys. It was the Dogtown era so we thought of ourselves as Dogtown skaters, Northern California style. Even after having watched Pipeline Masters at my friend's house in Berkeley, I didn't put two and two together: I was now a short bike ride away from the greatest waves on earth, which also drew the greatest surfers. Forty premium breaks, most of them iconic. Hale-ʻiwa, Lani-ākea, Wai-mea, Log Cabins, Off the Wall, Pipeline, Pūpū-kea, Rocky Point, Sunset Beach, Velzyland. Every kind of epic wave pounds the North Shore in the winter, the product of swells that originate off the coasts of Russia, Japan, and Alaska and freight-train over the wild, open Pacific. Flawless barrels. Solid twenty-five-foot marching walls of water. Clean, but complex and tricky, depending on the direction of the wind and swell.

Every surfer on earth ready to go for it wound up here sooner or later, cashing in their savings or selling their cars to show up for the action every winter.

At first it was no different from Cazadero or Berkeley in California, or British Honduras, just someplace my mom had perched for the time being. There were long sidewalks in Cement City, but we'd left our skateboards in California. I wasn't even immediately taken with the ocean. I wish I could report I was a natural waterman, that I paddled out and the ghost of Duke Kahanamoku cast a spell on me, conveyed to me from beyond the grave that I'd found my place, my driving passion, the thing I was born to do. But I can't.

It was our first day in Hawai'i. We dropped our stuff in our bedroom in the apartment and Mom and Darryl took us to Wai-mea Bay to swim. The sand was coarse, not the soft, sugary stuff I'd heard about. It was sweltering and humid, no trade winds rustling the palm fronds. Thunderheads scudded across the horizon, some atypical storm out there somewhere responsible for waves that looked huge to me. Overhead, maybe six feet. Maybe smaller. Liam and I swam in the shore break. The waves weren't breaking, really, but instead powerful swells surged in and out. We sat on the hard sand, our backs to the ocean, pretending to be race car drivers, waiting for the water to lift us up and drop us farther up the shore, so fast. For hours the swells pounded us, flinging us up the steep beach, then sucking us back out. This was so much fun!

After a while, seasick from all the pounding, I spewed a fountain of Doritos and bananas. It had been my lunch, and now it was chum.

My freak-outs never fazed me much. Throwing up my first day in the water had no effect on my desire to try surfing. Our mom knew that two boys could not hope to make a life in Hawai'i without surfing. She managed to scrounge up a board for us. She may have paid ten bucks for it at a garage sale, but a few days after we settled into the apartment, she showed up with a beat-up 12' board that must have weighed fifty pounds. It took both of us to carry it to the beach.

The next day we went on a recon mission around the neighborhood, just like we had done in Berkeley. Our apartment was on Apuhihi Street, which ended two blocks away at Waialua Beach Road,

Highway 82. The highway ran along the cane fields, far as the eye could see. But on the other side there was a row of little houses, and we spied a kid about our age standing in the driveway of one of them. Butchy Boy Wong. He invited us to come in. Inside, hanging on the walls, was his father's collection of hand-painted kneeboards with airbrushed seascapes, a kaleidoscope of blues and greens and white. He asked us if we wanted to take the boards out, and was sure his dad would let us.

We carried the boards to a beach break in front of Hammerheads, near Waialua. It was mostly dry reef, but Butchy knew a little spot where we could catch a wave. It was bright and sunny, no thunderheads on the horizon. The light breeze was offshore and there were tiny white-water waves, one to two feet maybe, mushy and weak, but we happily paddled out, each on our own kneeboard. We windmilled our arms to turn ourselves back toward the beach and within a minute or two I felt the energy of the ocean beneath me, raising me up, and I paddled as fast as I could and once the wave had me, without thinking, I popped to my feet. It felt similar to skating, but mind-blowing because the wave was doing all the work; instead of wheels, water pushed me forward making a little *shhhhhhhh* sound. I rode that wave all the way in, until I could just step off onto the sand, and from that moment on I was consumed, obsessed. It was love. I was stoked. The lifelong magic spell had been cast. In that ten-second ride I'd found perfect joy, and the sanctuary I'd craved, without even knowing it.

Summer passed. I turned twelve. Darryl was gone most of the time. Said he was in a nightclub act in town with Don Ho's daughter. Then one day he was gone for good, leaving our mom for some other woman, and she fell into a depression. Our apartment had a swimming pool, and she would lie out beside it all day long in her bikini, shiny with tanning oil, smoking cigarettes and crying. Eventually, the money ran out and we went on welfare. Poverty-stricken in paradise. We started using powdered milk on our Frosted Flakes. We got one pair of shoes a year—not as bad as it sounds, actually, since island kids all wore slippers, rubber flip-flops—or else we just went barefoot.

One day a few weeks before school started, on a day of waist-high swells at Hale-ʻiwa, we sat in the lineup with a bunch of kids with good boards. I'm not sure how at age twelve I could tell they were so much superior, but I could. The shape, the colors, the stringer— the thin line of wood that runs down the middle to help the board hold its shape—the fin or fins underneath—all different from the McNamara brothers' crappy, dinged-up longboard that they had to share. Also, they were much shorter and quicker, and made so you could carve across the face of the wave.

The only way I could figure out how to get a short board was to make my own. Once I watched one of our neighbors fix his own board, and bummed some cloth and resin from him. That night I dragged my board from the porch into my bedroom and sawed out the middle third, glued it back together, wrapped some cloth around the seams, and sealed it with the resin.

"What's going on in here?" My mom stood at the door to my room. She'd heard the sawing and smelled the resin from the living room. I dusted off my thighs and stood up. The room was a disaster. Pearls of foam from the board's interior littered the shag carpet, and I'd tossed the discarded middle section onto my unmade bed.

She puffed on her cigarette and I showed her how I'd shaped the tail so that it angled toward the fin. Without knowing it I'd made myself a rudimentary stinger. Say what you will about our mom—and everyone who knows her and the way we were raised has already said it—but she didn't mind a bit that I was shaping my own surf-board in my bedroom. She said cool, nodded her head, and told me to put down some newspaper so I wouldn't ruin the shag carpet.

FATTIES

THERE WAS ONLY ONE other haole in my sixth-grade class at Waia-lua Elementary School, a girl named Tina. (Conveniently, we had a fierce crush on each other.) Every white kid who moves to Hawai'i has stories about getting pounded by the locals. In the cafeteria on the first day a Filipino kid took notice of me. He pushed me, hard enough to send me stumbling. I caught myself, pushed him back. I wasn't a big kid. Normal-size, maybe a little on the skinny side. But I'd been sparring with black kids and Mexican kids at Malcolm X and LeConte since I was six, so I knew my way around a fight. In Berkeley, when someone pushed you, it wasn't "let's see where this leads." It was game on. When the Filipino kid shoved me the second time I cracked him and took him down in about thirty seconds.

After the fight the tough local guys took notice and we decided to form a gang, identifiable by our (mostly) matching leather jackets. I have no recollection where my jacket came from, which suggests either I stole it or my mom bought it at the Salvation Army. For about seventy-two hours we were the coolest kids at Waialua Elementary. Then the principal got wind of it, called us into his office, and said there would be no gangs in his school. Then he took away all the jackets. Back to puny haole misfit status for me, but luckily I was easy-going and got along with people.

The setup at Waialua was such that Liam and I couldn't just walk in the front and out the back like we had in Berkeley. The school was smaller and Waialua was a tiny rural town. We couldn't just lose ourselves at a big university or out in the streets. The only real way to stay out of sight was to hide in the cane fields, which we did when we weren't sitting in class or surfing till dark.

After Darryl took off we moved to a falling-down house on Haole Camp Beach. It was a one-story Hicks Home, a type of predesigned house popular in Hawai'i back in the day, smaller than the apartment, surrounded by a chain link fence and shrubby overgrown koa trees. Mom rented rooms to help pay the bills. One of our roommates, Norman Winter, opened Jelly's Bookstore in town.

The beach could be reached through a sandy path that ran along the carport, but most of the time the water was choppy, the waves an oily, kelp-colored brown from runoff. The North Shore faces true north from the western tip of O'ahu at Ka'ena Point to Hale-'iwa, where it takes a turn and runs northwest. Haole Camp Beach was maybe a mile due west from Hale-'iwa. From there, on a good day, we could see the waves pumping as far up the coast as Lani-ākea and sometimes even Wai-mea.

One night after Mom had gone to bed and Norman was still working in town, I pinched her car keys from the kitchen counter and drove her old Plymouth Satellite around the neighborhood, looking for bikes that had been left unlocked. We needed bikes and we were pretty sure our mom didn't have the money to buy us any. We'd seen guys steal bikes in Berkeley and saw that it was easy to ride one while wheeling another alongside you.

The next night Liam and I snuck out and went back to where we'd spotted bikes, mostly propped up by the side of a house or left on a porch. We also snagged some pot plants. There was a huge market for marijuana on Oʻahu. The kids on the corner whose parents were known growers—you could see a forest of lush starter plants from the street—had the nicest bikes, the nicest clothes, the nicest boards we'd ever seen. We didn't touch their bikes, but we were inspired.

Our mistake was riding down the same street three times. The sky was black and starry, immense. Midnight in rural Hawaiʻi must be among the darkest on earth. The little houses were all dark. The only sound was the trade winds softly rattling through the palms. We supposed the overgrown mango trees and kaiwe shrubs and koa trees would help conceal us. Down the middle of the street we rode one bike and ponied another, holding it by the handlebars, then returned and grabbed two more. On the second run we also stopped along the way to stuff some pillowcases with pot from a number of backyard plots. By this time we knew what good pot was, and this was the best stinky skunk hash we'd ever smelled.

Our yard was overgrown so we stashed the bikes in some bushes, tiptoed inside to our room, threw ourselves on our beds, and fell asleep, exhausted.

The next morning we awoke to pounding on the front door. We thought nothing of it. Could have easily been Darryl back from town for good, or one of Mom's other boyfriends or friends.

Sound of the door opening, a deep voice identifying itself as a police officer. "Are your boys here?" I sprang to my feet. Liam was still asleep, his arm thrown over his eyes. Our closet door was open, the pillowcases of pot tossed in on top of the shoes. I slid the door shut, put my ear to the door to listen.

"They're not here. They slept at a friend's house last night," said Mom.

There was some back-and-forth. Some woman whose bike had been stolen recently saw us through her kitchen window. She wanted us investigated, thought we were possibly the ones who took her bike. I shook Liam awake just as our mom opened the door. She took a big sniff, smelled the skunk of North Shore weed.

"The cops are out there. I told them you weren't here."

"We didn't steal that lady's bike," I said.

"You've got bigger problems than the bikes, mister. Come on." On the Big Island weed was an accepted part of life, like milk in the fridge. Mom, dad, son, daughter all growing weed and smoking weed together. On O'ahu it wasn't like that. A lot of sneaking around was involved, a lot of avoiding the authorities.

We were still dressed in the clothes we'd come home in. She dragged us out into the living room. The cop was a big Hawaiian, his partner a small Filipino lady with a perfect bun at the back of her head. "Officer, I didn't realize they were here. They'll show you where the bikes are."

We went outside with the cops and showed them where we'd stashed the bikes. They were Stingrays, BMX bikes. Kids' bikes. The big Hawaiian cop asked us where the other bike was, the one that belonged to the woman who'd called them out.

"We didn't take it," I said again.

He sighed, traded a glance with his partner. I have no memory of what happened after that: what they did with the bikes, how they got them back to their rightful owners, or whether they took us in.

Whatever punishment we received, we were unrepentant. It took me a while still to figure out that what goes around comes around, and that it was a jerk move to steal other kids' bikes. We did learn one lesson—instead of relying on the weed of others, we should be growing our own. We dropped a few plants into the front yard along the property line we shared with our neighbor between a row of shrubby koa and huge monkeypod trees that had probably never been pruned. Our neighbor's name was Mike Saguirdo, and we cracked ourselves up just saying it aloud. Our budding plants grew happily, well hidden beneath their leafy crowns and gnarled branches.

It was probably pot-fueled logic that inspired the tree house. One of the monkeypod trees overlooking the neighbor's house had limbs perfect for supporting a tree house, so we built one over a long weekend when the waves were flat; no point in getting wet. From our perch in the tree house we could see into Mike's windows. The first time we saw him he was at the kitchen sink, popping open a beer. He looked up and we waved.

He was pissed. He said we were invading his privacy. He was kind of a psycho about it, as if he was doing something he shouldn't have over there—maybe he had his own illegal operation. Who knew? He told our mom to tell us to dismantle the tree house and she said she didn't see what harm it did. Didn't all boys build tree houses? Then he told us to take it down, and we just laughed our asses off—probably stoned—hopped on our bikes, and sped away.

Time passed. Mike never came over to complain again. We sat up in our tree house and smoked fatties and read surf mags. We fantasized what our next boards would be. A neighbor back in Cement City gave Liam his old board, and now we didn't have to share anymore. Every once in a while we peeked over the wall just to see what Mike was up to, but we never saw him.

Mom supported our mania for learning to surf. She took us to nearby Army Beach, so called because there was a military recreation center and the entrance to Dillingham Airfield was across the highway. It sat at the eastern end of Ka'ena Point State Park, pretty and nonthreatening with its azure water, part-sandy and part-rocky bottom, and curving yellow-sand beach. In the winter the swell might hit fifteen feet, too big for me at the time, but mostly it was chest to head high, three to five feet, perfect for enthusiastic learners. We developed our skills in the shore break in half-foot white water.

One day we came back after a day at Army Beach to see that Mike had gotten his revenge. He had cut down the overgrown koas between his house and ours. The only one still standing had our tree house in it. He had carefully trimmed the stumps level with the ground, and also cleared away all the branches and debris, leaving our fat, glossy marijuana plants, now several feet tall, in full view of the neighbors and every passerby. That night in the dark our mom told us she didn't want any more trouble with the police. She shone the flashlight while we pulled them up and threw them out.

LOST AT THREES

THE FIRST CHANCE WE got Liam and I joined a Little League team. Waialua Little League was the oldest league in Hawai'i, and every pro scout who came to Hawai'i came to Waialua to watch the best teams play. Mom was thrilled. Every kid on the island surfed and it kept us from getting in too much trouble, but there was no future in it. Professional baseball—now we're talking some real money.

Aware of the league's status, our coach was humorless and strict. His first rule, issued the first day of practice as we stood sweating our asses off in the midday tropical sun at Pu'uiki Park, was to give up surfing. I laughed out loud. There was no way. But Liam was a good player and a tough competitor. Now that we were getting older, our personalities were starting to emerge. It wasn't just Garrett-and-Liam, joined-at-the-hip McNamara boys. Liam was more emotional than I was; he took things to heart. He also knew he was a much better player than I was, and that made him try even harder.

As for me—I kept surfing and kept lying to our coach about surfing. Then one day during warm-ups, as we were running around the diamond, I saw him get into some altercation with his son, who was also on the team. Coach lost his temper and gave his own kid a hard cuff on the ear. I thought, *You know what? I am outta here.*

I quit that day.

Liam kept on for the next three or four years. I would ride by the field on my way to Hale-ʻiwa, board under my arm, and I'd see him doing push-ups, sweat running down his nose onto the dirt, or jogging around the field, or up at bat. He was the star of whatever team he was on, and also made the All-Stars every year. He was convinced he was destined for the pros. At home he'd taunt me mercilessly: "You're going to be a surf bum and I'm going to be a pro baseball player."

Meanwhile, I would hang out every day with some of the guys I knew from the lineup at Hale-ʻiwa, where I now surfed most days. This was a big step up for me. At Cement City and Army Beach, Liam and I rode the tiny white water that curled onto the beach. We would watch the guys paddle outside to the lineup and we thought they were crazy risk takers. Hale-ʻiwa broke anywhere from a fun three feet in the summer to a scary thirty feet during the winter. When it was pumping I stayed inside and rode the white water like usual, but when it was small I paddled out. This was the first time I paddled out to the lineup proper, like a real surfer.

The lineup was crowded, and dozens of amateur contests were and still are held there. Along with Pipeline and Sunset, it's one of three breaks that comprises the Triple Crown of Surfing, something I couldn't even imagine participating in then, but I was having fun, and that was enough for me. More than enough. I didn't need to have professional baseball dreams, or any dreams aside from getting to spend as much time in the water as I possibly could.

· · ·

MY BEST friend was named Kui Aki. He'd been surfing his whole life. He happened to live next door to Roy Patterson, who glassed surfboards in his backyard shop and who also rented rooms to make ends meet—everyone did on the North Shore, it seemed. We called Roy's one-story shack the Wave Cave. It was covered in vines, huge brown centipedes crawling around everywhere, a block away from the surfboard factory in Hale-'iwa town. He rented to some military guys and also to Ed Barbera, an awesome underground shaper who was generous enough to shape a blank for me for fifteen bucks. Roy glassed it for free; this was the first nice board I had. It was time to abandon, in the bushes for someone else to find, the Frankenstein stinger I'd cobbled together.

It was summer after eighth grade. I almost never went home and Mom never came looking for me. Instead, I pretty much lived at either Kui's house or the Wave Cave. We would hit Hale-'iwa in the morning for a session then spend the rest of the day smoking fatties.

One day a guy named Mike strode into the Wave Cave and started passing around opium-dipped Thai sticks. He'd just flown in from Thailand. Roy knew lots of different kinds of people, and on that day there were a bunch of military guys there. We lay around philoso-phizing about the injustice of being stuck on the North Shore when it was so flat that a wading pool had more waves. Someone heard Threes (so called because it was the third named break off Waikiki) was breaking. We thought about that for a while, and then someone, maybe Roy, decided we should go and check it out.

I piled into his truck with the military guys. For some reason Liam and Kui stayed behind. Should have clued me in to my mascot status, me in the bed of the truck with the boards. It's an hour's drive, longer in traffic, straight through the middle of the island, green hills choked with ferns so big you can't distinguish them from the rest of the forest at eighty miles an hour. I lay back, closed my eyes. Felt the vibration of the wheels on the road. The sense of going, my favorite thing.

It was my first time surfing in town. Since we'd moved to Oʻahu I'd only ever surfed the North Shore and this felt like city surfing. We had to drive around in search of a place to park. The crosswalk to the beach was crowded with tourists with boogie boards and towels flung around their necks and little children with plastic shovels and pails. Haole tourists, but also a lot of Japanese with their fancy sunglasses and cameras.

Threes was a break featured in the movie *The Endless Summer* that a lot of the older surfers, including Roy Patterson, liked to joke about. He said if it was a real surf movie it would be called *The Endless Winter*, because everyone knew there were no real waves in the summer. He meant on the North Shore. I laughed every time he said that.

We paddle out. Way out, farther than I'm used to. Threes was a right break—really fast and really steep. I am so high. Salt water on my skin. Sun on my back. New friends in the lineup beside me. So stoked to be on an adventure with the Wave Cavers.

I feel myself lifting, paddle like a maniac, and pop up quick to keep from pearling. I catch a medium-size right and I whiz off toward shore. I paddle back out, catch another one. This goes on for hours. Sun slides down the back of the sky. I catch more waves in a row than I ever have before.

One by one the guys all rode in. I didn't pay too much attention. The lineup was crowded, and it took me a while to realize none of my friends were in it with me. I sat on my board and searched the beach, but saw no one I recognized. I rode the next wave in on my belly. I walked one way up Waikiki Beach, then the other.

They were gone.

I'm calling it a combination of the Thai stick, the stoke of the session, and the unfamiliar surroundings, but I freaked out. How was I supposed to get back to the other side of the island? All I had on me were my trunks and surfboard. No shoes, no change, no nothing. The sun set. I wandered around Honolulu until I found a phone booth and tried to call my mom collect, but the operator wouldn't put the call through. I started to cry.

There my memory ends. I obviously got home somehow. My mom has no recollection of the event. I've decided that Roy, who I always looked up to as a father, drove around the corner in his truck just as I was losing my shit, leaned over and opened the passenger side door for me, then smiled and said climb in.

THE DREADED 7

FOR A WHILE I crashed with a guy named Jensen and his brother Striker, who glassed surfboards, and they hung out with Fielding Benson and Jasper Warren. Together we were the Six Feet and Under boys. Anything above that scared the crap out of us. Or me, anyway.

I had no illusions about going pro or being an especially hard-charging ripper. Most of the guys I was getting to know had learned to surf not long after they'd learned to walk. Jason Majors, Brock Little, Kolohe Blomfield—guys I came to know at school or in the lineup—surfed circles around me, but I didn't mind. If there was one thing I excelled at, it was the ability to be in the moment and have fun.

Hale-'iwa was my home, my break. It wasn't super gnarly by North Shore standards, a semi-monster that could pump during the winter and was, in the early eighties, the site of the final event for the pro tour's World Cup. At three to five feet it was still a wave with a little mercy and offered a little something for everyone—nice walls, lefts and rights, and a good barrel.

By the time I started ninth grade Sunset was where it was happening. It was known to be a complicated, frustrating, completely addicting break. Framed by the Sunset rip to the west side and the Backyards rip to the east, there were Backyards and Outside Backyards, the Point, North Reef, Middles, West Peak, Inside Bowl and Val's Reef, Second Reef and Outer Reef, an amusement park full of quick waves that change direction on a dime, pumping even when conditions are poor on the rest of the North Shore. Everyone was up at Sunset, all the good shapers and all the cool guys: Ronnie Burns, Mike and Derek Ho, and Jason Majors, among others.

At Hale-'iwa we were light-years behind, with our ten-foot 50-pound boards, riding straight in on the white water. This didn't prevent me from riding my bike the few short miles up Kam Highway to check out the killer waves at Sunset. One day on the beach I met a friend from school, Matt Esnard, there with his sister.

Michelle was my age, blond and tan, and pretty in that classic beach girl way. We became boyfriend and girlfriend defined as . . . we held hands. I don't think I ever kissed her, way too shy. Way too backward when it came to girls and socializing with girls and making the moves on girls and getting involved in that way. With girls you couldn't have a friendly little skirmish, then smoke a fatty and go surf. Which was pretty much the range of my social skills. Our relationship consisted of me riding or hitchhiking up to Sunset and sitting on the beach with her.

Maybe I felt like I needed to up my game to get things to move to the next level. One day I rode to Sunset with my board under my arm. I had no intention of surfing Sunset. It was summiting Everest, it was a walk on the moon. I pretty much thought the paddle out alone would kill me. And yet here I was. With my board, a little light-as-a-potato-chip board made for me by Dick "Rozo" Rosborough, 6'2" maybe, perfect for my daily sessions, but not for Sunset.

The wind was offshore, swell coming from the northwest. I guessed it was five feet Hawaiian, a little over shoulder-high, an eight-to-ten-foot face. Part of the surfer's credo is always to underestimate the size of the wave. To do this they rely on the Hawaiian style of calculation, which measures the back of the breaking wave. It's about half the size of the face, the part that the rest of the world is interested in.

I ignore Michelle as I gaze out at the waves, studying them like the pros did. The peaks are coming more from the west now. I think. The peaks are shifty, with crumbling wind-capped lips. I couldn't believe I was really going to do this. I was a Six Feet and Under boy. My heart is pounding in my head, the adrenaline already surging, and I hadn't even gotten wet.

As I paddle out I realize I'm in the so-called Dreaded 7 situation. There are two good waves at Sunset. The six-foot-and-under wave breaks nicely at the point. The eight-foot-and-above wave breaks outside and offers three different takeoff spots, at Middles, Inside Bowl, or West Peak. The Dreaded 7 breaks between the two zones and is frustrating even for hard-core Sunset lovers. The Dreaded 7 wave is neither here nor there, and leaves you pretty much screwed. That was why I was alone out there. Surfers who knew better were out at other breaks that day.

Michelle sits on the beach, watching.

I say a prayer, paddle into position. At Sunset you are always paddling into position. So much paddling at Sunset. The water is dark blue out here, and so fast. One swell rises up and another is right behind it. I let a few waves pass and decide I can't just float out here all day. I paddle until my triceps and shoulders burn. As I feel the wave lift me up I pop to my feet. The wave jacks beneath me and I find myself sliding sideways down the face. Over I go, shoulder hits first, heels in the air. The water mountain looms up behind me. It's roaring and rumbling, and over the falls I go. I am pounded. The wave is so fat, pressing me down. My ears fill with water. I tumble past a reef head, try to grab on; pointless. I climb my leash and pop up for a breath of air before the next pounding, enough time to vow never to do this again.

HURRICANE

DURING LIAM'S OFF-SEASON WE hung together like old times, surfing every day, riding up and down Kam Highway checking the waves. Liam wasn't about to give up on baseball anytime soon, but he never lost his stoke.

I was fifteen and he was thirteen. A few days before Thanksgiving, Liam, our friend Dennis, and I were walking down a cane field road near our mom's house in Waialua. It was harvest season, and they'd been burning some of the fields. When they burned the fields the air smelled like someone was making caramel, and tiny ribbons of ash fell from the sky. It was windy. Dark blue clouds were moving in from the north. We were in high spirits because we'd been let out of school early for some reason we seemed to have missed, most likely because of the pot cookies.

That day I'd been up since dark for an early morning surf session. I didn't have time for breakfast but smoked my usual fatty in the bushes, and went to class. Lunchtime comes and a kid in our grade is offering around a shoe box lined with tinfoil, filled with pot cookies. Chocolate chip with walnuts. We ate them with milk at lunch. So wholesome, milk and cookies. Two or three cookies in and I sort of forgot they were pot cookies and ate until I felt full.

I was in a special English class for slow readers with Mrs. Wee, last class of the day. I didn't mind English per se. It was my favorite class after agriculture and woodworking. But if Hale-'iwa was breaking I cut out a lot. So when I was there with my butt in the chair and my book open on my desk, Mrs. Wee was glad to see me. Maybe she thought she was getting someplace. She was patient with me, knew I didn't care too much about her special class and all her efforts, and yet she was still kind. So when she told me to turn to page—who am I kidding, I don't remember the page number or the book—when she told me to start reading from the top, I really wanted to make her happy. I wanted to show her that she wasn't completely wasting her time. I looked at the first word, saw it was *the*, and felt helpless in the face of it. The? The? The. The. The. What in the hell kind of a word was *the*? I squinted at the sentence, but no words came out. The chocolate chip and walnut pot cookies had broken my ability to talk.

Also in my class for slow readers was a budding young psycho who lived on my street. He made Liam and me look like Boy Scouts. He broke into cars, marched into people's houses and took their stuff, dealt in hard drugs. A troublemaker, not just a regular wild North Shore kid.

"He's stoned, he's stoned," said Budding Young Psycho.

"It's okay, Garrett. You don't have to read today," said Mrs. Wee.

I hung my head, curled into myself a little. I'd let her down, and here she was giving me the benefit of a doubt I didn't deserve.

• • •

ON THAT dark windy day we hurried through the cane fields toward Changes, a secret spot with an excellent left. The wind picked up. There was the loud applause of palm fronds and the leaves of all the tropical foliage. We grabbed our boards and took the sandy path between two hedges of koa to the beach. I led the way, then Dennis, then Liam. Just as we emerged from between the hedges, a gust of wind caught Dennis's board and spun him around in circles and straight into the bushes.

Now it's awesome. Now we are excited. The clouds on the horizon are dark and the sets are rolling in at a quick clip. The waves are not too big, not yet, and thanks to a heavy offshore wind that's forcing them to hold their shape, they are neat and perfect. That wind has got to be 20 miles an hour, 30 miles an hour, and as we sit on our boards I hear a strange sound, *wah wah wah*, and I wonder if maybe I'm just hearing things. It goes on, it gets a little louder. *Wah wah! Wah wah!*

"Hey!" I call to Liam. "Hear that?"

"What is it? Whales?" he calls back.

A swell passes under us. We look toward the beach and there's a little yellow figure jumping up and down waving its arms. Our mom. Screaming her head off. She's wearing her yellow raincoat. We take the next available wave in. She's never been a woman to get panic-stricken, especially when it came to our safety. But as we slide off our boards, she stands over us wagging her finger. "A hurricane's coming! Don't you know any better?"

We laughed our asses off as she chased us home. Hurricane Iwa made landfall just in time for Thanksgiving. Kaua'i suffered the worst of it. The storm surge flooded the streets around Waikiki. In our neighborhood on the North Shore, big branches were sheared off the trees and some trees were pulled straight out of the ground. When our gas main broke we were forced to run to a friend's house, where we stayed until it was fixed a week later. The TV news said that President Reagan had declared a state of emergency. We were outraged that we had to go back to school on Monday.

DA KARMA

WHEN I WAS GROWING up in the commune, people talked a lot about karma, the you-reap-what-you-sow kind of thing. Were they talking about real seeds or something else? It was one of those things adults went on about, like the war and the Man and the establishment and whose turn it was to clean the bathroom. It was a part of everyday life, but didn't have a thing to do with me.

But it did, eventually. During the winter of my sophomore year, when it seemed that every sketchy thing I did—jacking some guy's bike or stash, cheating on a test, lying to my mom—was answered almost immediately with some bad wipeout, some head-bashing trip over the falls. I was also practicing my aerials and turns and wound up with stitches from head to toe. Even on small days. Even on ho-hum, waist-high waves, I kept getting hurt.

My surfing was improving rapidly, probably because of my skateboarding. But in skating the ramp isn't a fast-moving mountain of water shifting and changing beneath you, chasing you. It took a while for me to automatically factor in the moving water mountain and to accurately read a wave, to know what it was going to do by how it felt as it began to rise up beneath my board. I knew where exactly to take off and where to make my bottom turn. At Hale-ʻiwa, my home break, I'd memorized where the submerged rocks were, and how the waves broke depending on what direction they were coming from and what direction the wind was blowing.

I'm saying I knew what I was doing, so I shouldn't have been racking up so many stupid injuries, and yet I was. One day at the end of the winter, I pulled into a barrel and the lip crashed on my front knee. Just before I tumbled off the board, I heard a loud pop. The knee swelled to as big as a grapefruit, so after a few days I went to the doctor. He took some X-rays, checked out my ligaments and tendons, and could find nothing wrong. I could walk on it, but the swelling refused to go down. He told me to come back in if I heard it pop again. I switched from surfing to boogie boarding. For no reason at all one day I was sliding off my board and it popped again. I didn't return to the doctor, but I stayed off the knee all summer. During that time I started thinking about why this was happening to me. I thought about how I was raised, recalled the principle of karma. Was I paying my karmic debt for all the bad things I'd done? Was it because I didn't care what kind of person I was?

Truth was, I did whatever I wanted when I wanted, without considering anyone else. Liam and I stole from people who didn't need what they had as much as we did, or so we imagined. But then I got to thinking that perhaps that was an asshole thing to do regardless, and that karma had employed the ocean to slap me around a little, show me that what goes around really does come around, just like my mom said.

I stopped stealing other guys' bikes and tools, stopped shoplifting, stopped trading pot for test answers, stopped pinching the stray twenty from my mom's purse. Stopped doing things I knew I could get away with, even though they were wrong.

It came down to this, I thought: *change your actions, change your life.*

A few months passed.

There's a community center in Hale-'iwa that used to show movies once in a while. One night they were showing a Christian surf movie, *Shout for Joy*, about how Ricky Irons won the US Invitational Surfing Championships, then found Jesus. Liam and I stopped by after a long session at Hale-'iwa. The waves that day had been only waist high, but there was a long sweeping left and Liam and I didn't get out much together. We had stayed until it got dark, practicing our cutbacks, dropping in on each other, messing around in a way you get away with on a small day when most of the guys we knew from the lineup couldn't be bothered to get wet.

It was crowded, maybe two hundred people sitting shoulder to shoulder on folding chairs in front of the portable movie screen. Before the movie, the organizer lady passed out raffle tickets. After the movie a winner would be chosen. Throughout the movie Liam pestered me. "Hey, wanna trade tickets? Let's trade tickets."

I said no way. One in three hundred chances of winning, but I knew I was going to win.

The movie ended. The audience applauded politely. Someone turned on the overhead lights. I was standing at the back in my surf shorts, no shirt, no slippers, hair on end. Suddenly the girl who pulled the winning ticket was reading off its number. The one I refused to trade with Liam for no good reason at all. I won!

The prize was choosing a brand-new board by one of a bunch of top North Shore shapers. I chose one by Bill Barnfield, who was shaping boards for all the big Sunset boys, with a Shaun Tomson airbrush.

Shaun was my out-of-the-water hero. He was one of the hard chargers who showed up on the North Shore from South Africa and Australia during the 1970s, and won the IPS World Championship in 1977. I wasn't necessarily a fan of the way he surfed Pipeline—even though a six-foot face was my limit, I had lofty opinions about the methods of the guys up at Pipe. But he also ran a surfing clothing company called Instinct. He was the only guy who would come to Hale-'iwa Beach. Most sponsors and promoters focused on the big, showy, pedigreed breaks farther east—Wai-mea, Pipeline, Sunset— and the big surf stars who surfed them. We were the undersung, mostly unrecognized mutts of the North Shore. But Tomson showed up on the beach with free stickers and free shorts and T-shirts. My mom was a single mom, raising two kids. It wasn't easy for us. We just barely got by. His generosity made a huge impact on me.

From a garage sale board to the board I sawed into thirds in my room to the $15 blank given to me by Roy Patterson to this.

It was the first great board I'd ever owned.

GUSTAVO THE PERUVIAN

JUST AS I WAS starting ninth grade, we moved from Waialua to Sunset into a four-bedroom apartment that cost my mom $400 a month. Sunset is due east on Kam Highway from Hale-'iwa. Calling it a highway makes it sound grander than it is. Really, it's just a two-lane road that threads through the tropical jungle. The Sunset Beach Store was the lone outpost when I was growing up there, a little side-of-the-road grocery with two gas pumps.

The houses along the highway to Sunset are hidden by the trees and brush, as is the ocean. On big days the sound of the waves thunders. Sometimes you can feel the steering wheel vibrating in your hands. You make a sudden left into the dirt parking lot and there's Sunset Beach. Postcard Hawai'i. Azure water, frothy waves breaking on the yellow beach, palm trees swaying in the breeze. Standing in the parking lot looking out to sea, you can look back up toward the direction you've just come and see Kammieland and Rocky Point. Straight out from the lot there's Sunset's Inside Bowl, more treacherous than the usual monster because it often doubles up on itself; two waves become one, creating twice as much energy and a terraced step in the middle of the face, producing either the barrel of your life or cause of death. On a good day, looking farther to the right, you see the middle peak connecting all the way through the inside bowl. There's an outer peak that is completely dependent on the direction of the swell. When the swell arrives from the west, it just breaks and crumbles all the way in. When the swell arrives from the north it rolls in big and nice, and there are three to four good takeoff zones. Same with a swell from the northwest. On a perfect north or northwest day the waves start from way outside and you take off, and you can just ride forever from the outer peak through the middle bowl to the inside bowl.

From the parking lot Sunset looks like a bunch of disorganized mush, challenging but not too heavy. If you walk up the beach to the right, to the point, you can see the waves as they roll in. From that angle the waves look massive, heavy, hellish. It looks like you'd have to have your head examined to paddle out in that shit.

WE NOW lived within walking distance from the most epic power breaks on the North Shore. Velzyland became my new Six Feet and Under spot. Named in the midfifties after surfboard manufacturer Dale Velzy, V-land was a wicked right at the northeastern end of the island. Turtle Bay is technically the last break on the North Shore, but it's not considered part of the North Shore's Seven Mile Miracle. V-land, my new home break, was the last stop.

Mom enrolled Liam, now in seventh grade, at Kahuku, the neighborhood combo middle school/high school, but I was still at Waialua, and I took the bus there in the mornings. I didn't mind, because it gave me a chance to check out all the breaks on my way. Liam and I didn't see each other at all now during the school day, but I started seeing him on the beach. He wasn't going to classes that I could tell.

His deep commitment to baseball and pursuing a pro ball career was a thing of the past. Suddenly, my little brother was hard-charging, getting his education at Rocky Point and Pipeline.

On the North Shore, when you're not surfing, the main activity is hanging out. Actually it's the only activity. No malls, movie theaters, bowling alleys; not too many bars, and anyway, drinking at a bar cost money. We didn't have any. We started hanging out with a big, charismatic, and largely insane Peruvian guy named Gustavo. He was tall, black-haired even after all the time he spent in the sun, loud and passionate and sweaty. He loved to surf and loved to talk about loving to surf. He was also one of the North Shore's most successful dealers of cocaine.

Like Roy Patterson, he was another father figure, and we loved him.

Unlike all the other surf houses I'd known up until then—broken-down couch with springs that poked you in the butt; coffee table littered with surf mags, surf wax, rolling papers, maybe a bong; dishes in the sink that never got done unless some irate girlfriend happened past and couldn't stand it another minute—Gustavo's place had matching furniture and a polished floor swept clear of sand, and every high-end cool board you could imagine. And the boards weren't just stacked on a weedy lawn or leaned up against whatever vertical surface available. They were hung on a rack in a spare room. He also had a pretty wife who was friendly and a gracious hostess. We'd never met anyone like them.

We smoked a lot of pot with Gustavo, but when it came to coke, he kept it away from Liam and me. He was old-school conservative that way. We were grommets, still, sixteen and fourteen, kids that, in his view, shouldn't be corrupted.

One nothing-special day we were sitting around and he said, "Punky One, let's me and you go check out the waves." He called me and Liam Little Punkies.

I wasn't an idiot. I knew that check out the waves meant getting wet. When Sunset was up—and we already knew it was up because we could hear the thundering waves through the open windows—no one went to check out the waves.

I remembered clearly the last time I was at Sunset. I was scared and horrified by my fear on my little Rozo potato-chip board. I closed my eyes and could still feel myself slipping sideways down the face, the pounding that followed. Black water, lungs close to bursting, no idea which way was up, fingers and toes, hand and feet abraded on the lava rocks, bloody nose. Also, the end of Michelle, whom I totally failed to impress.

I may have invented some homework I had to do. I may have cited a time my mom needed me home. Gustavo just laughed at my patently bogus lies. "You're coming out with me today, Punky One. It's time."

He disappeared into the room where he kept his boards and came out with a 7'10" Pat Rawson Sunset Point gun. Rawson was probably the best gun shaper in the world. Certainly on the North Shore. He'd made boards for the current crop of top pros—Michael Ho, Triple Crown champ; Tom Carroll, World Surf League Champ—and now Gustavo was placing a white one in my hands. I'd been surfing daily for five years by then. I was sixteen, maybe 5'5", 125 pounds.

I followed him out of his house and down the road. There was a lot of traffic on Kam Highway. We stood by the side of the road. I was so nervous that every organ in my body felt like it was working over-time. Heart banging in my ears, palms are sweating, and boy howdy do I have to take a shit.

We crossed over, walked between some parked cars, and nodded to some of the Sunset boys, me with the white Rawson gun under my arm, designed specifically for Gustavo, who had a hundred pounds on me. The board was so much longer, so much thicker than anything I would have ridden, had I been in a position to buy my own Rawson, which never looked possible in this lifetime.

The wind is stiff and offshore. Navigating this shore break can be treacherous. We paddle over the West Peak, which breaks between the Bowl and Sunset Point and is generally easier to navigate, but more powerful. The rocker on the Rawson is perfect and makes paddling instantly easier, but I chalk this up to the adrenaline dump that comes from being scared out of your mind. There is no gliding forward at Sunset, no taking a paddle break, and I am relieved to have to focus on getting out and into position. Gustavo is off to my left. We see a set streaming toward us and he says, "It's all you, Punky!" The blue peak is there, suddenly, rolling under me. Maybe it's ten feet Hawaiian, so about eighteen to twenty feet regular, double overhead plus. It feels huge. I feel like I'm in a cartoon or a fairy tale. I rocket down the face. Wind in my face, roar of water in my ears. It's the same flying feeling I got from riding the trees to the ground in Belize. Same as jumping off the roof into the sandy barbecue pit in Berkeley.

I am going faster than I'd ever gone and now with a blue monster chasing me. I streak across the face. The ride is so long. I hit a big chop. Boom boom. Bones getting rattled. Brains getting rattled. There was still more to go. More speed, more water, more glassy water beneath my board.

Gustavo, in his wisdom, had put me on a board that was meant for that wave. Paddling was so much easier, maneuvering into position so much easier. It was harder to make a late drop—something I didn't do very well at the time anyway—and you couldn't really carve, but it was perfect for speeding along, going farther, faster.

From that day on, I started living for big waves.

WE HUNG out throughout the winter, but in the summer Gustavo went back to Peru, or maybe Indonesia. His coke business was fully operational in the off-season. Guys who couldn't afford to get off the rock occupied themselves pining for winter and getting high. Gustavo had a partner who kept things up and running, and a couple of mules who ran product up from Peru. The mules were also photographers. In the early eighties it was easy to smuggle drugs onto Oʻahu in a camera case with a false bottom.

Everyone on the North Shore who could afford to go somewhere else in the summer did. It was murder being stuck there. The ocean became a lake, and Kam Highway was choked with intrepid families in their rental cars who'd driven up from town to the wild North Shore to "surf." Liam and I nurtured our pot crop and spent hours rock-jumping at Wai-mea. A black lava rock formation juts into the Bay. Towers, the highest point, is about thirty feet up. We'd spend all afternoon smoking fatties and seeing if we could "bomb" the cliff. Aim your cannonball just right and you can splash the rock, and the tourists crowded on the top, waiting to go next. It smacked your ass pretty hard, so we wore pants with a pair of shorts over them to minimize the bruising.

Once in a while the surf would be pumping in town. The south shore got all the swells in the summer, but they'd have to be big enough to be worth the gas money and the crowds. One day late in the season the swell was in the eight-to-ten-foot range, so I got in my Toyota Celica and sped off down Highway 99 toward Waikiki. The car was used, but new to me, a dark red two-door hatchback with big tires on the back and smaller ones on the front, funny car–style. Best times in that car were roaring down Kam Highway, full moon visible through the open sunroof, cassette blasting, headed toward a party where we'd heard there would be cute girls.

Ala Moana Bowls was breaking that day, but the lineup was packed. Paddling out, three guys on longboards dropped in on the same wave, and chain reaction wipeout followed. But then the swell started dying and I ran into a guy we knew from Hale-'iwa—I can't remember his name now, maybe it was Arty or Marty. He was only a little older than me.

Arty or Marty's girlfriend lived in one of the high-rises near the Honolulu Zoo and was throwing a party. She'd invited a bunch of her friends, he said, and I should come hang out.

I strapped my board to the roof of the Celica and followed him to the top of a nearby high-rise. The apartment belonged to his girl-friend's mom. It was small and basic, but with a view of the zoo park-ing lot, and a little sliver of Waikiki. I struck up a conversation with a girl with long brown hair and brown eyes who looked as if she had pity on me when I started trying to make my clumsy and completely humiliating moves. At sixteen, still awkward, still shy, I still couldn't figure out how to make time with girls. I invited her out to the bal-cony "to look at the view."

As we stepped outside there was the sound of brakes squealing and sheet metal crumbling. Down in the zoo parking lot a van had crashed into a barricade and flipped onto its side. The cops' cars chas-ing it screeched to a halt and they leaped out, just like on TV. It was the end of the day and the parking lot was half empty. Tourists and people with families stood and gawked.

"Holy shit holy shit, this is heavy!" I was more stoned than usual, most likely. It took me a minute to realize that the van wasn't just any old van, but the one I'd seen parked most days in Gustavo's driveway. And just as that dawned on me, and just as everyone else at the party squeezed onto the balcony, a big brown guy with black hair squeezed himself out of the passenger side window, clambered over the door, jumped down, and ran. The cops chased him out of the parking lot and onto the street. It was Gustavo.

Later I learned that Gus was picking up one of his photographer mules, who'd just arrived. Both of them went to jail, and the mule ratted out everyone else in the operation.

PIPE

THERE IS A PECKING order in the lineup, strictly enforced. At most of the heavy surf spots it's this: hard-charging Hawaiians; any other Hawaiians who happen to be out; the biggest, meanest haoles who live on the North Shore full-time; any other haoles who live on the North Shore full-time who happen to be out; respected and respectful big-wave surfers who arrive from the mainland for the winter contests; and up-and-coming local grommets.

Nowhere is this more true than at the Banzai Pipeline, where the main wave breaks pretty much right on the beach, which is always crowded during the winter with photographers, contest organizers, sponsors, spectators, tourists, and guys like me who thought maybe they were finally good enough to give it a try.

Pipe is the most deadly break in the world. People break their backs, their arms, their legs. People get cut up, sliced, wasted. It's claimed more lives and injuries than any other wave.

The famous main wave that you see in all the Banzai Pipeline pictures breaks in about six feet of water. Pipe looks perfect but it's far from it. The reef is a disorganized series of jagged flats. There are caves and pinnacles and coral heads that cause big boils that can bump you right off your board, ruining an otherwise perfectly positioned ride and throwing you onto a lava spire that can impale you like a medieval torture instrument. This is the First Reef break. First Reef is maybe seventy-five yards from shore and creates the average six-to-twelve-foot Pipeline wave that arrives on a westerly swell. The ocean rolls in, hits the reef, and jacks up into the classic, glassy tube. You need to take off with absolute conviction because the wall is almost vertical and you've got to set your edge hard and fast. The barrel is deep and perfect and, if surfed correctly, offers a ten-second ride that drops you off on the sand so you can step off your board like you're crossing the street. There are two other Pipeline reefs in deeper water. Bigger swells, in the twelve-foot range, break on Second Reef, maybe a hundred yards out from First Reef. Monster waves break on Third Reef, three hundred yards from shore, a few times a year. When the swell chugs in from the northwest, the regular barreling left becomes an A-frame, creating a ferocious right called Backdoor.

The wipeout here is serious business. Getting tossed off the wave and onto the reef is like falling off a tall building onto pavement. Liam, who would go on to suffer several gnarly injuries at Pipe, wore a helmet.

The first time I paddled out at Pipeline it was eight to twelve feet breaking on Second Reef. This wave is just a little slower, bigger than the main break, and doesn't require split-second decisions. Safer. I stood on the beach and timed the waves—three to five waves in each set, three to five sets rolling in every five to ten minutes—then walked east up the beach and paddled out through the channel.

The waves exploded to my left. I paddled hard, gulping air, felt myself getting sucked down toward the next break and the beach. Once I made it through the channel I turned and paddled laterally to the lineup. The serious enforcers were all there. Gerry Lopez, Mr. Pipeline himself; Derek and Michael Ho; Johnny Boy Gomes; Ronnie Burns. They eyed me as I paddled up, said howzit. I knew I could easily sit here for hours. These guys were in charge of doling out the waves. If a good wave came, they were taking it. You had to earn their respect. If you called a wave and they let you take it, you needed to go, commit with all your heart, or you'd never get another chance. If you put your head down and went without permission, or if you dropped in on the wrong person, you risked an open hand, a crack, or being sent to the beach. It could get as bad as "get on the next plane, haole." This was mostly for newcomers, but it could happen to anyone.

I sat with my legs dangling in the water, so clear I could see the reef twenty feet below. I watched as one perfect barreling wave after another jacked up on First Reef, closer to shore. For a half hour or so I watched guys take off. No one paid any attention to me.

Finally, a wave rolled in and I was closest to the peak. The next surfer was yards away from me and wouldn't have been able to make it. I was in the best position to drop in. The dog pack looked over at me. No one made a move. The swell rose up beneath me. It was going to be big. If I pulled back I would lose the respect of every North Shore charger in the lineup and might never get another chance. Didn't matter whether I ate it, didn't matter whether I was swept over the falls or ragdolled all the way to California.

I put my head down, stroked as hard as I could, took off in the perfect spot, pulled right in, all authority, all commitment, no butterflies, but I'm too deep in the barrel, and within seconds the wave gobbles me.

Under I go for a good pounding. Had the presence of mind to take a big breath. The wave roars by overhead. My sinuses filled with water.

I pull myself into a ball, bouncing along, the reef below me speeding by as I'm pulled along. I grab my leash, try to climb it. Dark blue water turned light blue and I could tell I was nearing the surface. I popped up, just as the lip of the next fifteen-footer crashed down on my head. But I was able to get a little breath, and at that moment I understood that if I could grab just a sip of air I didn't mind the pummeling, didn't mind the rolling around, didn't mind the thought of all that wave energy passing by overhead, didn't mind being held down.

I was stoked. Same as if I'd just ridden the wave of the day.

I popped up, made it back to the channel, and paddled back out to the pack. So fired up. Johnny Boy nodded as I passed by. He was my friend, but out here he'd bash in the head of anyone who took his wave. Someone, can't remember who, said, "Wow, that was heavy. Good try, just a little too deep." I could tell I'd gained a little respect. Another wave came my way. Dropped in, too deep again, gobbled up again, over the falls, held under, lungs bursting. I climbed my leash up to the surface, popped out.

Still stoked.

Third time's the charm. I drop in just as I had before. Didn't change a thing, but this time I was in the right spot and my edge held. One second, two seconds inside the glassy blue tunnel, the white water applause sound over my head. After three seconds, I shot through the perfect barrel and the wave closed out.

A Japanese photographer named Denjiro Sato was sitting on a board in the channel. He was known for his work with Gerry Lopez and had shot my very first surf-mag photo. I was standing on the beach at Velzyland late one gloomy afternoon and he came up to me and said he'd just gotten a new flash attachment for his camera, and would I help him test it out. The waves were little and mushy, the sky was getting darker, and it seemed pointless. But then a long dark ridge formed on the horizon, an unexpected swell rolling in. I paddled out, lined up, and took off into a shitty little barrel that in Denjiro's photo appears to be a glowing, magical blue room.

On this day, at Pipeline, Denjiro's shots of me were the best yet, and found their way into *Surfing*, one of the most respected magazines in the industry.

PART II

Sunset Beach, Hawai'i, 1989.
(*Tomomi Mizuguchi*)

GOING PRO

THE WILLIS BROTHERS BECAME our board sponsors. Michael and Milton were identical twins who shaped boards for all the Sunset hard chargers and were the first guys I knew who loved to surf Outer Reef Sunset, where the waves were monstrous. They had assembled the heaviest surf team around—Johnny Boy Gomes, Jason Majors, Titus Kinimaka, the Moepono Brothers, and others.

Liam was a B-lister but I may have been a C-lister, there only because I was Liam's brother. That's pretty much who I was known as, Liam McNamara's brother, and most people thought I was the younger one. He was gaining a reputation as a hard charger, ferocious in the lineup, never one to back down. He shot off his mouth. He didn't care about the pecking order. I was known as being unafraid of a bad wipeout, but more easygoing, less of a threat. Still, they gave me this 9′6″ single fin that doubled my confidence. I could catch any wave on that thing.

Michael Willis lived in a little house at Sunset Point with his wife, Bellina. Milton lived just up the hill. They would issue us proper invitations to come over for dinner—not just wait for us to show up whenever, as happened with most surf houses. They would wait for the team to arrive, then they would barbecue. Bellina also served healthy food, vegetables and salad and fruit, and I remember thinking for the first time that maybe if I ate more than just Hot Pockets and Frosted Flakes, I might be able to take my surfing to the next level.

We'd sit on a couch on their front porch and watch the sunset. Peter Davi would come by. He was a commercial fisherman in Monterey and saved all year so he could spend his winters surfing Pipeline. Bellina fed us, would take one hit off the joint going around, then disappear inside, where it always seemed as if she was working on something. Unlike most of the girls I knew, she was high-strung, a go-getter, an organizer. She made Michael and Milton's fledgling board-shaping business work. She did the billing and made sure they sponsored surfers who might actually have a future, not just any random guy who had the wave of the day at Sunset the day before. Stoned and full of good food, feet up on the railing, trade winds blowing, red sun dropping into the sea, it still registered to me—that being high and stoked all the time was not a business model.

This was on my mind at the time. Business. Earning a living. Doing something responsible and grown-up to bring in a steady income, a real paycheck with taxes taken out. I was a senior in high school and earning a few Cs, but mostly Ds and Fs. One day my counselor called me in to her office midway through the second semester and said that if I didn't bring those Fs up to Cs, I wouldn't graduate. This seemed like a viable idea and I was contemplating it. My birthday was in August and I was young for my grade anyway. If I flunked senior year and had to repeat, I'd be the same age as everyone else. That would give me a full year to figure out what I wanted to do. I continued to cut school. The Cs dropped to Ds.

For the first time in my life I felt fear.

The surfers that I hung with at school were Chris Roberson, Chris Angel, Kimo Ukauka, Sean Wingate, Jason Majors, Alan Moepono, Rainos Hayes, Kip Orian, and others. We never talked about the future. Brock Little was in my class. He came from California like Liam and me. He was a loner, known for surfing the biggest waves the North Shore had to offer without a thought. Once, when I was coming home on the bus, I remember seeing him riding Wai-mea on his red board. He was out there charging twenty-foot waves all by himself.

I'd developed my own obsession with the Bay. I surfed dawn patrol at Wai-mea most days, getting up in the dark, smoking a stomach-settling fatty, driving my Celica to the church parking lot across the highway, getting my board off my car, crosssing the highway, and wending my way through a narrow path cut through the thick bushes that lined the highway. I dug the neon colors of the time. Green wet-suit shorts or red wet-suit shorts and a tank top, usually a fluorescent green or hot pink. I'd stop in the bushes, wax my board, and smoke my fatty. Somebody might come along and I'd share some with him. Then we'd cross the sand and paddle straight out.

Meanwhile, Liam and I had gained another sponsor, Randy Rarick of Surfers Alliance. Randy was one of the few guys who'd made the successful transition from professional surfer to organizer and im-presario. He was a semifinalist in the 1970 World Surfing Champi-onship, and a big name in North Shore surfing in the late sixties and early seventies. He was an all-around good guy, honest and fair, and wore all the surfing-related hats there were to wear: surfer, board shaper, promoter, event organizer, world traveler.

It was fall 1984 and a year earlier Randy had created an event called the Triple Crown of Surfing. Not unlike the Triple Crown of horse racing, which features three grueling races only a few weeks apart, our Triple Crown rewarded the best surfer to dominate the North Shore's gnarly, expert breaks. The contests were Pipeline Masters (Pipeline), the World Cup (Sunset), and the Hawaiian Pro (Hale-ʻiwa).

Randy lived at Sunset and I practically lived in the Sunset lineup, surfing there up to four times a day. One day he paddled up to me and we started talking. He said Surfers Alliance wanted to sponsor me—back then that meant T-shirts and shorts—and that he wanted to put me in the Triple Crown.

Liam and I had been entering the odd contest here and there for a few years. Most of them were little local affairs, where you signed up at a wobbly card table set up on the beach and first prize was a gift certificate to a local surf shop. Nowadays even the beginning heats on the opening day of major events are streamed online. Towering bleachers wrapped in the giant banners of Billabong, Vans, Hurley, Volcom, all the big names, are erected in front of the break, and traffic on Kam Highway is at a dead standstill on contest day.

All the top Hawaiians were there: Tony Moniz, Hans Hedemann, Dane Kealoha, and contest winner Michael Ho. I was only seventeen and in awe of all the talent. There were six surfers in a heat, but Sunset is a huge playing field, so spread out you can easily find your own wave. Everyone else had so much more knowledge and experience competing than I did, but I was devoted to this break. I rarely surfed anywhere else those days. You could say I had the home court advantage. There are three takeoff spots—a little bit in, a little bit out, and a little bit north or west, and usually you have to hunt around for them.

Since I was here every day I knew exactly where they broke and could get there before anyone else.

I wasn't surfing very well that day, and after my heat I left the beach, convinced I wouldn't be moving forward. My mom was on the beach that day watching, and had to track me down at another break when my name was called to advance to the next round.

At the end of the contest I wound up placing in the money round. I won $250! Back then, you could stock up on free T-shirts and surf-boards, but the day you tucked cold hard prize money in the back pocket of your shorts you were considered a pro.

My career had found me. I was going to be a professional surfer. I started going to class, raised my grades to Bs and Cs, and graduated in June with the class of 1985.

MAKING THE MOST OF THE JAPANESE INVASION

IN 1983 THE NORTH Shore became popular with Japanese people. Kooks and hard chargers alike showed up all winter long. The local heavies were not amused. The North Shore was already overcrowded with South Africans and Australians and Californians. Now this?

Liam and I didn't see it that way. We'd spent most of our lives being inconvenienced by the crazy ideas of others. We'd learned to set aside our feelings and see how we could work the situation to our advantage, turning what most people would view as a negative into a positive. Also, we'd made friends with a guy named Nick Nozaki, who'd moved to the North Shore to surf years earlier. He mentored us a little, by which I mean he let us come to his house on the afternoons there were no waves teaching us how to speak Japanese.

So instead of sitting on our boards cussing at the dozens of Japanese guys who'd suddenly turned up in the lineup, we were friendly. Asked them their names and where they were from. Easy stuff. They taught us a bunch of dirty phrases that Nick never would. There are more ways to say *masturbating* in Japanese than you might think.

We met Ken and Eito in the lineup at Wai-mea. They were in their early twenties and had quit their jobs in Tokyo to move to Hawai'i to devote their lives to surfing. They were looking for a place to rent. Liam went right home after the sesh and told our mom. Within a few days Liam and I had moved into one bedroom, our mom had given up her bedroom for the foldout couch, and we had two new roommates whose rent completely covered ours.

We took Ken and Eito down to Hale-'iwa on a waist-high day to show them a wave they might find more fun, given their current abilities. We tried to explain about the etiquette, about how you couldn't just take any wave that looked good to you even if you were in position to do so, that you had to be given permission from the heavies already in the lineup. We tried to explain how dropping in on someone else's wave was a good way to get punched in the head, or chased down the beach and sent home. Who knew how much they understood, since a lot of this was sign language mixed with pidgin English and our rudimentary Japanese.

We stood on the beach on a cold spring day and a huge set rolled in. Waves so big you could feel it in your molars when they closed out. "Go in, go in!" they said. "No go, no go!" I said. They sprinted across the beach, threw their boards in the water, and were immediately pounded. They dragged themselves out of the water, laughing.

Out of gratitude for what they thought was our kindness (not realizing the McNamara brothers were experts at making the best of any situation) they liked to take us out to dinner in town, mostly to the restaurants in the big resorts, where they would buy us big steak dinners and blue cocktails with hunks of pineapple skewered on plastic swords. Then they would let us drive their rental car home.

There was a house up the street from our apartment where some other Japanese guys lived. We introduced them to Ken and Eito and they would all surf together. Before school Liam or I would check the surf report and advise them on the good spots for the day. We felt as if it was part of our duty as landlords to show them the ropes.

In Japan, word spread.

More surfers showed up, and a lot of them were hard chargers, already famous in Japan.

Takayuki Wakita showed up at Pipeline one winter. Liam knew him from Paskowitz Surf Camp, where "Takita" had worked a few years earlier. We learned through the coconut wireless that he was a hard charger at Shonan, ground zero for surfing in Japan, a long stretch of coast with a big variety of beach breaks, reef breaks, and river mouths, commuting distance from Tokyo. He was sixteen and had saved up money from a factory job to come and conquer Pipe.

He couldn't afford an air-conditioned rental car, and so got around on a yellow Stingray sized for a ten-year-old.

Wakita wasn't interested in any other break than Pipeline. He was mellow, laid-back, and polite, but determined to master that break. Like everyone else he had to earn his place in the lineup. Even then my brother had a compulsion for taking people under his wing. Liam invited Wakita to live with him and taught him everything he knew. He literally sat Wakita down and said, "Grasshopper, here are the rules. Number one: Always wear a helmet. Number two: Go deep and sit near me. Number three: Don't paddle out and say 'ho ho' or anything else. Number four: Last but not least, never, and I mean never, pull back."

The takeoff spot for Pipe is small, and the lineup crowded. One day Liam showed Wakita a spot that he preferred, a little deeper and off the peak. It's a gnarly little section of heavy wave between Backdoor and Off the Wall, thicker and even faster than Pipeline First Reef and Second Reef, a short perilous left in a choppy wave field of rights.

Wakita took to surfing that section day after day. It became known as Wakita's Bowl. If life was fair it would be known as Liam's Bowl.

Japanese photographers showed up along with the surfers. Denjiro Sato, who had documented my own first successful day at Pipeline, was one. Not long after that day he took Liam and me to California for a surfing/photo trip. Started at Ocean Beach near San Francisco and surfed all the way down to Swami's in San Diego.

Ken and Eito moved out, to be replaced by other Japanese surfers who'd heard back in Japan about Liam and me and our willingness to show them the ropes.

For the next decade or so, my mom rented her extra rooms to Japanese surfers and photographers. Another time and place, our mom might have taken up with one of them, and one day without warning disappear to start a commune in some rural wooded Japanese valley where she would come up with some harebrained scheme to make ends meet. But by the time we moved to Sunset, she'd changed. She told us the North Shore was a fishbowl, and she worked hard to mind her own business and not start any scandals. She said her goal was to disappear into the middle class. She was still blond and tan, still had her figure and could still turn heads. She loved to tell a story about a guy who worked at the front desk at Turtle Bay Resort who mentioned to one of her friends that he'd like to go out with her. The friend laughed and said, "Oh no, she's far too straight for you."

She'd also been hired to work for a local clothing designer who wanted Hawaiian flowers painted on things—skirts, coats, and bags. The designer had advertised in the newspaper for artists, and our mom got the job. She made good money, maybe $60 an hour. She went with the designer to craft fairs in Honolulu a couple of times a month, and she was happy. We all were.

NAMI OKI (SURF'S UP)

I TURNED EIGHTEEN IN August that year. My Triple Crown winnings were long gone. It was summer on the North Shore, ocean flat, tourists slowing down traffic on Kam Highway, staring out at the water hoping to see a monster wave rear up, justifying their drive across O'ahu. Liam and I were renting rooms to make ends meet. Bored by the lack of swell, we were puffing ten big fat joints a day. I would wake up, take a few first puffs from the roach from the night before, eat breakfast, then smoke a stomach settler. Called friends on the south shore to see if it was worth going there just to get wet. Either drive there or not. Smoked another one.

At night we partied with our Japanese friends. Best thing you could say about that hot boring summer was that every day I had a chance to practice my Japanese. At night we'd find our way to Michael Willis's little house at Sunset Beach, smoke some more, and feast on Bellina's brown rice and vegetables. One day Michael called our apartment and asked my mom to send me over, very official.

"Guess what?" he said as I walked through the front door. "We're sending you to Japan."

As he explained it, the Willis Brothers had entered a partnership with a Japanese wet-suit manufacturer, and they were looking for a surfer to represent the brand. His voice was extra pumped. I had the sense that he was prepared for a discussion, for me to say no way, North Shore has the best waves on earth, look at all the Japanese surfers who come here, why would I want to go there. But even at that age I was never one to turn down an opportunity. Three days later I was on the plane to Tokyo.

FOR THE next four years I spent my summers in Japan. I was off the rock! After the Willis Brothers set me up with Hotline Wetsuits, other companies asked to sign me. Peakaboo Clothing. Murasaki Sports.

The first few times I went to Japan I went alone. Liam was only fifteen, still in high school, still somewhat unfocused, torn between baseball and surfing, and had also fallen for a beautiful, high maintenance, slightly older woman (who would go on to become Miss Hawaii).

It was red carpet first class all the way. I'd never been treated this way in my life. I'd always been the barefoot kid in the raggedy surf shorts, the bicycle thief, the one flunking the class, the little stoner who didn't apply himself.

A first-class plane ticket would be Federal Expressed to me. At Tokyo Airport a driver would meet me holding a sign that said *McNamara*. Take me to the nice home of Shinzo Tanuma, Hotline's CEO. He lived in Shonan, on Sagami Bay. Shinzo introduced me to the Sakino brothers, two of Japan's top surfers at the time and they shared some of their favorite secret breaks with me and I fell in love with all of it. The country, the Japanese people—so humble, so hospitable—and working with Japanese companies that treated me with a level of respect I'd never known existed.

After I arrived I usually had a few photo shoots with my sponsors. It took me a bit to adjust to the idea of using my face to advertise a pair of shorts or a light beer or even a surfboard. I still thought great shots of me surfing that appeared in an article about surfing were more important to sponsors. At one point there was an ad campaign that featured my mug on huge billboards throughout the city. That was a trip.

I had a routine in Japan. I was determined to take this seriously and I did. First thing in the morning I'd get up and do my exercises. Sit-ups, push-ups, and a stretching program a trainer had devised for me. I'd call Mitsunobu, who lived nearby, and ask him to take me surfing.

About thirty-five miles west of Yokohama are the Sakawa River mouth breaks. Both a right and a left, a fast and hollow eight-footer on a good day, the southern swell usually generated by a typhoon in the Philippine Sea. The right-hander reminded me of Off the Wall back home, but the water was milky and thick, probably because of the sandy bottom. Not the sparkling aquamarine glass I was used to.

I was always the only gaijin, the only foreigner in the lineup. But Sakino was good friends with Eka, the gnarliest heavy who ruled the break, and no one bothered me. After our sesh we'd go back to Shinzo's house and his wife would cook us dinner and we wouldn't talk, not even to dissect the rides of the day. We would then go to his workshop, where they shaped boards and designed wet suits, and I would learn that part of the business.

Typically I'd then fly to Niijima, a forty-minute flight from Tokyo. One of seven in the Izu Islands group in the Philippine Sea, Niijima is a tropical vacation spot for harried Tokyoites. Emerald green jungles in the center, volcanic cliffs overlooking white-sand beaches on the perimeter. It reminded me of Kaua'i. Habushiura, a long straight beach on the east side of the island, was the site of all the surf contests. The bottom was sandy and regular, producing A-frame waves with regular rights and lefts so perfect they appeared to come off some swell-producing assembly line. I thought of the break at Habushi as a very Japanese wave, beautiful and polite.

Best and the worst times in Japan were had on Niijima. The guest houses were all on the same small street, and all the pros who'd shown up for the contest stayed there. Derek and Michael Ho and Ronnie Burns were regulars. We'd meet up at the same bar, a little place called the Red Velvet Bar that seated no more than ten of us. Brad Gerlach was there the first year. He'd just beat Tom Carroll in Australia's Stubbies World Pro and was riding high. Carroll was one of the greats, a powerful carver who'd won the ASP (Association of Surfing Professionals, now the World Surf League) title in 1983 and 1984 (and would be the first millionaire surfer, having signed a humongous deal with Quiksilver in 1989). If surfing didn't work out, Gerlach could have been a comedian. He would get going on a story and before you knew it you were watching a first rate stand-up act. Sometimes I'd paddle out the next morning, my sides would be sore, and I'd wonder *What the hell*, and then realize it was from laughing at Gerlach for hours the night before.

I never did well at Habushi, losing in the first or second heat. In my memory the waves were always too small for a contest, knee high or less. This can't be right, but the waves were definitely a lot smaller than ten feet, measured Hawaiian, and I just had no interest in seeing how many turns I could carve into a little rolling beach break.

Still, I hated not doing better, hated not winning. I kept my disappointment to myself. I knew I didn't come off as being competitive. My reputation at that time was as Liam's easygoing big brother.

As was my way, I made the best of it. Turned the negative into a positive—my best habit among all the obvious bad ones. Niijima was on the world pro tour circuit. Sitting in the lineup day after day with the top pros was like going to the Harvard of surfing. I spent my days watching them working, learning from them, refining my approach.

One guy I studied was Tom Curren. He had been one of the first surfers on my radar. Like the weather, like God looking down on me, the specter of Curren had been there since the beginning. He won his first junior contest in 1978, the year Liam and I arrived on the North Shore. In 1985 when I went pro, Curren was world champ. Every surfer coming up in the eighties tried to copy the Curren style. When he popped up he planted his feet and there they stayed for the duration of the ride. He'd drop down his back knee a little, and use his hips and knees to carve a flawless line across the face. One day, someday, I would surf like Tom Curren. That was my hope.

MY BROTHER BECOMES
THE ONE TO WATCH

A FEW WEEKS BEFORE I turned twenty-two I quit smoking pot for good. It was August and I was in Japan doing my thing. One day after lunch I smoked my usual after-lunch joint and took a little nap that turned out to be a long nap, until late in the day. So late in the day that by the time I struggled awake, splashed some water on my face, grabbed my board, and drove to the beach, all the photographers who normally covered the break had packed up their tripods and had left for the day. It was just a normal small-wave day but it hit me then that it could have been a huge day. I could have missed some important opportunities. It could have been a day when someone snapped a shot of me that made the cover of one of the surf mags, a career-making shot that would have satisfied my sponsors for the rest of the year, perhaps even attracted new sponsors, and there I'd been, nodding off like an eighth-grade stoner.

My career as a professional surfer relied on my being photographed. That was how the sponsor game was played. While it was good to win prestigious contests, good to score a high ASP ranking, it was even better to be photographed riding an epic wave. It was required. Cutting across the face of a deep blue monster, being spit out of a heavy aquamarine tube. Tiny man on a board, roaring giant white-lipped wave. Every year sponsors reviewed their allocation of sponsorship money. If you hadn't been photographed dropping in on a monster wave in South Africa or getting deeply barreled in Tahiti or even grabbing some air on a neat little wave in Huntington Beach, there was always someone else who had.

Recently, that someone else was my brother Liam.

When I'd returned from my first trip to Japan in '85 I'd sat him down and said, "You have got to get your shit together. There are some major opportunities here!" He was sixteen and more or less fully on his own. Up and down the North Shore were friends and associates whose couches he crashed on. Baseball was a distant memory. Surfing he loved, but mostly he preferred partying. While I was gone he'd wandered down a road well-traveled by a lot of surfers. Cocaine was huge on the North Shore, and he'd started dabbling (thankfully something he gave up long ago).

Liam could be bullheaded. He didn't like to be told what to do. But on the day I sat him down he heard me. Since we were little, he's been quick to assess certain situations, whereas things dawn on me gradually. I told him about my trip, about the first-class plane tickets, the nice hotels, the days spent surfing and partying with the world's top pros, the free boards and wet suits and wax and hats and T-shirts and shorts, the accolades, the sense of purpose and fulfillment, the way you could make an actual living surfing. Something lit a fire under him. Next time Pipeline was pumping he was one of the first ones of the day to paddle out.

All of a sudden he was on it. He focused on surfing to the exclusion of everything else. He was done goofing off in the comparatively low-key breaks down the coast at Chun's Reef, Lani's, and Hale-'iwa, where we'd learned to surf years earlier. Where the lineup was more easygoing. He would only surf the breaks that attracted the top photographers. Go big or go home—that was Liam.

So, Pipeline, Rocky Point, and Sunset. Movie-star waves. He was out there every day. Maybe it was because he'd been training to be a teenage drug kingpin, but the gnarly Hawaiians who ruled those lineups didn't faze him. If there was one lesson we'd taken away from our childhood it was that no one was going to give you anything, and if you wanted something, you had to step up and work for it or do without. Had Liam waited for one of the locals to pass up a wave of distinction he'd probably still be sitting there.

Instead, if he felt it was time he had a turn, he took off on the best waves, usually the third wave of a set, and always meant for the inner circle of locals. He would paddle behind the heavies, and drop in on anyone else, never caring about the cost.

I think part of the reason Liam felt confident in stepping up his game was that over time we'd become friends with most of the heavies in the lineup. The Moepono brothers ruled V-land. Junior Boy weighed over three hundred pounds and surfed on the biggest board you've ever seen. Somehow he could still fit himself inside a tube, and his turns and cutback were WTF crazy good. When Junior hit the lip he would throw off so much spray you felt like you were being hit with a fire hose. He had three equally massive brothers. Alika, who weighed in at only 275, was a sweetheart, a gentle giant. Elliot was more outspoken and in your face. Alan was a year younger than I was and my best friend for a while.

Once Junior was angry at Alan for something and pulled his big hand back to slap him, but Alan ducked. I took that openhanded smack in the side of the head. Three hundred plus pounds of Hawaiian god chief of V-land power—it was a miracle I didn't walk away with a broken jaw.

Perry Dane was a haole local who may have had a squirt of Hawaiian blood. He was all about crowd control, would let you surf or not depending on his mood. You piss him off, he'd send you back to the beach.

The east side North Shore heavies were bigger, meaner, and more insular than any other locals at any other break on the island. They were mostly Hawaiians and Samoans, and if you were white, or not from the North Shore and at least on nodding terms with the regulars, every time you paddled out you risked getting slapped or sent in to the beach or both.

Maybe it was because Liam and I had had to figure out how to get along with a lot of different kinds of people from the time we were little—the people who came and went at the commune, our dad's friends and girlfriends and restaurant workers in Berkeley, Mad Bob and Luis and the various lunatics from the Christ Family—but even though we were haoles, we were accepted. We were V-land boys, the smallest white boys in the lineup, scrappy and willing to work for our waves. We were proud of our spot and our friends.

ONE DAY at Pipe the swells were pumping from the northwest. Three to four feet Hawaiian, a few feet overhead. A good time, but not the huge waves I'd come to prefer. Wind offshore, respectable A-frame breaking at Backdoor. When this wave is breaking two surfers can take off at the same time: one takes the left, which is Pipeline proper; one takes the right, which is Backdoor. It's the perfect wave for a regular-foot/goofy-foot brother duo. Regular-foot big brother Garrett takes off on the room-to-roam Backdoor right, goofy-foot little brother Liam takes off left and squeezes himself into barreling Pipeline left. Everybody wins. We'd done it so often our mom had painted a picture of that very scenario.

Liam and I paddled out together. We sat on our boards a few yards from each other. Farther down the lineup the usual suspects scowled in our direction. A few grunts and nods. Liam had taken to wearing a white helmet with a dark retractable visor. This was the late eighties, early nineties. Not every kid rolling down a city sidewalk on a bike or board was helmeted, wrist-braced, knee-padded. It was smart to wear a helmet at Pipeline, but no one else did. The visor made it so you couldn't see Liam's eyes, couldn't read him at all. The first wave of the next set gathered itself up and we let it pass, floated over the top a second before it broke at the peak. Second wave, same thing. Third wave came, bigger than the other two, but breaking a way that looked as if my right might be a longer ride, with Liam's left closing out after only a few seconds.

I nodded at him, angled my board right, and started paddling. Popped up and made my drop. Out of the corner of my eye, I saw a flash of red amid the steep curling turquoise face. At the last minute, he'd decided to go right after all.

My brother. Catching all the best waves.

No one charged harder than Liam. He wasn't a stylist, didn't have the sweeping elegance of Dane Kealoha or Tom Curren or the up-and-coming Sunny Garcia. Liam always looked as if he was working hard, but he attacked the wave with a seldom seen ferociousness, and people started paying attention.

In a matter of months he was getting deeply barreled on First Reef

Pipeline. First Reef Pipe jacks up the instant it hits the reef, so you've got maybe a second to figure out your strategy. Draw too high a line across the face and you'll get pulled over the falls. Too low a line and the lip will smash you onto the reef as it folds. Liam was able to carve the perfect line, as though he'd been born to it. Over at Rocky Point, he was working on aerial moves, practicing his ollies on a spacious left that rolled in during a west swell. He was doing it all, and I could only watch in amazement.

THE THIRD summer I went to Japan, in 1987, Liam came with me. We stayed with Shinzo Tonuma and surfed with the Sakino brothers at Sagawa River Mouth, my usual routine. We flew to Niijima, drank with traveling pros at the Red Velvet Bar. We surfed in some contests. Liam rocketed past me, a fire in him that wasn't in me. Peakaboo, my best sponsor, signed him before the trip was over.

"Five K a month, brah. Not bad. Just like you said," said Liam on the long flight home.

I didn't say anything. Peakaboo was paying me five hundred a month. I've never been much of a worrier, but since I'd injured my back I'd become one. Was my own brother going to snap up all my sponsors? What would that mean for me?

SOMETHING BAD HAPPENS

LIAM AND I DIDN'T have much to do with each other after that.

I didn't care to paddle out when Liam was in the water. He thought nothing about taking all the good waves when we were out together, and I wasn't about to get into it with him. Knowing when something was worth the fight was, for all my failings, something I knew in my bones. There was nothing to be gained battling him head to head. Even though many of my sponsors were signing him to bigger, better deals, I wasn't into aerial moves or obsessed with getting barreled at ten-foot Pipeline, his specialty. He continued to focus on Pipe and Rockies; I surfed Velzyland, Backdoor, Wai-mea, and Sunset. There was plenty of ocean for both of us.

I dreamed of monster waves, the moving mountains of water that showed up a few times every winter at Wai-mea, and at Avalanche, an outer break southwest of Hale-'iwa. On the other side of the lineup the reef drops off into the abyss. When a huge swell hits, Avalanche morphs into a deep blue peak, black diamond run–steep. Dropping in feels like jumping off a cliff.

I just let it go. I didn't know what I was doing, didn't have a scheme or a plan or a sense of what I might do in order to woo back all those sponsors. I just got up every day and paddled out and hoped that in time something would happen.

I sought out less crowded lineups at Sunset and Lani's. My old stomping ground, Hale-'iwa, where it was mellower, not too much gnarly energy, just Hale-'iwa boys having fun. Kerry Terukina, Marvin Foster, and Brock Little, my former high-school classmate. Brock was doing the stuff I dreamed of—in 1990 he came in second in the Eddie, getting barreled on a big, hollow twenty-footer.

The Eddie is officially the Quiksilver in Memory of Eddie Aikau. The event is celebrated internationally, and people travel from all over the world for the opening ceremony. A pure-blooded Hawaiian, Eddie was one of the most beloved surfers who ever called the Bay his home break, and also Wai-mea's first official lifeguard. During his ten-year-long watch Eddie saved hundreds of people and never lost anyone, even during the most massive, churning storms, when people who should have known better should have stayed on the beach. He is said to have surfed every major Wai-mea swell during those years. In 1978 he volunteered to crew on *Hōkūle'a*, the double-hulled voyaging canoe bound for Tahiti by way of the ancient Polynesian route. A dozen miles south of Moloka'i, in rough seas, the canoe started taking on water. Eddie leaped on his surfboard as the canoe was capsizing and paddled in the direction of Lā-na'i, in search of help. Everyone was eventually rescued, but Eddie was never found.

The first Eddie was held in 1984 at Sunset on a nothing-special eight-foot day. In 1985 the organizers moved it to Wai-mea, Eddie's home turf, and decided the one-day tournament would only go on if the waves were the size that met with Eddie's liking—minimum twenty feet Hawaiian, which means breaking wave faces of forty to fifty feet. Revered uncle of North Shore surfing George Downing calls the contest. Or, he says, he listens to the surf and the Bay calls the day. Every year the three-month holding period begins on December 1. If the twenty-footers fail to materialize before the end of February, the contest is scratched and it's better luck next year. The twenty-foot wave is a strict requirement, so strict that the Eddie has been held only nine times in thirty-one years.

The participants are chosen by a panel of experts—big-wave surfers, photographers, journalists, industry reps. Recommendations are forwarded to Quiksilver and the Aikau family, who make the final decision about who paddles out. Just to be invited is an honor and a dream come true.

I was standing in line at Foodland on a January day in 1990 and heard the checker tell the person in line in front of me that the Eddie was on. Foodland is the only grocery store on the North Shore, not far from Shark's Cove where Pūpū-kea Road meets Kam Highway. Every surfer who winds up on the North Shore, which is to say pretty much every big-name surfer in the world, finds himself or herself buying some orange juice or tortilla chips at Foodland now and then. The checkout clerks hear it all and they know everything. I left my groceries in the cart, jumped in a new-to-me VW Rabbit with a sunroof and crap transmission, sped down Kam Highway, parked on the beachside beneath the kiawe trees, and ran down to the sand. I could feel the crash of the waves in my teeth, in my chest. Surf was indeed up.

The contest is invitation only. Some of the Hale-'iwa boys had been invited, including Brock. The swells were huge, but the offshore wind was stiff and the waves were holding up nicely and marching in so fast, the way Hawaiian waves do.

The lineup was crowded. Regular contests are organized into heats where two or four—six at the most—surfers ride for a set length of time, usually an hour for big-wave contests. The judges take your top three rides from your two heats. You might get all three waves in one heat, or two in one heat and one in the other. Doesn't matter. There were thirty-three surfers in the 1990 Eddie, and since it was and is a one day tournament, they surfed their heats eleven guys at a time.

I arrived in time to catch Brock's second heat. First wave was a slab, thick, and rolling in so fast. Fifty-foot face easy. He took off with confidence, the wave rising steep behind him. So much moving water, threads of whitewash sucked up the face, and then the heavy lip beginning to curl. His line looked good until he hit some serious chop, was airborne, and somersaulted all the way down. The crowd on the beach went "Ahhhohhhhhhh!" and the wave closed out on him.

He popped up, retrieved his board, and paddled back out. Next wave. Same slab, same inconceivable amount of heavy open swell rearing up as it entered the Bay. Maybe he thought he took the wrong line before, because he took off deep, and lo and behold the wave pitched up and started to curl top to bottom. He shot into the tube and I couldn't believe what I was seeing. No one got barreled at Wai-mea. Pipeline, yes. Wai-mea, no. The wave wasn't built for it. The human body wasn't built for it. If you misread your line or couldn't keep your rail dug into the face and wiped out and got smashed by the lip, you were just asking to be paralyzed for life. That was the thinking.

Yet here was Brock shooting out of the barrel, foam ball spitting behind him. He tried to turn, but his gun couldn't hold the edge and he fell off. It didn't matter. Everyone on the beach was hollering and applauding, judges included.

•　•　•

I'M NOT envious by nature but on that day I sure did envy Brock Little. I became obsessed. Getting barreled on a twenty-foot wave was all I thought about, from the moment I woke up in the morning until I closed my eyes at night. I could imagine the glassy tunnel spinning round me, so hollow, so roomy I could stand up. Fingertips running along the smooth face. Long seconds of silence. Teardrop of pale sky at the end. Big white foam ball chasing me until I popped out, a half second before the wave closed and was gone. I no longer cared about sponsors and contests and photographs and whether Liam was viewed as the hard charger and I was viewed as the brother of the hard charger. This was all I wanted, my lone desire.

The week before Brock got barreled at the Eddie, I'd cracked my rib at Wai-mea. It's why I'd been lollygagging at Foodland in the middle of the day instead of in the water. I was trying to be smart, trying to take it easy and heal up.

It was easy to control the impulse to paddle out when the waves were little. A week later, on January 28, 1990, Super Bowl Sunday, another low-pressure system in the Pacific sent giant waves rolling into the Bay, set after set. I squeezed into my two wet suits, tossed my board into the Rabbit, and drove to Wai-mea.

I'm stoked. I've taken time off to heal and rest, spent three four five days out of the water. What more can anyone expect? I'm thinking I'm kind of invincible. Other guys paddle out injured; why not me? Liam's not the only hard charger. I wasn't showing enough respect for the ocean and her power, not respecting what she can do to the human body. But I wasn't thinking about that because I was feeling invincible after my wipeout. I paddle into the first wave, come down, catch it perfectly. It's fifteen to eighteen feet, not too big but really hollow. I'm roaring down the face, no boil this time. But the wave doubles up and jukes out midface, water streaked with foam and bubbles. I air-drop, make it. Come down and somehow another air-drop, make it. I get to the bottom and I look up and the barrel is there and it's hollow and ready, and I punch my board as hard as I can. But the fin cavitates— air bubbles collect around it—and my board won't turn. I fall on my face and the wave breaks on my head. I cannonball around in the darkness, come up, a couple more waves pound me, I come up again and I'm hungry for more. Yeah, right on! I climb up my leash and slide on my board and paddle back out for more. Exact same thing. Wave a little bigger, solid twenty-footer. Air-drop, make it, another air-drop, make it, get to the bottom, even bigger barrel, punch it, board goes straight, again fall on my face, again heavy twenty-footer breaks right on my back, square. Something bad happens. I think I've hit a finger of lava rock jutting up from the bottom, but it's my own heel knocking me in the head. Wave after wave pounds me, but all this time underwater doesn't matter: lack of air is nothing compared to this pain.

I'VE FALLEN AND I CAN'T GET UP

THE DOCTOR SAID I was lucky I wasn't paralyzed. I thought I'd broken my back, but the trickier diagnosis was a pair of severely herniated discs. The outside of two discs had been torn in the wipeout, and the soft inner part now pressed out through the fibers and into my spinal cord. Beyond that, medical mumbo jumbo. Beyond that, the floor is all there is. Me flat on it, staring up at the ceiling fan twirling round and round.

For two months I lay on the floor at my mom's house in Pūpū-kea, a few feet away from where I collapsed on January 28. As anyone who knows me will tell you, I have two speeds: full throttle charging or dead asleep. Flat on my back with hundreds of lonely hours to think is worse than any bone-busting skin-abrading lung-exploding hold-down.

And please let's not forget it was 1990. There was no i-anything, no laptops, tablets, or phones. I could hold a book or magazine up in front of my face, but I'd never been much of a reader, and anyway it gave me a headache. My mom sat at the kitchen table working on her painting projects and Liam was gone surfing. Our renters—no recollection of who they were—politely walked around me as though

I was the coffee table. At night my mom covered me with a quilt and in the morning she took it off. My biggest daily adventure was being helped to the bathroom.

Maybe because my life has always been unpredictable, I didn't stress out. The only thing we can count on is change. Why not go with it? Taking off on any given wave on any given day is a lesson in this. You eyeball the swell as best you can, take off and commit. You deal.

But I couldn't deal with this. Seemed like every day the mailman arrived with more bills I couldn't hope to pay. I had credit cards, a credit line. My little bit of pro fame had convinced banks I was worth the risk. Ha. To escape I turned my head to the side and stared at the TV. Daytime soap operas, game shows, *Beverly Hills 90210*. I took two codeine pills as often as the prescription allowed. I turned my head the other way and could see through the kitchen to the clock on the wall. Counted hours until my favorite shows. Counted hours until I could take my codeine again.

Time passed.

By March, winter big-wave season had passed and I was given the okay to walk around a little. My friend John Bryant had just become an acupuncturist, so every other day he came to the house and would practice on me. I joked that I could have a whole new career as a human pincushion. I found my way to George Cromack and his office in Hale-'iwa town, chiropractor to all the locals, specializing in wave-induced whiplash and spinal cord injuries. He graciously agreed to sponsor me in my rehabilitation. Together with Adam Salvio, my massage thera-pist, who worked on me for twenty bucks a session, they put me back together. My days revolved around my appointments, like some old geezer trying to shore up the ruins.

I had a few friends who didn't mind my coming over and lying on their floors for a change of pace. One was Peter Davi. A friend of his who made Hyde sandals and baked homemade bread was also crashing there at the time. He'd bake all day long and my mouth would water and I'd eat an entire loaf for dinner. Then I'd shuffle over to my friend Buddy McCray's place at Sunset. He had an extra firm futon, so I would lie on that for a change of pace. He would throw parties. Sometimes people would sit down on the futon, lean against my side, and then get up. It had finally happened: I had truly turned into a piece of furniture.

And then I'd go home. I never stopped to look at the surf; didn't want to see what I was missing, which was my whole life. Three months in and I was barely on my feet. One night, after a day of wallowing around on Buddy's futon, my balls felt a little itchy. I went to the bathroom, scratched a little down there, and pulled off what felt like a tiny scab. I held it up to the light and saw that the scab had tiny, wiggly legs. Turned out that one of my ex-girlfriends had slept on Buddy's futon the night before. I think I might have cried. I had a robust case of crabs and I hadn't even gotten laid.

My codeine addiction grew. I had started exercising by the end of the third month, walking half a mile, then a mile around our Pūpūkea neighborhood. I couldn't have told you how much actual pain I was in or wasn't in because I took a double dose of codeine round the clock. I was edgy and pissed if I couldn't take my next dose on time. "Give me my damn pills": pretty much the only thing I said these days. My mom, to her credit, gave me my damn pills and kept her mouth shut.

AROUND THE time I got hurt, a friend named Tom Tom Watawitz disappeared. He was a responsible, grounded guy, not the type to take off without telling someone. After I was up and around and practicing walking around carrying a surfboard under my arm, they found his body in a ditch beside Mililani Road, one of the highways that runs through the middle of the island. It was as if he'd been tossed from a moving vehicle, his head bashed in with a crowbar. They never arrested anyone, to my knowledge, nor could they even come up with a plausible motive. Tom Tom topped everyone's list as nicest guy around. Our suspicion was that he got in the middle of some heavy shit while doing a favor for someone he shouldn't have.

Surfers traditionally honor their dead with a memorial paddle out. Held at sunrise or sunset, we paddle our boards beyond the break, form a circle and join hands, share memories, throw leis or flowers into the center of the circle. It's a somber, special time.

I decided that Tom Tom's paddle out would be my first attempt at paddling since my injury. I would do it in memory of him. I remember driving down the hill to the beach listening to the Smiths. I am human and I need to be loved. I couldn't remember ever having been so sad, and thinking of it now, I'm crying.

We paddled out at Rocky Point just as the sun was setting. The waves weren't much, maybe one or two feet, but surely enough to hurt me had I got caught inside. We arrived outside the break and formed a circle. Tom Tom had been just nineteen, Liam's age. We said a few awkward words of farewell and threw our purple leis into the center. We raised our clasped hands, then brought them down. A moment of silence followed.

After it was done a small set rolled in, and on impulse I took off on the first wave. The wind had dropped and the wave was a tidy, smooth right, chest high. Easy peasy. I angled my board and started paddling. My arms felt leaden, my shoulders stiff, but I caught the wave easily enough. Was a little light-headed as I stepped off in the whitewash. I was more stoked than I'd been in months, but also tired and out of breath. Definitely in no shape to surf. Then and there I vowed not to surf again until I was a hundred percent.

I had been at the peak of my career before my back injury. I'd thought I could take on anybody because I knew I didn't need to be the best technical surfer or the most gifted athlete, I just needed to be the best paddler. In contests, the heats were stacked with six guys. If you could get yourself to the sweet spot on the best wave, it leveled the playing field. I felt that way at the time. I was probably very delusional.

Tom Tom's friends and family surfed or paddled back in. As I turned and looked back out to sea, I saw two humpback whales swimming through what had been our circle, among the floating leis and flower petals. One of them rolled on her side and waved her fin, and the other waved his tail for about ten minutes. It was the craziest thing I've ever seen.

"That's Tom Tom saying good-bye," I said to a girl named Kelsey, who happened to be standing right next to me. Every year there were one or two sought-after chicks on the North Shore who all the guys wanted to date, and she was one. Before my wipeout I'd tried to talk to her at a party and she had wandered off, completely disinterested. At the bonfire I sat next to her on a driftwood log and made more of my devastatingly witty small talk. I think she may have yawned. Then one of those gnarly half-a-foot-long brown Hawaiian centipedes crawled over her foot and began to make its way up her leg. I picked it up, casual as you please, and tossed it into the fire. She was in my arms in a heartbeat. That might have been Tom Tom, too.

I was back. Sort of.

DOLDRUMS

WHEN I WAS FINALLY able to paddle out with no back pain I took stock of my situation and found it pathetic. I was broke. My brother ended up with all my sponsors. Deep in my heart I wanted to focus on big waves, but it was the early 1990s, so the only big-wave contest was the invitation-only Eddie.

I thought back to the $250 I'd won in the Triple Crown when I was seventeen and figured if it worked for me once, there was no reason it wouldn't work for me again. The ASP ran the international pro tour—twenty-five big contests held all over the world—and if you wanted to stay in the game, entering them was what you did. The ASP tour has since become the World Champion Tour, and only top surfers in the world "make" it. But back then anyone ranked above 200 could pay $150 and was in.

Problem was, at that time the ASP was less focused on putting the best surfers on the most epic waves and more interested in trying to appeal to the mainstream public. People watched golf, the reasoning went, why not surfing? But to watch surfing you had to be able to actually see the surfers, which meant holding the contests on beach breaks, often in only waist-high waves.

I ignored my dream of riding monster waves and decided to be practical. Go back to what got me sponsors in the first place. Go back to what was the acceptable route to an acceptable career in the surfing world. Go back to what everyone approved of and paid attention to and applauded.

I focused on improving my small-wave style, got a YU board that was thick and short and flat, and started practicing my cutbacks. I believed I wanted to do this: what choice did I have?

I worked hard and started feeling more confidence. In smaller waves you've got to be nimble and even acrobatic, always doing what you can do to generate speed to keep the ride going. The adrenaline dump responsible for the big rush of big-wave riding—the rush that I loved like no other—was never guaranteed. I went to California, learned a few moves from San Clemente ripper Dino Andino, came home and started surfing Moku-lēʻia, at the western end of the North Shore, as far away from the big-wave action as you could get. Little waves, two-to-six-foot faces. Training like mad on them.

One time, at Hale-ʻiwa, during an early heat of the Triple Crown, I had surfed against my old idol Tom Curren, whose style I'd studied in the lineup at Niijima. We paddled out. I could feel my heart pounding. Woohoo, there's a chance I'm going to beat the great Tom Curren! I remember the day was hot and sultry, the waves barely breaking at about a half foot. I was sweaty with focus. I was so excited. I thought I really had a chance to beat him.

Instead, I got good and smoked. Can't remember what I did wrong. Other than not being Tom Curren.

I lived in a state of constant frustration.

Frustrated at the contests. It seemed as if the waves were always a foot high, practically ankle slop. The organizers would wait for weeks, and when they were finally forced to hold them, the wave of the day was chest high. These were no different from the waves Liam and I had learned on when we were children.

Frustrated at my finances. Endless money problems. The contests were held in Japan, Australia, California, and Indonesia. If I paid my bills at home I wouldn't have money to travel. If I spent money on traveling, the bill collectors came calling at home. Our sponsors paid for us, but most of my sponsors had cut me loose after I broke my back. Sometimes the tour would set us up with hosts who would give us a free place to sleep, but I still had to cover my food and airplane tickets. It was somewhat easier to surf in Japan. Sponsor-less or not, I still had friends there who would put me up and treat me like a king. That was a nice reprieve.

I fell back on the only guaranteed income I knew: renting rooms to visiting Japanese surfers.

After a year or so I managed to save up enough money to go to Japan to see if I could drum up some sponsorship interest. The executives at Hotline, Peakaboo, and YU, my old sponsors, were politely interested, so some of them agreed to throw a few hundred bucks a month my way. It was something.

I also set up another meeting with Murasaki Sports. I waited in the reception area with my new portfolio on my knee. Like all surfers my wardrobe consists of a pair of swim trunks, a pair of shorts, some rubber slippers, and a few T-shirts. For the meeting I'd bought some new slacks and a polo shirt. The tag at the back of the shirt scratched my neck, and I didn't like the feeling of shoes, also new, on my feet. In general everything felt wrong.

A secretary ushered me into the office of an enormous bald Japanese guy. I sat on the other side of his desk and asked in Japanese whether I might show him my portfolio. He didn't seem to know why I was there, even though he'd agreed to the meeting.

The portfolio contained a few of my favorite photos, as well as clippings of pictures of me from a variety of stories published in the surf mags. I thought it was more important to show me in an editorial context than an advertising one. I never showed any of the advertising campaigns I'd appeared in, reasoning that a new sponsor wouldn't much like seeing me working for someone else, same way you don't show the new girlfriend pictures of you with your arms around the old. I also thought it looked better if I'd actually earned the coverage—thus the emphasis on editorial—failing to consider that if one company saw that my image was successful in selling products for another, my market value was assured.

The executive couldn't have looked less interested. I kept trying to explain what I had to offer, wondering if he was getting it.

"If you sponsor me, I'll put your stickers on my board and do autograph sessions at your stores when I come to Japan."

"Stickers on your board?"

It was ridiculous. My Japanese was good but, it seemed, not good enough to convey why and how the romance and glamour of surfing would help sell his products, and how the photographs of me portrayed such romance and glamour. I thought for sure he was ready to show me the door, but then he said they would sponsor for me for $800 a month or so. It might not have been the end to my money troubles, but in my mind it was a huge victory, and we went on to have a great working relationship.

·   ·   ·

THE BIGGEST difficulty of that difficult time was watching people turn against my brother. Except for the winter, when everyone on earth who cares about surfing shows up on the North Shore, it's a small town, with all the small-town rules and prohibitions. Liam is at heart a lover and would give you the shirt off his back, but in the lineup he was a fighter. When he paddled out at Pipeline and Rocky Point he fought for every wave he wanted, and he wanted all the good ones. On a daily basis he was alienating the gnarliest guys on the North Shore, who also happen to be the gnarliest guys in the world.

He never backed down and his reputation suffered.

Since I was his brother, basically my reputation was in the crapper too. As time went on Liam had become more and more focused. When he paddled out he was committed. He never let a wave go that he believed was rightfully his. No matter who else was in the water, no matter who else called it. Liam didn't back down. But the heavies didn't like it and the kooks didn't like it and the traveling pros didn't like it and the surf magazines, whose revenue was based on the big ads sponsored by the big companies who sponsored the traveling pros, didn't like it.

Why? Because all summer long on the North Shore the ocean is flat. Everyone who could afford to go somewhere else went. Many of the locals, including Liam and me, lived hand-to-mouth and could barely pay our bills, so we stayed home. No waves, nothing to do except maybe partying. Then, in the late fall, the storms start percolating, sweeping down and across the Pacific. The waves finally come and thousands of people descend on the seven miles of world-class breaks that comprise the North Shore. From every part of the world they come. Surfers, managers, photographers and their assistants, corporate-sponsor executives and minions, surf-mag editors and writers, surf-contest muckety-mucks, groupies.

Every professional surfer on earth is there, and he somehow believes he deserves a wave because he's spent a lot of time dreaming of, say, Pipeline, and he's spent a lot of money to get there. And the photographers want to make their careers getting a great shot of him, and his sponsor, say Billabong, will feature the photo in a full-page ad in one of the big surf mags. A lot of people, not just the surfer, have a lot riding on him catching the wave of any given day.

But Liam has been here month in, month out, waiting. Pipeline and Rocky Point, the breaks he surfed religiously, the breaks he was working in an effort to have a solid career, were and are the most photographed breaks in the world. And, as a result, the most crowded.

This is where the challenges began for him. He was not about to step aside so that some pro who'd just stepped off the plane in Honolulu three hours earlier could take a good wave. Especially in contests, when all eyes were on him, he would go for it.

Writers writing their stories in the surf mags didn't help matters. Neither Liam nor I were sponsored by the magazines' big corporate advertisers. We didn't ride for Billabong, for example, so we were easy scapegoats. Stories need a villain, and Liam was as good as any, especially because he was unrepentant. Why shouldn't he be? There were California surfers who were blond and laid-back, and there were Aussie surfers who were radical and hard-charging, and there were noble and revered Hawaiians who could be as gnarly as they pleased because the entire world was encroaching on their perfect and unique waves, and there were eccentric South Africans and a few mysterious Tahitians, and there were drugs and there were feuds and choke outs and all the drama of any insular world, but there were no real bad guys. There were badasses, there were bad boys, but no bad guys. Except for Liam McNamara.

It was unfair. For refusing to play by the very specific rules of the lineup, he was offered up in the service of controversy and drama. He sometimes complained that the judges of the contests were prejudiced against him, and who's to say they weren't? His entry in Matt Warshaw's respected *Encyclopedia of Surfing* says he's "often mentioned as the sport's most disliked figure." I lived under his shadow, the brother of Liam. People who didn't know me disliked me. Even though I tried to stay out of the lineup when Liam was there, I felt the chill whenever I paddled out.

I STILL lived at my mom's in Pūpū-kea. It was another Hicks Home, three bedrooms with a screened-in carport that doubled as a Japanese surfer hostel, with three or four bunk beds. From the front the house looked more presentable. It was blue with white trim, and a little front deck that opened onto a patch of green lawn. I couldn't think of any reason to move. I crashed on the couches of various friends whenever I felt like it. During the winter months there might be a dozen surfers living in the garage and more in the house. We had bunks in the bedrooms and foldouts in the living room. Liam was also living there with his girlfriend, Brandee, whom he'd met in California and who had moved from Santa Cruz; and Brandee's mom, who claimed to be looking for her own apartment but as far as we could tell had no intention of leaving. And my girlfriend had also moved in. At one point there must have been twenty people living there.

My mom was obviously no stranger to communal living. As long as people kept the kitchen table clear so she could paint, and the kitchen counter relatively clean, she didn't mind. Then Barney Barron, Josh Loya, and Flea Virostko, buddies from Santa Cruz, started staying with us. They'd been staying next door at a pig hunter's house, and the pig carcasses hanging in the garage had gotten a little too gnarly, local style. Liam and I were stoked to have them. I don't think we charged them rent. So, all these surfers with their damp trunks and piles of slippers by the front door and boards stacked hither and thither, and the girlfriends and Liam's girlfriend's mother, each with their own special shampoo on the ledge in the shower, and the wet towels they left hither and thither and dishes in the sink, so many dishes in the sink.

Finally our once-upon-a-time hippie mom had had it. Every surfer who wasn't paying rent, out! Every Japanese who didn't have a bed, out! Girlfriends and their mothers, out! Liam and Garrett, grow up and get out! We thought she was joking about kicking us out. We laughed our asses off, we teased her about how she had raised us in a commune and we were just doing what we'd been raised to do, live with a bunch of more or less strangers in perfect harmony.

But she was serious.

Two weeks later we found ourselves a nice, remodeled house at Velzyland. While we were in the midst of moving, by which I mean we got the key from the landlord and dropped a bag of clothes inside the front door before we went out to surf an overhead day, Mom's house burned down, two weeks to the day.

The fire department said it was due to faulty electrical wiring in the garage. Miraculously, no one was home at the time. But all of the boards belonging to the renters and our visiting Japanese friends went up in flames, as well as our mom's paintings, the ones she'd been working so hard on.

TOW-IN NOW

YOU COULD ALWAYS TELL when there was no school because Sunset and Velzyland were packed with groms in their neon-colored rash guards and itty-bitty boards. V-land was grom paradise, very local, with a big buffet of rideable waves on offer. A lot of uncles (as Hawaiians traditionally refer to respected and beloved elders) loved that break, too, so sometimes the lineup was as crowded as a mall at Christmas.

If the surf was closing out inside, the outer reefs would be going off. From the beach you could see them, gleaming far-off white water curling in the sun, beautiful and empty. A pure waste of epic waves. But no matter how crowded the lineup got on the inner breaks, those outer breaks stayed empty. All wisdom, both the conventional and the un-, said they were pretty much impossible to ride. Even if you had the patience and stamina to paddle all the way out there, you could never paddle fast enough to catch them. The bigger a wave is, the faster it moves. Anything bigger than about twenty-five feet Hawaiian was thought to be moving faster than the human shoulder could rotate. And you had to be stronger than the average swimmer, comfortable in the wild, wide open ocean, willing to have a skyscraper-high wall of water crash down on you, delivering wipeouts that didn't just toss you around, but sent you down into the inky depths, thirty forty fifty feet down, into the abyss.

All this changed one day in 1992. I was standing on the beach staring at the break at Outside Backyards between V-land and Sunset when I saw a few specks of color moving in the water way outside. One speck moving across the face of the wave, while another floated in a raft or something like it, finally meeting up with the first after the wave broke. It was a bright day, high noon, and I rubbed my eyes. Thought maybe I was seeing things.

But no. It was Laird Hamilton, Darrick Doerner, and Buzzy Kerbox, in a fifteen-foot Zodiac with a 60-horsepower outboard motor, out there pioneering tow-in surfing. I didn't know that then, of course. Didn't know that it would change my life. Without thinking I ran home and grabbed my 9' Wai-mea gun. I was so stoked I wasn't thinking straight. I had an underdeveloped idea that I would paddle out and say howzit and ask Laird to tow me in. But when I made it back to the beach with my board I just stood there. It was a bright day and I shielded my eyes with my hand and stared with a dropped jaw.

I must have stood there for hours. I watched while the driver of the Zodiac towed the surfer along, water-ski style, getting a running start on the gathering swell. When the surfer felt he was at the right spot, he let go and it was on. The Zodiac driver drove back over the shoulder of the wave and waited, then collected the surfer when he was done and drove him back to the lineup.

Excitement brewed in my heart. At that time I rode a little 6′6″ or 6′8″ board. They were more maneuverable than longer boards and duck-diving was easier. But it was harder to catch the bigger waves, and I was in the middle of the pecking order as it was. Part of the reason I fell for surfing in the first place was the escape it offered. But as more and more surfers started showing up from all over the world, the breaks became more crowded. If I towed in, I wouldn't have to battle with the rest of the boys for every good wave. I wouldn't have to battle with my brother.

I WATCHED until the sun was dropping in the western sky, more stoked than I'd been in a long time. I envisioned those mysterious outer reefs, all empty. Avalanche. Walls. Hammerheads. Backyards. Phantoms. Suddenly, they were accessible. Everything would be more epic—the rides, the drops, the rush. All those big waves I loved? It was as if God had suddenly tripled the supply.

I made a pact there and then to start saving for my own Zodiac. A year later I bought a used one and refurbished it. It was black, and I painted a big red-and-white shark mouth on the bow. I went out a few times by myself with a few friends, but the Zodiac was big and bulky and hard to steer. It wouldn't go over white water. Then there was the outboard engine rumbling on the back, threatening to chop you to pieces, or that's how it seemed.

Another challenge with tow-in was putting together a team of guys you could trust. Paddling in was a loner occupation, and if you messed up you had no one to blame but yourself. Towing in was trickier. You needed to find guys with the right skill set who needed to be able to drive a jet-ski through often massive swells, and who would not just drop you at the right spot on a wave, but also had the guts and discipline to power straight into treacherous surf if you got pounded. Your life depended on it.

At the time, I was also into prone paddle racing—where you lie on a board and paddle a certain distance over unbroken swells. My top two competitors were Charlie Walker and Dawson Jones. They were also experimenting with towing-in and had just bought a brand-new Sea-Doo Explorer jet-boat. They invited me to Lani-ākea on a hot, windless day when the waves were triple overhead.

Driving was tougher than it looked. The goal was to put the surfer on the peak of the wave, but you could only guess at where that was, since you were always thirty feet—the length of the towrope—ahead of where your partner wanted to be dropped. Dawson was a pilot for Hawaiian Airlines. He would disappear for weeks at a time, and Charlie and I became tight partners. We took out the Sea-Doo and practiced until I could read a wave well enough to know with only a glance over my shoulder how it was breaking thirty feet behind me.

One glassy day during the second winter we were together, we towed out to Alligators, an outer reef with very fast water where twenty-five-foot waves are business as usual. That day it was twenty feet of perfection. We passed Ken Bradshaw, who was anti-towing—"if you can't paddle you shouldn't be out there" was his mantra—until he decided to try it; then he never looked back.

Dawson was driving. A deep blue mountain rolled beneath us and put Charlie right on the peak. We ride along the shoulder and see Charlie eat it. We cruise over to him. Charlie's treading water and the 'ski catches on something, or that's what it feels like. Dawson's gassing it, but the 'ski is struggling. We're a little inside the break now and a huge wave arches up. We're going to get crushed if we don't move. I look back at Charlie and he's got an odd, panicked expression. Then Dawson yells, "Abandon ship!" We dive off and the wave crashes right on the 'ski and it's a yard sale. The hatches are blown, the seats fly off. Everything that can come off the thing comes off, and the debris field looks like a plane crash. We're forced to swim in, but in this swell that means going over the falls and getting pounded all the way in to the beach. It's only when we're sitting on the beach, gasping, that we figure out that the towrope had been wrapped around Charlie's leg. Luckily it was one of those cheap old water-ski ropes. It snapped right as the wave broke. Had it been new, Charlie's leg would have been yanked off at the thigh.

A lot of us learned the hard way that you couldn't ride a fifty-foot wave you'd been towed into the same way you ride a twenty-foot wave you'd paddled into. The water moves too fast and the usual drop-to-the-bottom-and-turn maneuver usually does nothing but put you in a position to get pounded.

Marvin Foster was a local Hale-'iwa goofy-foot who'd been an idol when I was just learning. He was one of the first guys to grab the rail of his board and get barreled (the move became called a Marvo). Like a lot of North Shore boys, he had trouble staying out of trouble on dry land, finding himself in jail for one reason or another. He was eligible for a weekend pass, however, and one Saturday Himalayas was pumping, fifty-foot faces at least. I'd saved up and bought a four-seater Yamaha SUV jet-ski, with my friend Maeda Yasuo. The gunwale was wide and flat and I didn't even need a sled. I could just haul people up and drop them there.

I told Marvin what I'd learned the hard way, that once you dropped the towrope you rode across the face. "Whatever you do," I said, "don't drop down to the bottom of the wave. Set your edge and stay on the face."

Of course, I put him on the wave and the first thing he did was drop straight to the bottom and get completely pounded. He hadn't been surfing since he'd been in jail, and he'd also taken up smoking to pass the time, so he wasn't really up for this kind of beating.

The waves are fifty feet, fifty-five feet, and they're thundering in. There are some Brazilians sitting on their 'skis in the channel, and they can't believe I'm going in to rescue him. I fight my way through the crashing white water and haul him up—he's a huge, impressively tattooed Hawaiian—and his eyes are like silver dollars. Even though he was gasping and choking on seawater he saw how it could be. The next year he was in the tow-in surfing championships at Pua'ena Point.

NO MATTER how hard we fine-tuned our equipment or tested out different flotation devices, we were always light-years behind Hamilton, Doerner, and Kerbox, who moved to Maui where they continued perfecting their act at Pe'ahi, also known as Jaws, the giant outside break on the north shore of Maui. Just when we were figuring out we could use shorter boards—the reason you needed a gun in the big waves is that all that surface area, coupled with paddling, generated enough speed to catch the wave—Laird and Darrick and Buzzy had stuck foot straps on their boards. I didn't mind being behind the curve. I relished it, in fact. Tow-in surfing now enjoyed the same off-the-radar status that paddle surfing once had. There were no competitions, no battling over sponsorships, and the waves were empty. Total freedom, and I loved it.

Paddle surfing had felt more like an exercise in pure survival. You had a big board, had to sit out and wait for hours for the perfect wave in the open ocean, hoping to be in the right spot. Then, when the wave finally came, you had to paddle like a maniac. Once you caught the wave, you could barely turn your board on account of its size.

Tow-in surfing was another world. Just you and your friends out in the water having fun, riding wave after wave. You no longer needed a big board, and whoever was driving the jet-ski could put you in the right spot. There was an artistry to it. You could focus, now, on carving and flowing with the wave.

When I was a kid at school I used to draw in my notebooks. A favorite drawing was of a huge wave with a little surfer on the face making big, swooping turns. It was a vision, and a dream I'd never thought possible, and now I was living the dream. I'd become the little surfer in my childhood drawings.

FAMILY GUY

THERE WAS A GIRL named Connie who lived across the street from my mom's house in Pūpū-kea, the one that burned down. She was a local girl, dark-haired and petite, quiet and, to me, mysterious. Her mother was a Jehovah's Witness so she wasn't allowed to run wild like some of the other North Shore girls, but somehow she managed it. The first time we hung out I invited her over for some Häagen-Dazs. After we were married we joked that I'd angled for a booty call and instead found myself taking a walk down the aisle. It was 1994 and I was twenty-six years old, a real adult now.

We moved into a cool little house not far from Foodland. The only furniture we had was a Ping-Pong table and a bed. We continued the rental business. We could not pack that little house full enough. At one point in the winter there were fifteen surfers staying there. The Japanese sponsors I'd managed to woo back were paying the bare minimum, but between that and renting rooms we were doing well for ourselves.

Our daughter was born on March 9, 1995, and the joy of becoming a father took me by surprise, as I guess it does everyone. Ariana was dark-eyed like her mother, with a heart-shaped face and a wicked smile. I was smitten. Now that I had a family it felt important to try to be a better person. God had always taken good care of me and blessed me all over the place. Blessed me when I didn't deserve to be blessed. I'd slipped up a lot and still the blessings came, and I was not about to take my good fortune for granted.

I stopped partying and also, once and for all, stopped kidding myself that I had any interest in anything other than big waves. In that I had any genuine gift for surfing, it was on the outer reefs, riding the monsters. It wasn't that I was fearless, as some people said. I was afraid, but I didn't mind feeling that way. It was all part of the rush that made me feel so alive.

I gave up on the ASP tour and entered the few big-wave contests that came along, most of which were within walking distance from my house. I made the Triple Crown quarterfinals one year, and hoped I'd be invited to the Eddie someday. I'd managed to snag a couple of surf-mag covers and that pretty much constituted the rickety scaffolding of my professional surfing career—those few great photos. I tried to be philosophical and accept the good things that came my way. I wasn't winning contests but I no longer cared. I was never really a small-wave contest surfer, and the only thing that spoke to me now, the only thing that interested me, was the rush of riding big waves.

Around this time I was blessed again and found myself getting in good with the Brazilians. In the same way we'd shown the Japanese surfers the ropes when they hit the North Shore, we befriended the Brazilians who needed a place to stay. Taiu, Zecau, Jimenez, and Jorge Piceli were the first. I looked up to Taiu, who surfed with cool precision at Sunset and Wai-mea. (Later he would break his neck, suffering quadriplegia, in two-foot waves on a small sandbar.) More and more of them showed up regularly on the North Shore every winter, ripping on the pro circuit and winning a lot of the big contests.

Bad Boy was a sportswear company out of San Diego founded in the early eighties, specializing in apparel and equipment for extreme sports. In the early nineties Marco Merhej licensed the brand in Brazil—still does. Marco surfed the North Shore in the winter and was also a devotee of Brazilian jiujitsu, at the time an edgy, out-there form of mixed martial arts (MMA) more or less unknown in the States. Jiujitsu was huge in Brazil. Marco suggested Bad Boy sponsor Rickson Gracie (son of the founder of Helio Gracie), and all the jiujitsu guys started wearing Bad Boy, which led to their introducing an MMA combat line. People called Marco "Marcoting" because he was a master at marketing, so when he suggested to Bad Boy that they up their power surfing presence, they signed me.

Marco and I hit it off. Peak surfing months in Brazil are April through October, Southern Hemisphere winter. He'd fly me down to stay with him at one of his two beach houses at Maresias or Florianópolis. Marco dragged me along with him everywhere he went, even business meetings. He was a one-man operation. I saw firsthand how this sort of business worked. I learned the importance of marketing, something I'd never really thought about, despite my prior experience with my Japanese sponsors.

Maresias is known for its big-wave break and its nightclub, so when we weren't surfing we'd throw parties where we'd give away Bad Boy product, or we'd literally wander around town giving stuff to anyone who looked as if they'd wear it—surfers, tough guys, fighters, even the special forces guys. Law enforcement loved Bad Boy. They'd stop by Marco's little office for whatever swag was on offer. For a while, Bad Boy manufactured their boots.

Then in December 1995 my lifelong dream came true. I was invited to surf in the Eddie. Thanks to Eddie Rothman, the North Shore enforcer who insisted on putting my name in the mix, I would be surfing with the likes of Brock Little, Johnny Boy Gomes, Sunny Garcia, Derek and Michael Ho, Marvin Foster, Aaron Napolean, Titus Kinimaka—all the hard chargers I'd long admired and competed with for waves. Kelly Slater was one of the lone non-Hawaiians on the roster.

A few weeks later, on December 29, George Downing, who'd been tracking a big storm barreling across the Pacific, made the call. All the surfers were to show up Friday morning at Wai-mea. The weather report was calling for a high surf advisory. This usually meant the entire North Shore closing out, with waves big enough to break across Kam Highway at Lani-ākea. All signs pointed to waves big enough for the Eddie to go.

I showed up at Wai-mea before dawn. The sky was rosy but clear, not a cloud in the sky, but a salty mist hung over everything, the way it does when the waves are macking. The Bay was still in shadow, the sun yet to rise above the Koʻolau Mountains to the east, but you could already see the waves were flawless. Dark swells rose up in a straight line to form steep walls of water that broke neatly across the length of the Bay. The light wind was offshore, guaranteeing they would hold their shape. A set rolled in, twenty feet easy, and when it broke, sending white water thirty feet into the air, the ground shook.

By 8 a.m. the Kam Highway was bumper to bumper. Wai-mea Bay Park was packed with spectators, standing room only. By 9:30 the judges were seated up on their scaffolding and the army of photographers stood on the rocks, tripods in place, zoom lenses pointed at the break.

There were thirty-three participants that year, and we would surf in two rounds, each round comprising eleven surfers in the water for fifty minutes. Surfing the Eddie was a spiritual experience, celebrating the soul of a great Hawaiian, a great human, and also the gift of the perfect, magnificent waves right outside our front doors. But the judging was anything but perfect. Like everything cooked up and administered by human beings, it was subjective and inconsistent. There were seven judges who scored each surfer's ride based first on the wave's height, then on the takeoff, whether you got barreled, and whether you were able to pull off a bottom turn and a cutback or two. The high and low scores were tossed out, just like in the Olympics. Sometimes you're on a closeout and the judges throw you a great score, and sometimes you make a great wave and you're largely ignored. I've watched it over the years to figure out how best to surf it, and the only thing I've learned is that whoever Eddie wants to win that day will prevail.

I surfed in the third heat. Paddled out as fast as I could. A little impatient, maybe. Fifty short minutes to catch the hugest waves and deliver a ride that will wow the judges. I miss my jet-ski, my tow partners Charlie and Dawson. I paddle up and over the first set of waves. The sound of white water crashing is deafening. I'm grateful for it; it keeps me from thinking too much about when I broke my back on a much smaller day.

Once outside I paddle to the spot where I feel the waves will break, based on my predawn assessment from the beach. Sure enough, the first wave of the next set starts to rise up only a few paddle strokes away. I take off. The face is so steep. Air-drop. Feel weightless, my toes clutching the board so I won't lose it before I hit the trough. Boom. Wobble a little, turn, pump off the bottom, and get myself in front. The white water catches up to me, mammoth swirling mountain chasing me. I haul ass out into the channel. Not my best ride on a wave that was maybe only eighteen feet Hawaiian, but still I'm stoked. I catch a few more waves that round, but they're nothing to write home about.

I was psyched for the next round. It was completely possible to surf the wave of the day during the second round and take the whole thing. I didn't dare allow myself to imagine the bump my career would take if I won the Eddie. It was too much to hope for. During the few still moments of my life, when the baby wasn't crying or there were no waves breaking anyplace in the world I could get to at that moment, and I was out on the covered porch behind our house tinkering with my jet-ski, the feeling would seep in that my career, my puny hardscrabble pro career, was probably over.

In the early afternoon something happened that had never happened at the Eddie before or since: the pristine giant swell disappeared. With no warning the huge rolling sets just stopped, as if the sea was exhausted and couldn't heave itself up one more time.

George Downing conferred with the judges, and the contest was called. It was early in the season. The thought was that surely another Eddie-worthy swell would arrive before the end of February, but it never did. That day went down in history as the half-Eddie, and the prize money was split thirty-three ways. I think I won about fifteen hundred bucks. I was stoked. I'd learned how to do well.

GARRETT McNAMARA, SHOPKEEPER

IN 2000 I OPENED a surf shop called Epic Sports. It sat at the end of a row of small shops in Haleʻiwa Town on Kam Highway. Great location, right in the middle of town, an easy walk away from a popular breakfast joint, Cafe Haleiwa. Epic Sports wasn't limited to surfing gear; I also carried Bad Boy apparel, including their mixed martial arts line. Connie's brothers were handy and they helped me stain the cement floor and build the wooden clothes racks. Along one wall we built wooden shelves, where the T-shirts were displayed. In the back room I carried a good selection of surfboards. I couldn't afford to stock new boards, so I sold the used boards of my friends.

The first thing you saw when you walked into the shop was a big color poster of me tacked up on the wall over the register. It was the classic big-wave surfer shot—big wave, tiny guy—taken from a helicopter, so the wave looks even bigger than it was. The wave is just about to break behind me, the heavy lip forever poised against the sky. Me, frozen in time, doing what I loved.

The photo was taken at Avalanche on Christmas Day 2000. I'd taken my WaveRunner out with Kalani Foster, Marvin Foster's younger brother; Ross Williams, one of those really good surfers who never won any contests but hung with the right people and is now one of the faces of the WSL; Kelly Slater and goofy-foot Rob "Mr. Smooth" Machado, who were at that time in a band (along with Peter King) called the Surfers. Rob had never towed in before but he was determined to do it that day, even though we only had my board. Watching him take off and ride a wave with his feet shoved into the straps fitted for my regular stance was like watching someone dance with his shoes on the wrong feet. We'd laughed our asses off.

That story was my big talking point. I suppose it should have made me wistful or nostalgic or downright sad. But I sold more stuff over the telling of that particular tale, and that in itself gave me a feeling of accomplishment.

Opening the shop was the best idea I had at the time. On May 3, 1997, our son Titus was born. When the baby came Connie and I decided it was time to stop renting rooms to traveling surfers, which left us relying on my always unreliable sponsorship money.

This was a great opportunity to provide some financial stability for my little family. I was still riding for Bad Boy, which was enjoying a moment. The popularity of MMA was skyrocketing, both on the mainland and in Hawai'i. Because they already sponsored me I was able to get a deep discount on inventory. Epic was the only place you could buy Bad Boy on O'ahu. Also, Connie was an excellent seamstress and could whip up everything from sundresses to bikinis for the ladies' department. It was a real family operation and I was proud of it.

I rented another house behind the store so I had an office. We moved our Ping-Pong table there from the house. Guys liked to congregate at Cafe Haleiwa for breakfast, and my hope was they'd then mosey on next door to the shop and hang out a little, play some Ping-Pong, before heading off to surf. I wanted it to be a gathering place as well as a surf shop. I even envisioned setting up a jiujitsu dojo.

Business wasn't bad. I was able to pay the bills and that felt good. I didn't mind the routine. In the morning I'd get up with the kids. It took some time to break the habit of waking in the dark before dawn to make my daily morning phone calls: I called one number to check the buoy readings and another to check the wind. I'd dialed those numbers thousands of times over the years. After I got dressed I'd walk down the road to Starbucks. Because it was located inside Foodland I'd always run into people I know; surfers, a lot of the time, heading out for a morning session. I'd never been a coffee drinker before, but now I needed a double shot of espresso with sugar and a splash of milk to cool it down, just to get my day started.

Then I drove to Hale-'iwa in my old Ford Taurus, past Wai-mea, past Chun's and Jocko's and Lani's, my all-time favorite break before I quit trying to be a professional surfer. I'd try not to slow the traffic down by crawling along at a few miles an hour, watching the break, just to see it firing, then over the rainbow bridge and into Hale-'iwa. I would park in the back; then, if I had time, walk over to Cafe Haleiwa where my favorite breakfast was Breakfast in a Barrel—an egg and potato burrito with cheese, spinach, and green salsa. Then another double shot of espresso to prep me for my day.

The days when friends would hang out and also the weeks before Christmas were the best. Time flew and I got caught up on the coconut wireless gossip, who was dropping in on who and getting cracked or sent in to the beach because of it, and what new tow-in teams were killing it and what new gear were they using. The Maui boys were still leading the tow-in charge, and they favored a big 155-horsepower

Yamaha WaveRunner. I got in a few sessions here and there, when I could talk someone into watching the counter for a few hours.

I made a lot of friends as the proprietor of Epic Sports, people I would never have known otherwise. I loved my repeat customers, and the people who would come in and say so-and-so had sent them. I liked feeling as if my efforts were appreciated, and this helped me focus on all the good things going on in my life. It's hard work to stay positive all the time and look at the bright side, but that's always been how I wanted to live my life.

There were challenges: regular businessman challenges. There were four parking places directly in front of the shop, and for some reason my landlord didn't like anyone to park there unless they were actively shopping. This discouraged my friends from dropping by, and also discouraged business by making it look like business was dead.

The days I had no customers were nine hundred hours long. Sitting there with the door open, trying to look welcoming, and people passing by, tourists all summer long, carrying giant rainbow-colored cones of world-famous Matsumoto Shave Ice from just down the street, peeking in, looking at me like I wasn't there, then passing on. Even though I paid dearly for air conditioning, I'd still leave the door open so the shop would look inviting.

On those slow days I had plenty of time to think. You can only wipe down the glass display cases so many times. Only straighten the surfboards in the back room so many times. But you can wonder countless times what you're doing with your life. My thoughts spooled out differently depending on the day. Same old hamster wheel, just every day a different hamster. Some days my thoughts were ambitious—

maybe I could open a string of shops, put one in Honolulu and maybe even in California somewhere. The next day would ache to be in the water, just to get wet. I'd get depressed thinking about my WaveRunner sitting on the back porch under a blue tarp.

I really missed the rush of surfing. I missed it so much that on one of my last trips to Brazil I smuggled in three hundred kilos of T-shirts and shorts just to feel my heart racing. Two luggage carts piled high with eight bags of Bad Boy stuff. I took every article of clothing out of its plastic bag and pulled off all the tags and laid my own dirty clothes on top of each bag. The customs fees I would have to pay for all this merchandise would be more than the plane ticket to pick it up. As I made my way through the line at JFK, I entertained myself trying to think up a plausible reason why I would be traveling with eight giant bags of clothes, but needn't have bothered. The customs officer waved me right on through.

ONE DAY on my way home from the shop, I decided to stop by the house of a friend who was having a party. It was a mistake. A big one. But I stayed. And it started a habit that would last for years: Escaping boredom and my reality by partying. Connie hated it and begged me to stop. So the usual thing happened. It got ugly. Partying ruined my marriage, or rather I should say I ruined my marriage.

I would promise to stop and I *would* stop for four, five, six months. Then there would be a big party at one of the surf houses down at, say, Pipeline celebrating some surfer's Triple Crown triumph or other pro tour contest, and I would go, and Connie would get pissed and I would promise her again that I was through, that I wouldn't go to another party and, in that moment, as I looked her in the eyes and the words came out of my mouth I meant it. But there was always another party. I felt ashamed, and mad at myself, so I started hiding it, sometimes sneaking out the window after she fell asleep. I started lying to Connie, and then lying to myself, and at the age of thirty-three that was my life.

PART III

The author, in the most memorable ride of his life, surfing Jaws (Pe'ahi) on the north
shore of Maui, Hawai'i, 2002.
(Ron Dahlquist)

BLUEPRINT

IT WAS EARLY AUGUST 2001. I sat on a tall stool behind the counter and stared for a long time at the poster on the wall beside the register. With little trouble I could summon up that moment, soaring down the face of that wave. For just a moment I pretended money was no issue. Would I rather be that guy on the wave or this guy behind the counter?

Tiny guy, big wave. That was me. This wasn't me.

This guy sitting behind the counter was a guy many degrees removed from his life's true purpose.

Here's how you know the truth of a thing: once you've formulated the thought in your head, once you've admitted it to yourself, no other thought rises up to contradict it.

When I decided to open the store I'd bought a copy of *Small Business for Dummies*. It advised me to make a business plan, so I thought, that's what I need to do. Make a plan for following my life's passion, for that's what surfing was.

But I'd been convinced that I could never make enough to support myself and my family doing it. I'd never forgotten that when we moved to the North Shore and Liam started playing baseball, our mom thought being a pro ball player was a more realistic career goal than being a professional surfer. That's how unlikely my dream was. And I'd lived now for more than a decade struggling to make ends meet, so I knew from experience how hard it was.

And yet, I suddenly believed if I put in 100 percent on my end, God or the universe or the unseen entity that observes and participates in human endeavor, whatever you want to call it, would clear the obstacles in my path. That if I believed in myself, it would believe in me too. I hadn't heard of the concept of manifesting—not yet—where your thoughts and the vibes you put out into the world help create the reality, but that's the idea that had revealed itself to me that day.

I grabbed a flyer someone had left on the counter—he was selling a boat or a board or something—turned it over, and started writing.

At the top I wrote: *HOW TO KEEP SURFING*.

How could I possibly create a life in which I could keep surfing, which also meant make enough money to keep surfing?

Below this I wrote: *Win the Eddie and Jaws Tow-In contests.*

The Jaws Tow-In World Cup was a new big-wave contest that would run for the first time in 2002 at Pe'ahi, with a first-place prize of $70,000. There were big-wave contests for paddle-in surfers, but this was the first tow-in competition, so the world was watching. The Eddie first-place prize money was $50,000. Neither of these purses was huge, but they were respectable and they would elevate me to a place in the surfing world where I would look more attractive to sponsors than I ever had in the past. The biggest hurdle was getting invited to participate. Neither contest was an all-comers meet, where you could just show up and pay your dues, like in the old ASP days. This was something of a hurdle, since I hadn't been surfing in over a year. Why would contest organizers even think of me, much less vote for me?

None of these thoughts were conscious when I was making my blueprint. These were two competitions that arose in my mind unbidden, contests I longed to win and that I knew I could win. I would never be the best surfer out there, but I seemed to possess one skill that few others did: I wasn't fearless on the big waves, but I took the fear in stride. I knew firsthand that those colossal waves could crush me, but I had confidence in my ability to endure massive wipeouts and hold-downs, and this made me willing to take risks other surfers weren't.

The blueprint branched out. What did I need to do to accomplish my goals? Quickly I wrote three headings: *Train Hard, Eat Right, Focus Focus Focus*; and then under each, the actions I would have to take. I made a training schedule, a menu, and wrote down a few ideas about how I could keep my eye on the prize.

When I was finished my plan looked like a family tree.

I CHOSE August 10, my birthday, to start my program. A few days before I sat Connie down and told her about the blueprint, about what I'd plan to achieve. Her response was guarded until I told her that my plan (obviously) included saying no to partying—I was even going to give up coffee—at which point she said she was in.

I cleaned out the kitchen of all junk food. I did most of the cooking at home so it wasn't a problem to stop serving musubi (Spam with rice) and potato chips and Coke, and start broiling fish and making salad. I wasn't a vegan or even vegetarian, but I would eat lean and clean. Tuna, brown rice, and baby greens, mostly. Lots of avocados. Some chicken every once in a while, and when I really felt ambitious and needed a change, I'd whip up a batch of vegetarian chili.

My training was a do-it-yourself regime that made sense to me. I had no fitness trainer or surfing coach. I awoke in the dark and lifted weights under the covered patio behind the house.

Then I rode my mountain bike up Pūpū-kea Hill and to the heiau at the top of Puʻu-o-mahuka Road. Three hundred feet up a steep and winding one-lane track through the jungle sits the Puʻu-o-mahuka Heiau, the biggest heiau, or temple, on the North Shore. Once there were buildings here made of stone and coral, places where Hawaiians practiced their religion. After the death of Kamehameha the Great in 1819 the Hawaiian system of religion was outlawed by his son Liholiho, and the heiau was burned to the ground. All that remains is the huge rectangular foundation, outlined with boulders of lava, with a stupendous view of the yellow sands and milky green waters of Waimea Bay and Kam Highway snaking along beside it. When the waves were pumping you could see the swells marching in straight, blue corduroy. In the distance on a clear day you can see Kauaʻi.

Once I reached the heiau I was winded and drenched with sweat. I read the informational plaques while I caught my breath. Four powerful Hawaiian gods were worshipped here: Kāne, the creator of all things; Kū, the god of war; Lono, the god of fertility; Kanaloa, the god of the ocean. All seemed auspicious. I would imagine I was marching around the heiau with them, receiving infusions of their mana, their power.

During the first weeks I thought I was going to give myself a heart attack. It was a mile up and a mile back. My legs ached as I stood on the pedals and crawled uphill. The air was heavy and humid and didn't seem to want anything to do with my lungs. My head pounded from espresso withdrawals. I kept at it, and things got better. Titus had turned four that spring, and after a while he would ride up the hill with me, charging along on his little BMX bike.

Sunset Beach Elementary School, more or less directly across from Pipeline, on the other side of the highway, had a quarter-mile track where I ran after work. There were four benches along the long stretches. I'd do wind sprints between the benches, then sit down and hold my breath while doing sit-ups, push-ups, and dips. The point was to train myself to be comfortable with not being able to breathe during the beatings I would take after a wipeout. To surf the big waves you not only have to be in great shape, you also have to be able to feel relaxed during a hold-down.

Sixty-foot waves can hold you down for half a minute or more. It can seem like an eternity, but if you're popped back out and not hurled upon reef or rocks, it's probably not enough to kill you. The problem comes when the wave has also flung you down, say, forty feet. The interval between set waves can be as short as fifteen seconds. If you're struggling in the dark far below the surface, unsure which way is up, you might not make it up between waves for a life-saving gulp of air.

Sometimes I'd run three or four times around the track, then do my breath exercise. I also went free diving and cave diving. In the summer, when the ocean is flat, there are also a few spots where you can run from rock to rock along the bottom. Shark's Cove, at the Pūpū-kea state park, between Pipeline and Wai-mea, was the perfect spot. Eventually, I trained myself to hold my breath for four minutes and thirty-three seconds.

Whether lifting weights or riding my bike or running the track, I kept at the forefront of my mind the goals I set out for myself. I envisioned standing at the podium after I'd won the Eddie. Since the Jaws Tow-In contest had never run before, I couldn't imagine myself after I'd triumphed. Instead, I put myself at the end of the towrope amid the wild, churning, deep ocean waves of Pe'ahi. My partner on the perfectly tuned-up jet-ski would slingshot me into the perfect spot on a massive dark blue behemoth and down I'd go, rocketing across the face, the roar of the wave crashing behind me. I'd have three perfect rides, then get barreled on the fourth.

I would always be having the time of my life.

Usually while I was training I'd listen to music and focus on my breathing. I was praying. I was focusing. I was manifesting. I was meditating. And always in a spirit of humility. I was realistic about my surfing ability. I did honestly think most everyone was better than me, but I trusted in this plan, and on my ability to see it through. And every day I thanked God in advance for the way he was going to bless me.

Pretty much everyone I knew thought I was crazy.

I hired a few people to help me at the store. When the waves were good I would be in the water at least three hours a day, sometimes as long as eight. Every morning I got up in the dark, long before Connie and the kids. Depending on the size and direction of the swell, I would either ride my bike to Wai-mea, or drive five minutes to Sunset. If it was pumping, I'd get in a short session before my workout. Otherwise, I'd train in the dark, then surf later in the day.

There's nothing like paddling out while dawn is breaking to make you grateful for everything.

One day near the end of the year I paddled out at Lani's. That underappreciated break is still one of my favorite rights. It was rarely breaking, but when it was on it offered one of the longest rides on the North Shore, with three possible barrel sections. You paddled outside at the point. Soon a long wave would roll up and offer the smoothest ride back to the beach. My shoulders felt good paddling out. I was breathing easy, clearheaded and at peace. The swells were maybe twelve feet; the wind onshore so the waves were a little mushy. I didn't care. I felt grateful, even though the only thing that had changed was my intention. I still was tied to the shop, still had no money, still struggled with the urge to escape, but I could not have been happier.

That night when I got home there was a letter for me. A heavy, creamy envelope from Quiksilver inviting me to be an alternate in the 2001–2002 Eddie. I was number seven on the list.

JAWS

I LAY IN BED listening to the windows rattling. Middle of the night, pitch black, morning of January 7, 2002. Whenever the surf was huge the windows rattled with every set wave that crashed at Wai-mea. A low rattle signaled twenty-foot swells. Higher pitched, and I knew we were talking thirty plus. This meant sixty-foot faces. This meant macking waves big enough to make surfing and meteorological history.

I breathed deeply and worked on not getting too excited.

The energy I'd been putting out there since late August must have had a trickster vibe. In the first week of January a huge storm slammed into the islands, delivering mammoth swells to the northern shores of both O'ahu and Maui. Something I never counted on when I wrote my blueprint—that the Eddie and the Jaws World Cup would take place at the same time on the same day.

I'd found my tow-in partner for the Jaws contest only a month before. Rodrigo "Monster" Resende was a renowned Brazilian big-wave surfer who also rode for Bad Boy. He let it be known that he wanted to get into tow-in surfing, and since the contest was sponsored by Studio Mega/Brazil it made sense, strategically, to partner up. I knew that if I was towing in with a Brazilian my chances of being invited were that much better, and sure enough, our team received an invitation.

Rodrigo showed up on the North Shore around the first of December. A lot of Brazilian surfers have big personalities, are loud and outgoing, but Rodrigo was humble, quiet, and focused. He didn't try to cover up the little detail that he had never driven a jet-ski before.

Okay.

First thing was to teach him how to simply drive the 'ski. We hooked the jet-ski trailer to the back of the Ford Taurus and drove to Hale-'iwa harbor. The surf was tiny that day, shoulder-high, dribbling in from the west. We backed the 'ski in the water. A family with two little children wearing neon pink life jackets stood and watched.

Just around the point, five minutes from the harbor, there was both a right and left breaking wave that had a short bowl section near the end. Jaws was a violent, racing right with a towering C-shaped bowl that could crush your skull during a bad wipeout, but with a bit of imagination—okay, a lot of imagination—this wave was Jaws-like. The small size worked to our advantage from a training perspective. On big days you're riding down this mountainous swell and you have some time to get situated. On little days the waves just pop up and you've got to act fast. It's more difficult to tow-in properly to a small swell because there's less wave face to work with, and you've only got one shot to get it right before the wave breaks.

We sat together on the 'ski, bobbing in the channel. I taught him how to steer the jet-ski, and how to gauge the thirty feet of rope so that he could place me right on the peak of the wave.

I slid onto my board, fed my feet into the straps, and picked up the towrope. A little crowd had gathered on the beach. I'm sure they wondered what on earth we were doing, towing into two-foot waves.

"Imagine this is Jaws!" I hollered.

Rodrigo turned around and looked at me, confused. "Ah, come on Garrett. What are you talking about?"

"Look! There's the right and a little left, just like Jaws! Put me on the right!"

Rodrigo gunned the 'ski, dropped me on the wave as if he'd been doing it all his life, at the perfect place on the little bowl. He nailed it on the first try. We did it a few more times just to make sure he had the hang of it. "Amazing," I said, "you're a total natural." He thanked me, but thought he should train more. At the event there would be a safety crew on call among the swells, so Rodrigo wouldn't be responsible for saving my life, just getting me where I needed to be.

I felt confident.

Cut to: two weeks later.

At the end of December, the Jaws contest organizers put the competitors on forty-eight-hour standby notice. Surfers were traveling from all over the world, and this gave them time to get themselves and their equipment to Maui. Rodrigo and I grabbed a flight from Honolulu that afternoon.

Next morning we arrived in the predawn dark at Maliko Gulch to launch our jet-ski and saw immediately that the waves were junk, maybe twenty-five feet blown out from an onshore wind and barely breaking. As the sun came up we drove out through the channel into the open ocean. A wave breaks on an outer reef a half mile from shore and it's fast. When Jaws is macking, the faces can be in the seventy-to-eighty-foot range, moving, conservatively, twenty miles an hour. The surfer is also moving down the wave at twenty miles per hour, which means he's actually jetting along at thirty to forty, sometimes even fifty, miles an hour, depending on the wave.

This is much faster than the speed he might be going on an average overhead beach break wave.

Rodrigo gunned the jet-ski and dropped me on a medium-size wave to practice. He positioned me right at the peak. I took off, and just as I was making the drop the wave suddenly hollowed out, removing water from beneath my board. I face-planted and tumbled to the bottom.

I'd watched footage of guys surfing Jaws in the past and I always thought, *What the hell are they doing on the shoulder? There's a freakin' barrel behind them and they're lounging around waiting for what, exactly?*

Now I knew. They were trying not to get killed. After that first wave, I could feel my heart banging with fear. I was scared shitless. My goal instantly readjusted itself from winning to just surviving. I didn't know what I was going to do.

The contest was scratched. The junk waves blew out into ten-foot mush. Rodrigo and I flew back to O'ahu. I kept training. I wasn't sure about winning the Jaws contest anymore. I tried to let go of my terror, but occasionally my prayers would include one that the three-month holding period for the Jaws contest would pass without another significant swell. I turned my focus to winning the Eddie. I knew I could win at Wai-mea. My own backyard. I could see the back of the wave from my front yard. I'd already broken my back there. I'd already eaten it on the biggest wave I'd ever encountered there. I'd surfed it so many times I felt as if I could do it with my eyes closed.

THEN CAME the first week in January and the window-rattling swell, and both contests called for the same day.

The night before I was up every hour calling to check on the buoy and wind readings. Every hour the forecast was updated, and through-out the night both the wind readings and the projected wave heights increased. I prayed that at Jaws the swells would ease off, peter out to nothing special. I lay down on the top of the covers. Closed my eyes and tried to breathe, then hopped up and checked again. I called out to Jesus, Buddha, Lightning Amen, Universe, whoever was up at that hour, to give me a sign. Meanwhile, the windows were rattling at a higher pitch. It was huge out there.

I was convinced I could win the Eddie, but there was a detail I kept conveniently overlooking. I was an alternate. The year before I had also been an alternate and had the depressing experience of being called in to compete, donning the neon bright jersey, paddling out to the lineup, nodding to the other six guys in the heat, then being called back in. The alternate on the list before me had been running late. I was devastated. What if that happened again? What if I passed on Jaws in lieu of the Eddie, then sat on the beach again? Also, what about Rodrigo? He'd come all this way, trusted me to take the lead on what was more or less my home turf. We were partners.

ONCE AGAIN we arrived just before dawn. Roy Patterson, my old mentor from the Wave Cave, had moved to Maui years earlier and let us borrow his 'ski for the contest. It was the Cadillac of jet-skis, with running lights and fishing rod holders and a nice sound system.

We turned off Hana Highway onto a winding, potholed road. It's a dark tunnel of jungle foliage that runs alongside a river. The way is usually clear, but this time, as soon as we turn off the highway we hear cracking, scraping, clonking sounds of kukui nuts and debris hitting the undercarriage of the truck. In the headlights we can see all kinds of crap—plastic milk jugs and boat bumpers and big branches. The water had surged all the way up the road.

The air was heavy, funky smelling. Salt, mixed with the smell of the earth. Eerie.

A steep, busted-up concrete ramp lead to the water. You had to line the trailer up with the ramp just perfect. If you started down and a set wave rolled in, the 'ski would be pulled off like a toy. Lots of guys lost 'skis, and even vehicles, to the surf all the time. Big waves broke on the truck, on the trailer as we inched it down the ramp. We worked quickly, timing the waves and launching the 'ski without a problem. The lack of calamity put me in a good mood.

The contest began with a ritual blessing. We stood in a circle as dawn broke, put a hand on the shoulder of the surfer next to us as a local Maui holy man distributed ti leaves for luck, one for each of us and one for our 'ski. He said these waves were big and serious and that we must make it our goal to take care of one another out there. Rodrigo gave my shoulder a let's-go pat, and we were off.

Out there it was wild and busy with jet-skis and sleds and photographers with their big waterproof-casing-enclosed cameras in little boats, and the safety crews with oxygen tanks and backboards in their larger boats, and helicopters overhead darting around like big tropical birds. The whirling blades drowned out by the roar of the waves.

There were two one-hour-long rounds. Each team had one hour to surf, switching places at the halfway point. Rodrigo surfed the first round and I surfed the second. The best three waves of each surfer would be scored and added to the best three of his partner. The team with the highest score would win.

Straightforward enough, but everyone knew that making six of these monsters in sixty minutes—that's ten minutes per monster—meant making no serious mistakes. A noninjury wipeout would sap your energy and slow you down, and valuable minutes would be lost as your partner zipped over to where you'd be gulping down air and trying not to feel dizzy, and then you hauled yourself onto the sled and quickly got your shit together to try it all again. If your feet slipped out of the straps and you lost your board, good luck finding it. Oh wait, there it is, bashed against the rocks.

In the interest of general safety, I'd also made our flotation gear at home, cutting the "flotation" pieces out of life jackets and using wet-suit glue to secure them inside our suits, and then wore life jackets on top of that. We were ahead of the curve, but obviously our DIY approach was no comparison to the custom Body Glove survival suit I wear today.

It was windy. The dark blue waves were raked with massive chops. Our plan was to play it safe and make our first three waves. If there was time left after that we would focus on catching another wave and pulling into the barrel.

I put him onto three perfect waves, maybe in the fifty-to sixty-foot range, and he surfs them flawlessly. I have no doubt they'll be among the highest scored all day (I am right).

As I put him on the fourth one, he takes off and pulls in high but the barrel, which is usually perfectly round, takes on a weird oval shape and pinches shut, clamping down on him, and he's sucked up and over the falls and disappears into the pounding, white water.

I watch from where I sit on the jet-ski just outside, looking for the tiny human head, a dark bead of color among the acres of aerated, foamy water.

He is under for a long time.

I spot him but have only seconds to rush in and grab him—a mountain of white water from the wave behind me is bearing down. I gun the 'ski, make it to where he's bobbing around, and pull him onto the sled. I give the 'ski some gas, but nothing happens. I try again even though I know what's happening—the 'ski cavitating in the foam; the impeller flooded with aerated water.

I'm a little panicked, mostly because I'm aware that this isn't my jet-ski, but a ten-thousand-dollar Cadillac and prized possession that Roy was generous enough to let me borrow. I grit my teeth, gun the 'ski again. It goes nowhere.

When you're in the foam it's like being stuck in the mud with an avalanche coming right at you. The white water closes in all around us. Rodrigo is out of breath and completely exhausted, but being the selfless champion that he is, he slides off the sled and gives Roy's 'ski a push, hoping to shove me out of harm's way. But the wave eats him, then grabs me and tosses me twenty feet into the air. I now bless Roy Patterson for having a 'ski with all the bells and whistles—he'd also sprung for foot straps. High up in the air, I grip the handlebars and use my feet to keep myself attached to the 'ski. I can't think of anything else to do, knowing that most likely I will fall over and, in this surf, it will be the end of me, and definitely the end of the 'ski.

I have no other explanation for what happens next other than the hand of God reaching out and setting me back down in the front of the wave, perfectly level and pointed toward shore. The second I land I press the gas, the 'ski sputters to life, and I'm out of there.

I can't believe what just happened.

In the meantime, thankfully, Rodrigo has been rescued by the lifeguards.

·　·　·

WHEN MY turn comes I breathe to calm myself and focus on what's in front of me. The first swell is twenty feet—a forty-foot face—nothing giant, but solid and respectable. I let go of the towrope and angle down the wave. After I've gone, I don't know, twenty yards across the face I can see the wall of water hollowing out in front of me, the lip heavy and threatening. I feel the urge to pull in now, but the plan was not to pull in until the fourth wave. Instead, I feel a rush of fear and kick out, bailing out of the wave back over the lip.

The humiliation is instant and absolute. I thought to myself, *This is the biggest contest I've ever been in, the biggest waves I've ever surfed, the biggest purse on the line, my career on the line, and I just wussed out.* I haven't given them a thought all morning, but suddenly I remember the thousands of spectators lining the cliff. I feel the eyes of every one of them boring down on me. From a half mile out to sea I can see their thought bubbles: *Garrett McNamara—total wuss.*

And it wasn't even a big wave.

To say I've lost my mojo is an understatement. Rodrigo speeds back around and I pick up the rope. We circle back around and we wait. I hate waiting. I hate feeling like I've let Rodrigo down. Let myself down. And even worse, I've jacked myself out of the moment. I can't focus. The hamster wheel in my head is whirring. *What am I going to do? What did I just do? What am I going to do next? How am I going to do this?* I remind myself what I know to be true about fear, that it's something we manufacture. It arises when we're stuck in the past remembering something bad that's happened, or projecting into the future, imagining something bad that will happen. Right now, in this moment, I know I know how to do this.

Finally another set arrives and the wave Rodrigo puts me on this time is twenty-five feet, fifty-foot face, and he puts me in the perfect spot. I torpedo across the face, almost get barreled twice—it takes everything I have to resist the urge—and finally make it to the channel and kick out.

Confidence surges with the adrenaline. *Okay*, I think, *let's do this.*

My second ride is similar to the first. Find the sweet spot and surf like it's a race to some invisible finish line.

But my wussing out on what would have been my first wave has indeed cost me. The minutes on my heat are ticking down. Rodrigo tells me we only have a few minutes left. The next set is cruising toward us. He guns the jet-ski and moves to put me in on the wave.

I shout no no no. Rodrigo guns it and we zip back over the shoulder. We wait, maybe twenty seconds, a long time. The second wave gathers itself up and again Rodrigo drives on the gathering peak. Again I shout no and again we move off over the shoulder. The third wave is usually the biggest one of the set, so I'm banking on that.

Rodrigo taps the face of his waterproof watch and gives me a what's-going-on-here shrug. We're running out of time. I point at the next wave, rising up huge and glistening, and he slingshots me into position. It's on. The squirt of confidence I'd gained on the second wave reassures me, calms me down, nudges me back into the moment, and now my hunger wakes up.

IT ISN'T the biggest wave and doesn't have much to it, but I'm able to fade for a while and do a snap and a cutback. Offshore wind is blowing a little stronger and I can hear the sound of the horn blowing, signaling the end of the heat. I execute a sharp cutback. I am aware of the mountain of wave on my back, but I'm not scared shitless racing out to the channel. I surf the whole thing as though I own the place, then I kick out at the end. I can't believe it. I've made it in the nick of time.

Rodrigo picked me up and we rode back to the gulch where we put the 'ski in that morning. The contest was over, and the judges were tallying the score. I felt optimistic. Our performance was solid if not inspired. Now we struggle to get the 'ski out of the water, same situation as that morning only in reverse, waves crashing on our backs and on the trailer and truck. I'm relieved for the distraction.

I can't remember how, exactly, we found out that we'd won. There was no formal announcement over the loudspeaker. I think a contest volunteer may have found us as we pulled the jet-ski from the water. I do remember my reaction. I walked away from the crowd and looked out at the waves. I asked for a phone and called my wife and I burst into tears.

At that moment, I thought about my months of hard work; the predawn workouts; the lean and clean eating; the mana and power I'd tried to embody as I walked around the heiau; the blueprint I'd written on impulse that day in the shop, listing, confidently, the winning of this contest as one of my goals.

I'd made the right choice choosing Jaws over the Eddie. I was only an alternate, and there was no guarantee I would have been able to paddle out. Even so, amid a little controversy, Kelly Slater had won the Eddie. At first Australian Tony Ray had been declared the winner. Tony was the tow-in partner of Ross Clarke-Jones, and one of those guys who lived and breathed big waves. Then Kelly Slater asked to see the judging sheets and, wouldn't you know it, someone had counted wrong. Tony's celebration was cut short when the announcer came back on and apologized. The winner was Kelly Slater. How easily I could have been in Tony's shoes.

HOUND OF THE SEA

THAT NIGHT I FLEW home. For the next week or so, people came into the shop to congratulate me. When I was shopping for groceries at Foodland they congratulated me. Sunset was pumping a little later in the month, and when I paddled out the boys (who I once thought of as the gnarliest locals) nodded and asked howzit and threw me the shaka. Definitely had the feeling that I'd gained some new respect.

I was proud of myself for making my blueprint and, along with Rodrigo, earning the win at Jaws. But it was unclear how it was going to help me with my ultimate goal: keep surfing. Sponsors didn't flock to me. I fielded phone calls from Red Bull, which I signed with (and left years later, after it came out that energy drinks were hard on your heart and in general bad for your health), and Quiksilver, which I didn't. (They offered me $2,000 a month and I thought I was worth more than that.) I also signed with No Fear clothing, and Xcel wet suits.

I was trying to be a better businessman, but a high-school diploma and *Small Business for Dummies* can only take you so far. The shop was doing all right, but I wanted to close it, and soon.

I was thinking about a Web site for the shop, and thought maybe

I should have one for myself too. It was 2002 and the concept of personal Web pages was just catching on. I didn't know a lot about it, nor did anyone I know. Surfers didn't care much about the Internet except when it came to predicting storms and the big swells that came with them.

"Claiming"—publicly acknowledging that you totally owned that monster wave or heavy-lipped barrel or snagged the wave of the day during a historic swell—was frowned upon in surf culture. Depending on who you were and how heavy the wave was, you were sometimes permitted to raise your arms for a moment of stoked triumph after a barrel spit you out. But after that it was best to underestimate the size of the wave and let others marvel about your epic achievement behind your back. It occurred to me that having a Web site was probably the digital version of claiming. But my instincts said that I needed to put myself out there if I wanted to succeed, instead of waiting for people to come to me. And anyway, Laird Hamilton, who people generally admired, had one and it seemed to be working for him.

The shop's Web site was hosted by a company called GlobalHost. The main office was in Haleʻiwa, above Coffee Gallery, and I'd seen their ads around town. One day during a slow afternoon I called and told them who I was, and said that if they cut me a deal I would consider them a sponsor and wear a GlobalHost T-shirt or run a banner ad on my Web site or whatever they thought was fair. The guy I spoke to asked whether he could call me back. I assumed he had to check with someone before setting up my new account.

A few minutes later the phone rang, someone named Lowell Hussey calling. He was on the board of directors at GlobalHost and also happened to live on the North Shore, near Log Cabins, just down the road.

"We'd be happy to host your Web site, but how about we also build you a better one, and why don't we meet and we can talk about management."

I said sure, because when do I not say sure? I was a little unclear as to what he meant about management. Did he mean managing my Web site?

Turns out he meant managing me.

LOWELL HUSSEY was one of those start-up guys who makes a fortune by the time he's thirty-five, then "retires" to pursue his passion, which usually involves making a few more fortunes. (Lowell was thirty-seven.) He had an MBA from Harvard and was a former senior vice president of marketing and programming for Time-Warner Cable. Solar energy, Web site hosting, digital communications—Lowell was into it all. He'd also volunteered to help big Kahuku High and Intermediate School, at the far end of the North Shore, eastside, start up their own e-commerce site. In their second year they were pulling down $150,000, mostly in T-shirt sales (their football team had been back-to-back state champs.) The kids were fully in charge and the profits were fed directly back into school programs. He would go on to build a few more companies, start a couple of charities supporting animal welfare, and introduce American football to Poland.

I put on pants and an aloha shirt and went to the meeting. Lowell was a big guy with a firm handshake and a lot of master-of-the-universe-type confidence. Most managers of professional athletes have no idea what to do with surfers, even now. Most surfers resist anything that gets in the way of surfing. Which pretty much means anything. We don't like to be counted on to be somewhere at a certain time because our passion and our reason to get up in the morning always depends on those massive storms tracking around the planet. Our daily lives are literally as changeable as the weather. Team sports and tennis matches are scheduled years in advance; the best we can do is have a three-month holding period for our marquee events. We are the only professionals in the world who have so-called big-wave clauses—if there are giant waves pumping somewhere on earth, we reserve the right to take off and not attend the event, the opening, the premiere, the fund-raiser, the whatever it is we've been contracted to do.

Maddening.

But Lowell Hussey was stoked by the challenge of helping me figure out how I could keep surfing.

We worked together for a few years and he taught me everything about business, specifically the world of marketing. How corrupt it was and how cynical it was and how political. All these things I had no desire to know and still wish I didn't know.

I was a little kid who grew up in a commune. I never had a father who came home and read the *Wall Street Journal* and talked about what went on at the office. Never had family holidays where the businesspeople talked about buying low and selling high. I was a boy raised on too much pot and no sex, no killing, no materialism.

Business, it turns out, is all about numbers. It is only about numbers. Only about profits. Bottom line is all that matters. Shareholders are all that matters. Everyone else is completely expendable. A corporate-sponsored surfer whose role it is to use a product to make it look sexy and glamorous by association, and whose only value lay in being photographed carving a beautiful line across a glassy turquoise wave in an exotic location, can be replaced in a heartbeat by a younger, blonder, smoother surfer who is photographed on a bigger, glassier, bluer wave in an even more exotic location. Chew you up and spit you out and on to the next guy and the next and the next, and that was how it worked.

This was no surprise to me. Hadn't I seen this in my own life when I broke my back? Out of commission for a single surfing season at the height of my so-called career and my sponsors fled, rats on a sinking ship. Didn't even have to look too far to find the next big thing—my own brother stepped right up. Lowell made me see that winning the Jaws Tow-In World Cup was all well and good, but unless I changed the way I thought about myself and what I had to offer the world, I would very soon find myself in the same position I'd been in before I bought the shop. Maybe now I'd be negotiating for $5,000 a month instead of $500, but I was still replaceable, probably by the next guy who won the next big contest. Also, staring down the barrel of thirty-five. Also, as Lowell kindly reminded me, not blond, not blue-eyed, not only not smooth, but rough around the edges. I found myself telling him something my dad once told me, that the original Celtic meaning of the name McNamara was "hound of the sea." Lowell laughed and said, Why not?

The only way to become irreplaceable was to distinguish myself from everyone else. To make myself recognizable as a big-wave hell-man named Garrett McNamara. The one and only. The hound of the sea.

Oh, I had a hard time with this. This went completely against the unwritten surfer code of ethics. We accept sponsorship money to wear the hats and T-shirts with the corporate logos, but we don't want our faces on anything. We don't want our names on anything. Maybe a limited edition surfboard, maybe. If a Japanese company wanted to stick my mug on a giant billboard looking down on the traffic of Tokyo, that was their business.

The bigger cajónes we have, the bigger waves we ride, the more we risk our lives, the more humble we're supposed to be.

I told Lowell all of this one day over breakfast at Cafe Haleiwa.

"I totally get your point," I said, "but I don't think I can do it."

"Let's try an experiment," he said.

Before I could ask what kind, he reached down and picked up a poster leaning against his legs and unrolled it. There was a glossy picture of the Jaws barrel and my name across the bottom in bold black letters. It was against everything I thought I believed in.

He'd had a limited edition made for $2 apiece. I signed maybe two hundred. We placed them in surf shops all over O'ahu. Unsigned, $5. Signed, $10.

They sold out quickly. Suddenly, my name was everywhere. I'm still not sure if I agree with the tactic, but it worked.

TEAHUPO'O

THE SUMMER AFTER RODRIGO and I won the Jaws Tow-In I could afford to get off the rock. The only place I wanted to go was Tahiti, where I had some unfinished business.

Teahupo'o is a half mile out from a tiny village on the southwestern coast of Tahiti. The wave is a rampaging left, a heaving slab of glass that doesn't break so much as collapse onto a coral reef so sharp that a side order of massive lacerations are served with every wipeout. Added bonus: the fire coral, abundant here, ensures that your open wounds will sting for days, then possibly get infected.

There's no real height to the back of the wave here, and in pictures taken from behind it looks like a moving waterfall instead of something that rises up and spills over. So much water is sucked up from in front of the wave it bears the distinction of being the only one in the world that breaks below sea level. Sitting in the lineup as every set rolls in feels as if the entire ocean is moving toward the beach. But however unusual the wave may seem, it's basically just a ridiculously huge closeout with a nearby channel that offers a last-minute avenue of escape.

Every aspect of the wave is life or death from start to finish. Surfing it puts your nerves on permanent edge. Once, in 2005, after a nasty wipeout I felt what I thought was a huge strip of my own thigh meat hanging from my leg. I reached down and touched the skin, but felt no pain. For a long moment I thought I must have brushed up against some poisonous coral that contained a neurotoxin. Then looked down and saw it was only a neoprene strip from the leg of my wet suit.

When Laird Hamilton surfed what came to be called the Millennium Wave at Teahupo'o in August 2000, after he emerged from the explosive foam ball at the end of the barrel, he sat on his board in the channel and wept. The cover of *Surfer* showed him just before the fat lip rolled over, and in the lower left-hand corner it said "oh my god . . ."

A few years earlier, Liam and I and a couple of up-and-coming kids made the trip the week before the Billabong Pro Tahiti contest. A bunch of other Hawaiians showed up as well, including Danny Fuller and Hank Gaskell. Everyone else was there to practice for the contest, but I was there to get barreled and have fun. It rained for three days—a steaming tropical rain with crashing thunder and lightning that sounded like a Star Wars lightsaber fight, so heavy and loud that Liam was practically in tears. But on the fourth morning the sun rose so we drove out to the break before dawn.

I was jittering with anticipation and fear. I had wanted to surf this wave for so long. I'd tried to get here ten years before, when only bodyboarders talked about the massive, freakish wave at the end of the road in the little village of Teahupo'o. I'd saved up money for a ticket from Honolulu, bought two weeks' worth of spaghetti, canned tuna, and mixed nuts at Costco, then was turned away at the airport when it turned out I didn't have enough money to bring along my surfboards. It was seven hundred dollars, more than my ticket.

I went home, and Scott Ostrander, the guy I was supposed to travel with, wound up on the cover of *Surfer*.

We drove the boat out to the lineup. The water was so clear. If you paid attention to the reef, you could see green-and-blue parrot fish, and bright orange clown fish poking around the coral. But no surfer wants to think about the reef. Instead I watched the freakish, thick slabby waves. They were the perfect size—not monsters—and I went for an eight-footer, the first of a set. It was a bad choice. It was like I was in an elevator and someone cut the cord.

The next few waves tossed me around some more and I wound up in the lagoon. By the time I paddled from there all the way around the reef and back out to the boat, I was tired. I decided to take a little break, get some water, and climbed aboard. Suddenly, seemingly out of nowhere, a ten-to-twelve-foot set rolled in. I forgot all about my thirst. Liam was still in the water, and I watched while he frantically stroked away from the curling wave. I've never seen anyone do this. One of the first lessons of surfing is to paddle *toward* the oncoming wave, but here was my brother paddling like mad toward shore, trying to outrun it. I understood the logic. The wave here is that heavy. Better to be thrashed in the white water than sucked up by the wave and smashed onto the reef. I prepared to go rescue him, but he managed to escape the worst of it. I didn't realize I'd been holding my breath.

There were also a few locals in the lineup that day, notable Tahitian pro Manoa Drollet and his friend Briece Taerea. Everyone was surprised by this sudden twelve-footer. Manoa and Briece duck-dived, and Manoa made it but Briece was sucked over the falls upside down and backward and slammed headfirst onto the reef.

From where I stood on the boat I saw Briece's board tombstone.

As I watched Manoa paddle to the board, I grabbed my board and started to paddle over in case someone needed help. Just as I reached Manoa he pulled up the leash till he reached Briece's limp body. His face looked as if it had been gone over with a meat tenderizer. He had a hole in his head. One massive gash had ripped apart his jaw.

Somehow I managed to get his body on the boat, where I administered CPR. Someone else's hands were reaching in, holding together the bottom of his face. Briece started breathing on his own, but he never came to. He was wheezing and coughing up bloody foam. Then he stopped breathing again. I kept doing CPR, kept pumping his chest until my shoulders ached. My own feet were in shreds from my earlier reef dance. I was sloshing around in Briece's blood. When we reached the shore someone ran to call the paramedics. We put Briece in the back of someone's truck and I jumped in with him. Once again he stopped breathing. I started back in with the CPR. We bounced down the narrow, rutted road toward the nearest hospital and were met halfway by an ambulance.

Briece was breathing when the paramedics, who spoke French to me, and whom I couldn't understand, loaded him in the back of the ambulance. I remember patting the top of his foot before sending him off. They put an oxygen mask over his face. We would learn that he'd broken two bones in his neck and severed his spine. He died three days later from a lung infection and cerebral edema, swelling of the brain.

TWO YEARS later it's a different story. Everyone's towing in now. It's busy out in the lineup. Jet-skis, boats in the channel loaded with photographers. The waves were twelve to fifteen feet. One set nearly capsized a boat in the channel. I should have been scared, but I knew I could feel Briece's presence. I had done my best to save his life. I thought about our blood mingling at the bottom of the boat. We were blood brothers.

The best waves of the day came right to me.

I made five covers, including *Surfing*.

BARRELED

AS THE MONTHS OF 2002 passed I forgot how scared I'd been during the Jaws contest, how my goal then had been simply to survive. Fear was slowly replaced by a desire to feel that rush again. Like any other junkie, I now lived with a twitchy, obsessive need to return to Jaws. It was far from my favorite break. I wasn't sure I liked it at all, but during the next giant swell I was determined to show up and get barreled on a sixty-footer. Hell, a seventy-footer. I wanted the wave of the day, the biggest monster barrel Pe'ahi could deliver, and I wanted to get so deep inside it I could set up housekeeping. I may have forgotten the fear, but I hadn't lost sight of how I'd run across the waves to the channel during my heat, fleeing the massive barrels breaking behind me.

Getting barreled is the peak surfing experience. My memory has never been the best, but I still recalled Brock Little's epic tube ride at Wai-mea in 1990, and how for a long time that was all I wanted. Now, this was all I wanted, and I wanted it bad.

At the end of November, one of those once-in-a-lifetime swells rolled into Jaws. There are storms that bring larger than average waves in all winter long, but once in a while there's one for the history books. This one came from Siberia, 60-knot winds, forty-five-foot swells heading straight to Hawaiʻi. By the time it reached Jaws on November 26, there were twenty-five-to-thirty-foot swells—fifty-to sixty-foot faces.

I couldn't escape feeling I had some unfinished business.

My new tow partner was Ikaika Kalama. There are a few so-called royal families of surfing that produce generation after generation of great watermen. The Kalama name can be traced back three centuries, with roots on Oʻahu and Maui. I never felt my age much, but Ikaika was just twenty-three years old and already an accomplished surfer and respected Hawaiian waterman. We flew to Maui and looked up Roy Patterson, hoping he might once again lend me his ʻski. When he heard it was me he said, "Not *the* Garrett McNamara. *Again*." That Roy Patterson, always clowning around.

"Yeah, bro, I'd be stoked to take you out there," he said. He showed up at the gulch. He was just as I remembered him, big bulging eyes, going full speed, as if he'd just had ten cups of coffee.

We put in at five o'clock in the morning, early birds catching the worms. It was still dark. We needed flashlights to see. The gulch was more eerie than before. Waves had rolled all the way into the valley and the ground was drenched, the air heavy with salt, debris scattered everywhere. Smell of wet earth, leaves rotting, gas fumes. We put our flashlights down and pulled on our wet suits.

It's tough as hell to get the ʻski in the water during the day, and in the pitch dark it should be impossible. But we get lucky and between sets we're able to feed it right between the rocks. We drive out to the break. We're the only watercraft as far as the eye can see. The moon has set and the sky is dark, the water is dark. We cruise down the coast. The only light is the occasional blink of our red running lights.

Later we would hear that the crowd assembling on the cliff to watch were tripping to see us out there navigating the swells in the dark.

The sky turned from black to dark blue, same color as the sea. An orange glow in the east. Light enough.

Roy asked who wanted to go. Ikaika, as usual, said "You go first." Roy whipped me into a few waves, clean and glassy, just perfect. No chop, no bumps, the white water a tidy line atop the lip. Usually Jaws was brutally windy—Ho'okipa, about five miles to the west, is the windsurfing capital of the world—but this morning there was no wind.

I caught a few waves. Perfect rides from start to finish. Couple of under-the-lip snaps but alas, no barrels. Now it was Ikaika's turn.

I floated in the channel, resting, watching the sun climb the early morning sky, trying to be grateful for this day and this life. I watched while Roy towed Ikaika into fifty-footers. They were so smooth and glassy it was like we were surfing in a wave tank in Hollywood.

Every tow-in team that could get itself to Maui would be there, so we wanted to grab whatever waves we could before the crowds showed up. Tow-in surfing, once thought to be some weird surf nerd fad, had become huge, and the paddle-in problems we once avoided—too many boards and bodies on too few excellent swells—had caught up with us.

While I floated there in the crowd, Dane Kealoha drove by. Dane was the son of a pure-blooded Hawaiian and a fierce power surfer, a North Shore god in the late seventies, early eighties, a huge gnarly wave-ruling presence when Liam and I were still surfing straight on the white water at Army Beach. He made the Pipeline Masters finals four times, the Duke Kahanamoku Invitational six times, and won both of them in 1983. Dane had one of those faces that looked as if it was carved in stone, and a crazy mop of curly hair. He kept to himself, silent in the lineup and scowling on the beach. I worshipped the guy.

He sat astride a little Yamaha old-school jet-ski.

"Hey, Uncle Dane!" I hollered.

He scowled in my direction.

"You driving anybody?"

"What, nobody driving you?"

"No, you like tow me?" I said in the Hawaiian pidgin I'd naturally adopted over the years.

He answered by throwing me the rope. The handle landed right in my hands.

"Can you drive?" I was so stoked to be towing in with the Hawaiian hero, my idol, the great uncle, I had bumbled my words. He gave me a classic Dane Kealoha black-eyed glare like, *What the hell, stupid haole, you're asking me if I can drive? Of course I can drive!*

"No, no, no, please, please, yeah I know you can drive! Let's go!"

His answer was not to drive over and give me a slap, which was one possible scenario, but to turn away from me, gun the 'ski, and drive back toward the lineup.

This had to be one of the most crowded days in Jaws history. It was like *Waterworld* out there, at least thirty tow teams, which means about fifty 'skis and fifty boards and the photographer power boats and a few safety boats for good measure. We're rising and falling in the huge swells and everyone's zooming around jockeying for position. I have to consciously take some big deep breaths and tell myself to relax.

Uncle Dane was intense, but he was chill. We would be fine. We would take our time. We would respect everyone. We would be humble. We would go to the back of the line and we would wait.

We were approaching the crowd as a set started rolling in so I was prepared for Dane to drive down past where the peak was likely to form, so that we could wait our turn. But Dane is royalty out here and royalty does what royalty pleases. Suddenly he makes a big, showy U-turn in front of God and everyone and I thought, *All right, this is it then; we're going.*

He eyeballed the wave, gunned the 'ski, and slung me right into the spot. For the past two years I had been surfing Backdoor, training for just this moment, getting barreled while towing in. That was my sole purpose in putting in, I guarantee you, the most hours out there. I chose Backdoor because every time you paddle into a wave there's a late drop that requires you to fall in, then pull in under the lip at the last second and drive through the barrel. It was a break that forced me to put it all on the line to get the ride of my life.

It isn't just the thought of massive sixty-foot walls of fast-moving water bending themselves over you that fuels the impulse to either kick out (as I did on my first wave during the Jaws contest), or make a madman run to the channel, fleeing the exploding white water behind you (second and third waves). It's also the thought of what's inside the barrel. As the wave breaks and the lip starts to close out, the mix of air and water creates spit, which sounds like something only a little annoying, but it feels like being on the receiving end of a fire hose, blinding, stinging, and sometimes with enough force to throw you off your board.

I drop the rope and take off. I'm flying down the face of the wave. I get to the bottom and start to turn. I can easily play it safe and run for the channel, but I can see the lip folding over, and way up ahead, the wave starting to bend. Everything is coming together. The barrel I have been dreaming of for years, all the hours at Backdoor and at

Pipeline. I stall and fade back to the left a little. The lips starts to fold over. I wait and wait. At the last possible second I turn under the lip, and it hits me, brushes the top of my head, *tsh tsh tsh*. Later my wife will call these three kisses. They blind me, these water kisses. I'm traveling through the barrel of my dreams but I can't see a thing. My world goes silent. I imagine myself in the eye of a hurricane. Even though I can't see I think, *I'm making it! I'm making it! I'm making it!* Suddenly I feel myself getting sucked back up the face. I'm starting to fall backward when I hear a roar. What must be a gale-force wind lifts me off the water. Luckily tow boards have foot straps. I stay on my board and the wind flies me through the air, out the end of the barrel, and lets me down in front of the wave.

I put my hands in the air, not as a claim. I put them up to God, in thanks for this gift.

Buzzy Kerbox was in the channel and saw the ride. "It's not going to get any better than that. You should call it a day."

Uncle Dane drives up and says, "Oh, brah, thought I was going to have to come rescue you, trying to figure out how I was going to do it on this turtle."

Kelly Slater came by and said, "That was the heaviest thing I've ever seen."

It was the best feeling I've ever had in my surfing life.

DRYLAND LIFE

IN LATE SPRING 2003 I was finally able to close the shop and "keep surfing."

Earlier that year Ikaika Kalama and I took first place at the Jaws Expression Session. I also caught two of my most famous waves, epic barrels at both Jaws and Teahupo'o, which earned me two covers of *Surfing* magazine in one year and countless other magazine covers. The wave at Jaws was by far the best barrel I have ever experienced. Inside the tube I was blinded and couldn't see anything. It felt like the hands of God lifting me up and placing me neatly out of harm's way. The Teahupo'o session was right after Briece passed away and I could feel him looking after me, every perfect wave kept coming right to me. It gives me chicken skin just thinking about it.

I was proud of myself, felt so grateful and so blessed. But life on dry land was exasperating and complicated. Like every surfer I know, I secretly believed if I could just be in the water every waking moment, life would be perfect and trouble-free.

I'd made my goal, was making my name and doing all the things Lowell advised me to do, and yet still I had money troubles. I paid my bills, but anything extra had a way of disappearing to things that didn't serve me and my family. Sometimes I just sat down and scratched my head. How had I not anticipated this? I'd gained more sponsors and was earning more money than ever before, but my expenses had also kept pace.

My full-time job was now chasing the world's biggest swells. Everything depended on it. Supporting our family of four, my mental health, the "Gmac brand" (as Lowell called it). Before, if I couldn't afford to drop everything and jet off to Brazil or Australia or Tahiti at a moment's notice, no one much cared. I was small potatoes. My sponsors were cool with the occasional nice photo of me surfing here and there on the outer reefs. Now that I'd upped my game and public presence, now that I was sponsored by bigger corporations with bigger expectations of me, I couldn't risk passing up any monster swells. They didn't come around that often. Sometimes entire seasons would pass with no historic waves. Sometimes my sponsors would foot the bill, but mostly it was on me to get myself and my boards to the swell. The cost of last-minute plane tickets was out of control. I'd bought used cars for less.

That summer, to makes ends meet, I took a real job where you show up at a certain time, put in a set number of hours, and go home. It was the first straight job I'd ever had, the first one where I didn't have to figure out how to drum up business. I was on the pickup crew at the military base. A government job, $35 an hour with benefits. That seemed like an incredible amount of money. Our task was to do the detail work left undone by various contractors with fat military contracts. First night we had to relocate a big propane tank that had been installed in the wrong spot. I got to man the jackhammer. Freed the tank, moved it to the right place, re-poured the busted-up concrete. Regular guy work.

When a monster swell was predicted in the Southern Hemisphere the boss let me have the time off. How could I beat that? But I was grumpy when I got home from work. I was that guy who walked straight to the fridge and got a beer, then turned on the TV and yelled to the wife in the other room, "When's dinner?"

I felt too tired to train when I came home after work, so I eventually stopped training altogether. I started partying a little. Just a little! Connie wasn't happy. How could she be? She'd thought my wild ways were behind me. She was proud when I wrote my blueprint, trained like a maniac, cooked our healthy dinners, and was in bed every night at 8:30 like a third grader. Now, when I wasn't at my job, I was glued to the computer checking the swell forecast—something, with the explosive growth in both storm tracking and computer technology, I could now do twenty-four hours a day—or in a strategy meeting with Lowell Hussey; or dropping everything on a moment's notice, leaving before the birthday party, the holiday celebration, the eagerly awaited vacation, on a plane flying somewhere for a ton of money to meet my next monster wave.

Meanwhile, Liam had suffered a terrible wipeout at Pipeline. He was crazy in love with that wave, but it was a punishing mistress. He'd already endured fifty stitches in his head from being dragged along that brutal, shallow reef during what would have been a normal wipeout anywhere else (except Teahupo'o, where the reef was sharper and even shallower).

In October, a month to the day before I got barreled at Jaws, he took off on a normal faster-than-you-can-blink Pipeline wave and dropped in a second too late. When his board pearled he was flung into the air, bounced once off the face, then was smashed onto the reef. He broke his right femur and had to be airlifted to Queen's

Hospital in Honolulu. During a long surgery the doctors put a rod in his leg that extended from his knee to his hip. Just like me, Liam was now a family guy. His wife, Brandee, owned a clothing shop of her own on the North Shore, took care of their two kids, and was also now taking care of my now out-of-commission brother. He was pissed and frustrated and no picnic to be around. Connie and I tried to help out when we could, picking up kids from school events and taking them overnight sometimes. His doctors were not optimistic that he'd be surfing anytime soon. There was talk that this might be the end of his Pipeline career. But they didn't know my brother. Two and a half years later, in 2005, he would land a wildcard entry in the Billabong Pro Tahiti at Teahupo'o. Three years after that he'd be back at Pipeline, up to his old tricks.

One November day late in the afternoon, Second Reef Pipe was firing so I took my stand-up paddleboard out, just messing around. I was alone out there. Then I saw someone paddle up. Liam. We claimed and bragged and razzed each other like we always did. When the next set came in Liam called his. I cackled like a movie super-villain. He started to drop in but I swooped past him on my red paddleboard. Got totally tubed, poised my paddle out like an Uzi.

Liam was pissed. Liam was back.

JEFF CLARK, the big-wave legend who discovered Mavericks when he was a teenager back in the seventies, invited me to a contest there. I'd never been to that legendary Northern California break and never wanted to go. Everything I'd heard about the place scared me to death. The irony of being so fearful while riding for No Fear did not escape me. Mavs is a heavy, spooky wave in every sense of the words. It felt like a break that had intent, and that intent was to kill you. The water is cold and khaki green, and the visibility is nil. There is no beach, only dark, jagged rocks. The outer reef is a jigsaw, which in turn makes the wave complex, with a hollow opening section that roars into a near vertical bowl, then slows and flattens, then gets steep and fast again. Merciless. On a December day in 1994 the great North Shore pro Mark Foo drowned there on a nothing-special fifteen-footer. No one knows quite how he died, but most people think he was held under multiple waves by his leash, snagged on a rock.

My childhood fear of roosterfish had evolved into a fear of sharks that had only been heightened by watching *Jaws*. (For years after that I didn't want to take a bath at night for fear a shark might find its way into the tub.) There are sharks in Hawai'i, obviously, but I've never given them a thought. In my mind, they only bit surfers elsewhere. Mavericks, just north of Half Moon Bay, is also only about thirty-five miles from the Farallon Islands, one of the world's most active great white shark breeding grounds. So no. Had no great need to surf Mavericks. Except that now I'd become a fool for giant waves, the bigger the better.

People often ask me what it's like to surf a seventy-foot wave. At the rare times when the conditions are calm, when the sea is glassy and there's no wind, it's like cutting butter with a hot knife. When Liam and I were little we used to draw tiny cartoon characters squiggling all over a wave that was as big as the paper. That's what it's like on a glassy, windless day. You rip across the face with complete freedom, the sound of the wave wooooshing behind you, and it breaks.

But smooth and glassy is the exception. Normally you have wind, and a lot of it. So there's wind, there's chop, there's usually a little bump left over from the day before. Add to that your speed. You're going so fast. Everything is rattling—your board on the chop, your teeth in your head—and your feet feel always on the verge of sliding out of the straps.

The go-to comparison is snowboarding down a black diamond run studded with moguls while being chased by an avalanche. It's even trickier than that: if you want to get barreled, your goal is not to escape the avalanche but to taunt it. To wait for it, let it get just close enough so that you can tuck yourself inside its breaking curl. It's a flirtation, a dance. I used the word *taunt* here because it's the best one that comes to mind. I don't mean it to sound disrespectful of the power of the ocean, because no one knows better than me that the ocean will always win.

I can't recall how that contest went, but I fell in love with Mavericks. It was at Mavericks I came to terms with fear. One cold sunny day I was floating on my board and I realized that if a shark was going to cruise by me and mistake my gamey human ass for a turtle or seal, then so be it. At that very moment I was doing what I loved and there was no shark in sight, so why ruin it with worry? Fear is something we create, because we're stuck in the past or envisioning the future. If we stay in the present there is no fear. It's a challenging task. We have our memories, we have our active imagination, but as long as you stay in the moment, there is no fear.

I would go on to get myself to Mavericks for the next decade, every time that huge, complex wave decided to show up there. Mavs never loved me back. Once, on a foggy, windy day of twenty-foot plus swells I took off on a monster, attempting a snap beneath the lip to set up for the upcoming steeper section. The lip crumpled and I cartwheeled down the wave, and as my board flew past me, the fin slashed my arm. Through the gash in my arm you could see white muscle. Went to the local emergency room and sixty stitches later I was good to go.

Early in 2016 I paddled into a sixty-foot El Niño bomb—what *Outside* magazine dubbed "one of the heaviest waves a human being has ever attempted paddling into"—and suffered a wipeout that nearly killed me. I hit the wave and suddenly everything got brighter, a sign something was broken. I'd smashed my shoulder into nine pieces. Two surgeries later, and a handful of titanium pins later, I'm still recovering as I write this.

GLACIERIZED

I SAT ON MY board in thirty-five-degree water staring up at Childs Glacier, 190 miles east of Anchorage, Alaska, as the crow flies. It was the summer of 2007. My tow-in partner Kealii Mamala and I wore 6-mm wet suits, booties, gloves, and hoods. We'd been floating in the brown, ice-strewn Copper River for five hours, waiting for the glacier to calve. It was forty stories tall and—depending on the light—white, gray, or an aqua, and threaded with brownish veins of dirt, rock, and debris. When it calved, the thunderous crack could be heard from miles away. Up close, I could feel the crack and boom in my chest.

Our boneheaded idea was this: After a gargantuan pillar of ice neatly calved, separating itself neatly from the glacier and slid into the river, it would produce a rolling tsunami-style wave whose ride would be long and sick and life-changing. No one had ever done it before. It would be epic.

While I was at Teahupo'o in 2002 I met a photographer named Ryan Casey. His father, George Casey, was a documentary filmmaker who directed some of the first IMAX movies. He was nominated for four Oscars, including one in 1998 for *Alaska: Spirit of the Wild*. Ryan was a gofer on that production. He was a kid, maybe fourteen. One of the locations was Childs Glacier, fifty miles up a middle-of-nowhere river called the Copper, where wild black bears and brown bears co-exist and bald eagles are like house sparrows. Ryan said the local Alaskans liked to joke that they're so common the native Alaskans eat them for dinner, and like so many other things they taste like chicken.

Ryan and I worked together for several years, trying to develop TV shows and shooting footage for future documentaries. He showed up at a lot of the big swells at Mavs and Jaws and Teahupo'o. He was easygoing and professional and I grew to trust him, trust his judgment. One night he called me at home, off-season, out of the blue.

"Garrett, Garrett," he whispered. "I've got a great idea."

I said okay. I didn't have to be in the room with him to imagine the lightbulb clicking on over his head.

"Are you alone? Anyone around over there?"

"Kids are asleep and the wife's out; well, I'm not sure where she is but she isn't here."

"You can't tell anybody this, this is top secret. Promise me you won't say a word."

"Okay."

"Give me your word."

"You have my word."

"I have a wave for you, a new wave no one's ever surfed before." He went on to tell me about when he was with his dad in Alaska back in '95 and when they were filming Childs Glacier, he noticed that when the giant hunks of ice crashed into the river they created a nice rolling right, really clean, that went on forever. His brother Sean was the camera operator and Ryan, who had just discovered surfing himself, kept telling Sean to sneak some shots of the breaking wave. IMAX film is stupid expensive, and you don't just shoot off some footage for fun, but Ryan pestered Sean until he gave in and rolled camera for maybe fifteen seconds.

I said sure. Within five minutes a QuickTime media file dropped into my in-box. The pale green glacier was a wall of ice rising up behind a chocolatey wave that reminded me of Hale-'iwa when it's big and perfect. I was intrigued and excited and liked thinking outside the box. I'd heard of surfing in the Great Lakes and surfing the long wakes of giant cargo containers and thought, *Why couldn't this be like that?*

I assured Ryan that my current tow-in partner Kealii Mamala could keep a secret, and that I wanted to ask him to join the team. When it came to issues of safety, Kealii was conservative and reliable and the perfect guy for this kind of mission.

I got out a piece of paper and made a blueprint. First we needed a scouting trip to see the wave up close. Make sure the footage Ryan's brother had shot reflected something that happened on a regular basis, not once a decade. Also scope out the terrain, figure out where we would stay, where we would wait in the river on the 'ski, and where we might catch the wave, and feel for ourselves how freaking cold the water was. Then we had to figure out how to get everything up to Cordova, 160 miles southeast of Anchorage, then up the Copper River to Childs Glacier.

My main concern was the water temperature, which turned out to be the lesser of our eventual challenges. Kealii and I outfitted ourselves with 6/5/4-mm Xcel wet suits and 7-mm high-top booties and gloves and we flew up to Alaska. We drove a rental truck to the Miles Glacier Bridge, also called the Million Dollar Bridge—when it was built in the early 1900s it cost $1.4 million—and stood there with our boards, fully suited up, and looking down at the brown river with its hunks of ice floating by.

The clearance seemed about sixty feet, so we jumped in, just to get a sense of what it was like in the water. It took us about ninety seconds to realize this was a dumb move. The current was strong and pulled us straight toward the glacier. We floated downstream and caught up to a big flat grayish chunk of ice, maybe 10′ × 10′. It was drifting slowly, an invitation to climb aboard. There we were in our thick wet suits, our surfboards beside us, riding an iceberg. We joked about how there could be a caveman in this berg. We started to laugh—was this sick or what?—when it snagged on the bottom and started to spin while also breaking apart. We leaped off.

CHILDS GLACIER is the most active calving glacier in Alaska. We stood on the riverbank just opposite and watched while boulders of ice crumbled near the top, followed by a massive slab or pillar that would crack off and plunge into the water. True to Ryan's promise, a smooth peak, right and left, with maybe a twenty-foot face—it was hard to tell from that distance—would peel off and roll away. We consulted with a guy named Luke Borer, owner and operator of Copper River Cruises, who we'd been told knew everything there was to know about the glacier. We grilled him for one long afternoon, asking him every question we could think of about how it behaved under various conditions. How different sizes and shapes of ice affected the river and the waves, where the peaks of the waves formed, and so on. I was gung-ho and optimistic. Putting a positive spin on the situation was a long-time habit for me. I didn't stop to think of the negatives of the venture.

Once we were back on the North Shore I contacted my sponsors. We needed underwriting. No one was particularly interested. Some didn't think we'd actually be able to do it, and others just didn't get it. To show their support of Gmac, Fearless Big-Wave Rider, they gave a little. Not too much. Ryan and his dad, George, came up with some of the money. And Steve Luczo, CEO of Seagate Technology, had become a friend. After a tough personal time he'd discovered surfing, which changed his life, and he was also a guy who possessed a charitable aloha spirit. So I pitched him the idea, told him we needed about thirty grand, and that we'd also give him some points in the movie.

After the financing was in place, we assembled our gear and flew to Alaska. We talked two race-car drivers we knew in California to trailer up the jet-skis. Took them two days, all the way up from San Diego.

We camped at the recreation area. On the first morning we put our 'skis in the river and drove toward the glacier. In the weird early light it was aqua-colored and rose up and up and up. It towered over us, a many-blocks-long skyscraper of shifting, unstable ice, groaning and creaking like it was alive.

After an hour or so there was a loud crack and a mass of ice slid down the face into the river. Kealii gunned the jet-ski as the white water exploded and the wave began. But he hung back, trying to place me on the wave without getting any closer to the glacier than we needed to be. It didn't work.

We sat in the water for another hour or two. I'm still warm but I can feel the cold of that water around me, feel it encroaching. Next time the glacier calves—thunderous sound of the giant slab crashing down—Kealii drives closer and the moment I drop the towrope I finally and fully see the reality of the situation: I'm surfing a few yards away from a four-hundred-foot-tall glacier and I'm attached to nothing. I remember something Luke Borer said that hadn't registered at the time. Sometimes the ice "books"—a slab just falls off the face of the glacier like a book falling off a shelf. I envision myself squashed like a tomato. I imagine my family wouldn't even have a body to bury; I'd just be pulp at the bottom of this freezing river.

Even though I'd lost friends to the ocean, and had endured my own hold-downs and torn ligaments and stitches, waves were like familiars. You could learn a wave, understand how it worked, predict its behavior, know it like you knew a friend.

Now I was staring at death. If that thing calved on me I was dead. It was the heaviest rush I'd ever experienced.

After what seemed like the longest ride of my life—probably three seconds—Kealii picked me up and I lost my shit.

"We're out of here! I'm over this!" I wanted to pull the plug that minute. For once I didn't care about my sponsors or the generosity of Ryan's dad and Steve Luczo, or even if Kealii wanted a shot. I made Kealii take me back to shore and I called Connie on the satellite phone. I was sobbing.

"This is too much, I've got to get out of here. It's not worth it. What am I doing? What am I doing?"

I don't remember whether Connie talked me off the ledge or I just calmed down on my own. But eventually I collected myself, and Kealii, who is level-headed and usually drives me a little crazy with his caution, patted me on the shoulder. "No worries, Garrett. We can do this. No worries at all. It's all good." Then he started a fire and cooked some chili and we ate it and I calmed down.

For the rest of the week I was like a cat in the water. The river is littered with ice, everything from cubes to chunks the size of a mini-fridge. Also debris and rocky pinnacles on the bottom, and sandbars and rock bars and icebergs that for whatever reason have submerged and have attached themselves to the bottom. It was a nightmare. If any of that—cubes, mini-fridges, debris, sand, icebergs—gets stuck in the impeller, the 'ski's useless. The current was completely unpredictable. In some spots, it sucked you toward the glacier.

Kealii ended up getting the best ride, a solid ten-footer. For a native Hawaiian he sure felt at home in that godforsaken place.

I wanted to get barreled—because when do I not want to get barreled—and after sitting on my board up to my neck in frigid brown water for seven hours I got a big floater, then pulled into a tiny barrel, actually kind of just a little head dip, shampoo job.

I was stoked. Kealii was stoked. Shakas and high fives and happy as hell and we were never, ever going back.

I WAS now forty, and I'd learned a lot about myself that week. About risk versus reward, and how risk for risk's sake wasn't worth it. Also, about my level of deep comfort in the ocean, even among the monster waves, maybe particularly among them, and the true measure of my passion for surfing, that old and glorious pasttime of Hawaiian royalty.

But something else happened, too. The massive adrenaline dump of that first day, when I thought I was going to be killed, had ruined my capacity to feel the big rush. Rocketing down those long, near-vertical faces felt as exciting as a drive into town. Someone suggested I was simply desensitized. That I had ridden so many huge waves for so long that my perception of danger had been somehow recalibrated, so what the nervous systems of others viewed as a fight-or-flight situation was, for me, just another day at the office.

This was a turning point. I always surfed for the rush but now the rush was gone. Every once in a while, flying out of a giant, smooth barrel at Teahupo'o, I'd feel a little tingle up my spine, but nothing compared to the full body *Woohoo!*-claiming-arms-raised-thank-you-God-life-is-good rush of years gone by.

After I got glacierized I was never the same. Surfing, I knew, would take on a different meaning. I just had no clue what it would be.

ENCHANTED EVENING

IN APRIL 2010 IZZY Paskowitz invited me to a Surfers Healing camp in Puerto Rico. It was a tough time to get away. Connie didn't want me to go and I couldn't say I blamed her. We had an eleven-month-old baby, Tiari, born April 23, 2009. I'd also just signed a deal with a surfboard company to design a signature line of stand-up paddleboards (SUPs) and was also working on developing some rental property on the North Shore—another effort to secure some financial stability for the family—so dryland life was more chaotic than usual.

But I never said no to Izzy. Volunteering with Surfers Healing was pure and uncomplicated and it offered its own kind of rush. Izzy was a longboarder I knew from my early days on the tour. He was the son of Dorian "Doc" Paskowitz, who founded Paskowitz Surf Camp back in the seventies, one of the first schools dedicated to teaching beginners. Izzy's upbringing had been as crazy and dysfunctional as mine—he and his eight brothers and sisters lived with their parents in a camper and followed the waves, a pure bohemian existence with no schooling, lots of punishing health food, and enforced togetherness. Now Doc was in his nineties and had passed on the directorship of the school to Izzy.

Surfers Healing came about when Izzy and his wife Danielle's middle child (they have three), Isaiah, was diagnosed with autism. The only place Isaiah seemed calm and happy was in the ocean, and the only time Izzy and Isaiah truly bonded was during a surf session. It occurred to Izzy and Danielle that maybe this wasn't unusual, that perhaps there was something about the buoyancy and rhythm of the ocean that was therapeutic. Add the chance to ride a wave or two and that's a peak life experience for everyone—kids, their parents, and the surfers who are lucky enough to be able to help.

Going out in the waves with these kids was so emotional it was overwhelming, every day on the beach a roller coaster of tears of joy and tears of sorrow and feelings of giving and receiving. One sunny day I took a big seven-year-old named Jason out at one-foot Hale-'iwa and while we were riding the white water in together he shouted "I surf! I surf!" His parents heard this and wept. They said it was Jason's first spontaneous expression of pure joy.

The first time I worked an event it wasn't obvious to me that this was a great idea. Most of the kids don't want to go in the water, and they really don't want to lie down on surfboards. I watched while the more experienced guys wrestled with the kids, who yelled and kicked and sometimes bit. But the guys steadied the boards in the shore break, held the kids in place, and once they got past the white water something amazing happened: the kids would calm right down. Their world had become defined by the curved boundaries of the surfboard, and the rolling water and shushing of the shore break were comforting. Something in them settled down enough so that the other parts of their personalities could emerge, the part of them that was a kid in the water with a surfer and a board, about to have the ride of their lives.

As we caught a wave and pulled the kids to their feet, they'd gurgle and shriek with joy, and their parents, standing together on the beach, would be in tears.

At a clinic in Montauk a mother came up to me and said her son had been in "training" for weeks. She'd bought him a belly board and had been in the water with him every day, floating him back and forth between the lifeguard towers. This was a kid who, despite his disabilities, was eager to try to surf. After the clinic was over I worked with him until dark, until he could pop up by himself. After that, I made it my goal at every clinic to try to find the one child who was truly interested in the sport. I knew that for most of the kids this was just a fun day away from the usual difficulties and frustrations of their lives. But if there was a remote chance of making a surfer for life, I would take it.

I SHOWED up at Jobos Beach, on the northwest coast of Puerto Rico, where the Surfers Healing gala was to take place, in a new pair of camo cargo shorts, a V-neck shirt, and a new, signature driver hat I'd designed with Peter Grimm: dressed up, for me. I was early and standing around the bar with a few others when I saw her.

Across a crowded room, just like the song says. Well, semi-crowded.

She was dressed in a flowy sundress with her hair half-up, half-down, and I thought to myself, *whoa*. It wasn't as if I had never appreciated a pretty girl during my travels, but normally if I spied one I'd direct my friends in her direction. I'd never cheated on Connie and wasn't looking to now.

Then someone I recognized approached her. They talked a little and she laughed and it looked as if they knew each other well. It was Ernie Alvarez, a well-known Puerto Rican SUP champion. Maybe he was her date? Ernie moved off, headed back across the room, but I intercepted him.

"Ernie, who's that?"

Ernie grinned, clapped me on the arm. "Oh ho *ho!*" he said. "Nicole Macias. You should meet her."

He gestured over to the young woman. She came over and I now saw that she also had a beautiful smile. Warm eyes, lovely skin, gorgeous smile. I think that was probably the moment I fell in love, but it moves around a little in my memory. No—the truth is I was in love the second I spotted her.

"Nicole, this is Garrett McNamara."

She smiled politely. I could tell my name meant nothing to her. Turned out Ernie was not her date, but a friend of her father's. I gave her a chaste little peck on the cheek, which is a thing I do when I meet a woman. I don't know where I picked it up. She accepted the kiss, but was looking at me like *who's this old guy giving me the once-over?*

I lost sight of her during the sit-down dinner and the speeches and the auction and all the rest of the gala business. Afterward, there was a reggae band and I saw her again, standing alone near the bandstand. There was an empty couch near where she stood, so I went and sat down.

"So, hey, do you surf?" I called to her. So smooth.

"What?" She had to sit down next to me to hear.

"Surf. Do you?"

"Yeah," she said. "Do you?"

"Yeah, I surf," I said.

She told me how she was there for a stand-up paddle race, and was helping out at the gala as a favor to a friend of her father's.

I asked her what she did. When she said she was a teacher I fell a bit harder. Beauty and brains and a desire to serve. I told her I actually surfed for a living. She didn't believe me.

I went to the bar and brought back some tequila shots. We danced. That is, we sort of bobbed back and forth, side by side. I told her about an after party I'd heard about. She said she thought we could get a ride with Ernie and his girlfriend in his florist's van—that's how Ernie supported himself and his surfing, delivering flowers. But when she excused herself to go to the restroom, I ran away—out the front door and down the driveway. The night sky was thick with stars and the air was still. It was humid but cool. Problem was, I was staying at that hotel, so where did I think I was going? I had no clue. But I knew if I didn't get out of there quick something was going to start that I would have to see all the way through, and it would be amazing and cataclysmic and bring joy and pain and rearrange a lot of people's lives and open up new vistas and I was scared and didn't know what else to do.

"Hey, where are you going?" It was Nicole. That sweet voice. Calling after me.

I sauntered back up the drive as if fleeing into the night was a normal thing to do. We stood in the glare of the yellow lights beside a potted plant. All the guests from the gala had pretty much cleared out by then. Except for a few guests coming and going, we were alone.

"You know what? I've got to tell you something. You're a nice girl and a nice person but I'm married."

"I am too," she said.

"I know you're not," I said.

"Yeah, well, I am."

Then she launched into a speech about how she believed that everything happened for a reason, and that she had a feeling we were meant to be in each other's lives, but maybe just as friends, probably just as friends. I took this all in and then we said good-bye, and I thought that was the end of that.

The next morning I started my long trip back to California, where I was involved with a charity event for the Red Cross. I landed in Fort Lauderdale, my connecting flight to Los Angeles was oversold, and the gate agent was asking for volunteers to get bumped to a later flight. The night before, Nicole had told me that she lived in Fort Lauderdale. Her parents also lived there and her dad, Carlos, was a SUP distributor. Since I was now selling my own paddleboard line it felt like a wise decision to try to meet him and discuss my boards. Also, my own dad lived in Lake Worth near Palm Beach, and I hadn't seen him in a few years.

I hadn't had much contact with him during my late teens and early adulthood, but after my kids were born we began to rebuild our relationship. After my mom took Liam and me to Hawai'i he and Nancy circled the drain together, locked in a crazy relationship built on drugs and alcohol and their inability to call it quits. Finally, after maybe a half dozen years together, they split up. He moved back to New York and got a job managing the bar and wine cellar at the legendary French restaurant Lutèce on East Fiftieth Street. The only way he could succeed at his job—and he was determined to succeed—was to go cold turkey. No booze, no pot, no hard drugs. The one thing he and my mom had in common was a loathing of cold weather. He hated New York winters and would grab a flight south for a hundred bucks. Little by little he started investing in real estate in Florida. After September 11 he moved there for good.

On impulse I volunteered to rebook my flight. I congratulated myself on my excellent business sense. That's what this was, business. And Nicole Macias was a good contact to have. I'd traded phone numbers with Ernie the night before, and texted him about a half dozen times, trying to get her number. She had her paddleboard race that day so I didn't expect to hear back from her. I called Ernie this time and he picked up. My heart was pounding as I asked for Nicole's number. He was driving. I heard his girlfriend say something in the background, and then suddenly I was talking to Nicole.

I asked her how her race went, told her I'd been bumped off my flight and would love the chance to meet her dad. She gave me his number. Then an hour later I received a text from her. She was sitting at San Juan Airport and had missed her own flight back to Florida. I was frantic. We texted back and forth like hysterical teenagers. We could both feel how heavy it was.

"I'm scared to see you," I wrote.

"I'm scared to see you too," she wrote back.

THE NEXT twenty-four hours were easily the most emotionally fraught and awkward twenty-four hours in my life. And I say this as someone who grew up in a commune and wandered the country in a white robe when I was in grade school. I was desperate to see Nicole, but I called my dad and he picked me up at the airport. We sat on his couch in his house in Lake Worth and drank espresso. Nicole texted me that she'd managed to get on a flight standby.

Turns out there's a version of the coconut wireless in south Florida, because by the time Nicole landed, word had gotten out that Garrett McNamara was in town, planning on hitting the lineup in Fort Lauderdale. I'd had no intention of doing anything but angling it so that I could be with Nicole for even just a little while. But she wanted to go surfing, so we went surfing. Her dad, Carlos, showed up and seemed genuinely happy to meet me, and I tried not to hope too much that this was a good omen. There were a few other dudes in the water, too. The swell was—well, who can remember? Nicole wore her hair in little pigtails and had a white bikini—I'm going to say the swell was shoulder high, the water warm and Atlantic green, and Nicole was the only one who caught any decent waves.

Rory, one of the local known guys in the lineup, was married to the director of the floor show at a Polynesian restaurant. He decided that they needed to take me there. The Mai-Kai is a Fort Lauderdale institution, with tiki torches and tropical rum drinks and chicken teriyaki. We are shown to our table and Rory sits across from his wife, Ui. Carlos and Rose, Nicole's parents, sit across from each other, which leaves Nicole and me to sit across from each other. It feels now like a triple date. I wonder where Nicole's husband is. I don't ask.

Carlos knows a lot about surfing—turns out Nicole has a younger brother who surfs—and we pretend to talk swells and boards and wipeouts but all the while Nicole and I keep eyeing each other. My mouth opened and words came out and food went in, but really, no one existed at that table but her. After dinner Nicole and I went to an Irish pub for a nightcap. Then she drove me back to my dad's house in Palm Beach.

Neither of us said a word about seeing each other again.

"There's a good chance I might be at this charity thing in Las Vegas next weekend." I was being as cagey as I could possibly be. We were both married. I couldn't ask her to meet me out there. At that moment I would have given anything for a centipede to crawl up her leg, so I could snap it in half and fling it away and make her jump into my arms.

The air conditioning whirred. I looked out the window.

"My best friend in the whole world lives in Vegas, actually," she said. "So let me know if you go."

I went. She met me there.

NAZARÉ, MEU CORAÇÃO

AFTER OUR WEEK IN Las Vegas, Nicole and I knew we wanted to be together.

Nicole stayed in Las Vegas for a few weeks after I left thinking things over. She really was married, to her college sweetheart, and even though they'd been having trouble, she wasn't sure she could leave him. She thought of herself as being responsible, and she was responsible. She told me stories about playing teacher when she was little, and how her joy was making her friends write papers that she would then grade. She never went through a wild period in high school. Running off with me didn't fit in with her image of herself.

And yet.

My plan was to sit down with Connie and have a heart-to-heart talk about how things just weren't working out and hadn't been for a while. That wasn't just an excuse for my actions, although of course it was that, too. We'd become completely disengaged with each other. She always thought I was cheating when I was away, which I wasn't, and I didn't have a clue as to what she got herself up to when she wasn't home. I'd stopped asking years earlier. Still, I never thought we wouldn't be married. Years earlier I was flying the red-eye to a wave somewhere and watched a movie about a Boston mob boss. Matt Damon played an Irish criminal who one night tells his girlfriend, "You know, if this isn't gonna work you're gonna have to be the one to leave. I'm Irish and we can live with things going wrong for our whole lives." I laughed out loud in the middle of the dark cabin, flying over the ocean. I thought, *That's me.*

I hoped to ease into the conversation with Connie, who had already sensed that something was wrong. I hoped it wouldn't hurt too much. I hoped and prayed it would go smoothly.

It didn't.

Does it ever?

NICOLE AND I spent the summer in LA. The more I got to know her the more I realized that she was a rare woman, that there was God blessing me again when I didn't deserve it. She had worked her way through both undergrad and graduate school, sometimes holding down two jobs—she has a bachelor's in health science and a master's in environmental education—and also worked for a time as an environmental educator for the Fort Lauderdale chapter of the Surfrider Foundation. She taught science to gifted middle schoolers and was chosen from a thousand candidates to participate in NOAA's Teacher at Sea program. She is also a surfer herself, routinely placing in the top three in stand-up paddle contests.

I say all this so you'll know that when she asked if she could help organize the business side of the Gmac operation I couldn't say yes fast enough. One day when the surf was nonexistent she watched me "work"—shooting off single-word answers to e-mails, writing haphazard to-do lists on my laptop that I then deleted rather than saved, losing track of where I was supposed to be and when for some big meeting about something or other—she couldn't stand it another minute, deciding that she needed to do us both a favor by managing things. She was a visionary, like Lowell Hussey, but whereas Lowell focused primarily on succeeding in business, Nicole believed that you could be happy and fulfilled and live your passion while devoting yourself to giving back to the world.

Nicole's first order of business was reading my e-mails to catch up on everything I had going on. There she found a five-year-old thread between a Portuguese bodysurfer named Dino Casimiro and me about a big wave that breaks on the beach of an ancient fishing village called Nazaré. He'd attached some pictures—huge thick-looking A-frames. I'd written back and said it reminded me of Jaws. There the exchange had stopped. I'd never been to Europe, and can honestly say I'd never given the waves of Portugal a thought.

"What do you think about this Nazaré place?" she said. "You want to go?"

All surfers dream of discovering a wave, pioneering it, and putting it on the map. There are two types of discoveries. Waves no one has heard of before in some crazy, tough-to-get-to spot in Ireland or Tasmania or Brazil or Micronesia; and waves, usually on outer reefs, thought to be completely unrideable. Before Laird Hamilton, Darrick Doerner, and Buzzy Kerbox towed into Jaws in 1995; before Jeff Clark paddled out at Mavericks in 1974; before Greg Noll proved to even the locals that twenty-five-foot Wai-mea could be ridden in 1957, those waves were part of the great unknown.

We thought it looked as if this Nazaré place might be both.

Nicole worked her magic—everyone I know is jealous not only because she's beautiful, smart, and kind, but because she's a genius at making stuff happen—and within a few months we received an invitation from the Portuguese government to fly over and check it out.

Before we left for Portugal, Nicole and I met Alan, Bill, and Michael for dinner. Before the waitress even passed out the menus we were reliving the past. We argued about who decided to introduce our parents and which was the best, most gnarly bike ramp we'd ever built, and about that day Benet the Rastaman caught us spying on him and Nabia having sex in his backyard canopy bed. They accused me of being the instigator, the one who always wanted to climb up things and jump off.

Alan is still Sir Lancelot, tall and lanky, now a father of three and one of the higher-ups at Guitar Center. Bill is a fast talker, articulate and smart. He was working as a restaurant consultant and has writing aspirations. Michael is a successful BMW salesman, with a full team working under his guidance. We joked that he really was the golden child. We've all had our troubles, but against all odds we seem to have turned out okay.

NAZARÉ IS an hour's drive north of Lisbon on the central coast of Portugal, an old fishing village and local tourist destination, one of those little coastal towns packed with vacationing families in the summer and stone-cold empty in the off-season. There are whitewashed buildings with red-tiled roofs, narrow cobblestoned streets, a broad yellow-sand beach, wooden frames loaded with mackerel, and sardines drying in the sun. The town is most famous not for a monument or historical landmark or cathedral, but for the women, who still wear the traditional seven layers of petticoats under black knee-length skirts. No one knows why seven. The reasons are lost to time.

Some say each skirt stands for the number of waves a fishing boat must crest before it is safe.

When we drove into town on a stormy day in November, the streets were empty. We were told to be prepared for the widows with rooms to rent. During July and August they line the streets in their lawn chairs, cardboard signs advertising the size and price propped on their knees. But we saw only a few of the hardy ones, or the desperate ones.

We went straight to the lighthouse, constructed in 1903 atop the centuries-old Forte de São Miguel Arcanjo built to protect the town from marauding Norman and Moroccan pirates. It sits on a point between the Praia do Norte, where you can watch the big swells roll in, and the main beach and village to the south. We sat in the car and looked out at the ocean. It was a stormy day. The wind howled around us. It felt strong enough to blow the car away. I pushed open the door and got out. The wind roared, almost took my hat. My eyes watered. I made my way toward the cliff, and there I saw the biggest waves of my life. Dino Casimiro, who'd first emailed me, wasn't the only Nazarean who thought the wave here was something special. Two young guys who worked for the mayor were also interested in finding a way to put their wave on the map. Paulo "Pitbull" Salvador, a bodyboarder who also ran a local surf school, and Pedro Pisco, a non-surfer who nevertheless knew a ginormous wave when he saw one, both worked for the mayor. They'd come up with the idea of inviting a respected big-wave surfer to check out their wave, see if it was rideable, and whether it'd be possible to hold a big-wave event here. Since I was on the search for the elusive—some said mythic—hundred-foot wave, it was a match made in heaven. We quickly realized we could make one another's dreams come true.

Dino, Pitbull, and Pedro met us at the lighthouse along with Jorge Leal, who would become our trusted videographer, and gave us the tour. People are a little wary of the ocean here. When the Atlantic storms came in the winter, it felt like earthquakes all day long. The waves gobbled up the broad yellow beach and flooded the streets. People died in the shore break every year. There was even a spot called the Reef of Widows where the wives of fishermen would wait for their husbands' return, only to watch their boats capsize and break apart in the surf, and the men drown.

Surfers hungry for new challenges may not have known about these magical mystery waves, but the Portuguese navy surely did. But before I could put a toe in the water we needed to get a special license and special insurance to prove that we had working jet-skis and also adequate safety backup, both in the water and on land. This required many conversations and meetings. To their credit, the navy didn't think we were totally insane to want to surf here. They showed us their charts so we could understand how the swells worked and eventually, after our first season surfing here, they put out two buoys so we could monitor their size.

IN THE same way the North Shore of Oʻahu is first landfall for every mighty northern Pacific storm, Praia do Norte is the most westerly point on the European continent, landfall for northern Atlantic storms and all the huge eastbound swells that roll uninterrupted across the ocean for thousands of miles. Those prevailing north/northwest swells would produce familiar nothing-special big waves, if not for the undersea canyon to the south of the lighthouse.

Nazaré Canyon is three miles deep at its deepest point and runs a hundred or so miles east from the open ocean to less than a half mile from the beach, where it angles north, running past the cliffs and the lighthouse. When the swell comes from the west-northwest the energy of the wave is funneled through the narrow deep canyon until it hits the end, and the depth changes radically and suddenly from thousands of feet deep to about sixty. Here the waves jack up crazy; they're the tallest teepees you've ever seen. Some rise up as huge mountains and, as they roll, meet another slab section. As the widows could tell you, the biggest trick is getting out of the shore break and onto the beach. You think you've survived the waves, you're standing in the shallow water, and then you get sucked back out. People die there every year just standing on the beach. If you combined Jaws, Puerto Escondido, and the Wai-mea shore break and put them all on steroids, you'd get Nazaré.

Nicole and I stayed for a month in a small, dark, but comfortable apartment in the middle of town. We became close friends with the Nazareans who'd invited us. We shared meals, threw birthday parties, did favors for each other. I didn't go to college, but Nicole said our camaraderie felt similar.

Many of the restaurants were closed for the season, but there was a bright place with a blue awning on the Avenida da República, the main street that ran along the beach, Restaurante a Celeste. Not long after we arrived we went there for lunch—clams (Ameijoas à Bulhão Pato) with *migas* and potatoes cooked in garlic and olive oil, and for dessert, *arroz doce*, rice pudding. The food was excellent and we struck up a conversation with Dona Celeste, the owner and chef, who bustled out of the kitchen in her chef whites, complete with toque. She, too, believed in the power and magic of the wave, and agreed then and there to sponsor us.

Over time, Celeste's would become our headquarters. I conducted interviews and meetings there and when I wasn't surfing, sleeping, or driving to another part of Portugal for a meeting or to give a talk, we hung out there. When Thanksgiving rolled around, Celeste researched recipes for a traditional American meal and set about cooking one for us. I pressed her into letting me help her with the feast, and it was the most meaningful Thanksgiving Nicole and I had ever celebrated. Celeste would go on to spoil us rotten, keeping pace with our dietary needs, going so far as to learn a number of vegan dishes, which she feeds us all winter long. There is a huge language barrier, but so much love expressed just the way she looks at us. She speaks to us with her eyes.

WE SPENT the winter of 2011 in Nazaré documenting our search for the biggest wave on earth. More preparation went in to this than you might imagine. There were dozens of logistics to tend to, basic training, and learning the break. It was a team effort. Pitbull spent hours at the warehouse, organizing and performing maintenance on the jet-skis and safety equipment. Pedro and others would spend time talking to the media, in an effort to get some press.

In late October 2011 a storm popped up on the Atlantic weather map. I monitored it obsessively and called in some reinforcements, in the event she decided to show herself.

I still needed a tow-in partner. Before then I'd paddle out by myself, exploring the break around the lighthouse, on either a big-wave gun or paddleboard. I still hadn't found a tow-in team in Nazaré I felt I could trust 100 percent. The bigger the waves get, the more crucial it becomes to work with someone who will without hesitation risk his own life to save your own. Kealii, my current partner, was in Hawaii and unable to make the trip. I was introduced to a Portuguese guy, the only surfer who could both drive a jet-ski and had knowledge of the break. He could put me on the wave with no problem, but was a little hesitant to rescue me in the impact zone.

Renowned Irish big-wave charger Al Mennie was up for the task, as was his partner, Andrew Cotton, a part-time lifeguard and plumber based in Croyde, England. Both were known to be fearless and determined. The first day in the water the waves were big and a little disorganized. It was gray and windy with some serious chop. Andrew put me on the wave and after I wiped out, without any hesitation, he came straight over to pick me up. He pulled me onto the sled, then took off at full speed toward the beach. At the last second, he executed a perfect-ten spin, flying us over the white water. Right then he gained my confidence in his ability.

Cotty, as Andrew was called, was dying to be a full-time professional surfer. It's not like England is a hotbed of surf culture, so he couldn't figure out how to make it work. I recognized myself in him. He wasn't the world's most gifted surfer, but he was passionate about big waves. One day during our third year working together I would sit down and tell him about the blueprint concept. How if you write down your goals and commit to them, anything is possible. As I write this he's quit his plumbing job, is sponsored by Red Bull, and has gained a reputation as one of the world's up-and-coming big-wave surfers.

IT WAS clear this was going to be a monster swell. At 9 a.m. on October 31 the wind was light, WNW, and the buoys were reading eight meters, or twenty-six feet, which translates to a fifty-foot face, at least. That was my minimum these days. That's what it would take for me to drop everything and jump on a plane. Lucky for me, I was already here.

Since my revelation at Childs Glacier that the rush I once lived for wasn't really happening anymore, I wasn't interested in getting in the water for anything less. I suspected that if the surfing rush was going to return, it would be for the biggest wave in the world.

I'd been training since my birthday in August. I'd given up alcohol and coffee and ate mostly fish and vegetables again. I'd lost twenty pounds. I was forty-four years old. I had a hundred scars; some intense learning experiences; and an extraordinary new lover, partner, and friend.

I got up in the dark and Nicole stirred and got up with me and together we performed our morning ritual of reading and writing together. Then we ran to the lighthouse to check the surf.

The people of Nazaré had been generous to us, even though the town was struggling. The local fishing industry had fallen on hard times—local waters were overfished—and the national economy wasn't great either. Also, a complicated and unfair public policy saw that Nazaré received government subsidies based not on the hundreds of thousands of people who used the roads, bridges, and beaches during the high season, but the fifteen thousand year-round residents who lived with the crumbling infrastructure.

Nevertheless, with the help of our new friends at City Hall, we managed to secure two beat-up, used Sea-Doos. A local fish broker generously leant us a warehouse to store them in. We made a deal with a Portuguese multimedia group called Zon to produce a documentary (it wound up being three) of our exploits.

The swell was in the sixty-to-seventy-foot range, a bit bigger than we'd anticipated. The waves were glassy and smooth. Long rights coming from way up the beach to the north; the weather was sunny and mild, with an offshore breeze.

We got underway at 8 a.m. Pitbull stationed himself on the cliff with his binoculars, and Nicole took her place on the roof of the lighthouse with a walkie-talkie. She and Pitbull would be our eyes, reporting on the incoming swells, pointing us to a promising, possibly perfect wave, and directing us to the location of a downed surfer. Jorge Leal positioned himself on the beach with his video camera, poised to film the day's rides. French documentarian Thierry Donard happened to be in Nazaré that day and sprung for a helicopter to catch some aerial shots.

Al Mennie, Andrew Cotton, C. J. Macias (Nicole's brother), and I drove out to the lineup. We surf all day, sticking mainly to the second and third peak. We have no desire to surf the first peak. This wave breaks so close to the cliff that if someone wipes out it's nearly impossible to rescue him. It was a textbook fun day in the world of big waves—long steep rides down fifty-foot mackers—but nothing for the history books.

Just as we're about to head in for the day, I put Al on a wave and he goes down almost immediately and loses his board. He's carried into the break zone, a chaotic churning war zone of white water. I power my way into it and haul him onto the sled. The white water roars around us. It's nearly impossible to escape. A wave looms up in front of us, a sixty-foot wall of glassy blue. I gun the 'ski, but we're too late and the next thing I know we're speeding vertically up the face and I'm staring at the late afternoon sky, and then we're going backward over the falls.

I abandon ship. Al holds onto the sled for dear life.

Cotty has to come in and rescue us both.

MOST MORNINGS I wake up at about 5 a.m., amped to get up and have at it, but the next day, after that last wipeout, all I wanted to do was cuddle in bed with Nicole. I had zero desire to leave the warmth of our little room, squeeze into a cold wet suit, and brave the ocean.

As I drifted back to sleep, I heard someone pounding on the door. It was the boys, bringing news that it's already firing. Again, in the sixty-to-eighty range, peaky A-frames, less organized than the day before, coming from a more westerly direction.

When you're on a team you have to make sacrifices. I told them I'd be happy to drive the 'ski, put them on as many waves as they wanted, but I wasn't up for surfing myself. I was tired, and my entire body ached. I told them—as if they needed to hear this standing in front of my door at five-thirty in the morning—that we should only surf when we feel like it. Only surf for the right reasons. Only surf for love. We should never be doing it for records, for sponsors or publicity.

It was sunny again, but a little chillier. Winter was definitely on the way. We launched from our usual spot at the harbor, a five-to-ten-minute ride from here to the break at Praia do Norte.

The boys were right. The waves were immense, dark green and peaky and a little disorganized. I was happy just to be on the water. I put Al on a wave while Cotty drove the safety 'ski. His ride was flaw-less. At the end the wave crumbled and flattened, and he kicked out over the low shoulder.

When it was Cotty's turn Al drove the safety 'ski. On his third wave, Cotty wiped out and lost his board, an avalanche of white water sending it straight into the beach. The impact zone looked even more treacherous than the day before. Cotty told us to forget about it, and instead of trying to retrieve the board we drove back out past the lineup to regroup.

Al and Cotty were done for the day, but together they convinced me that we couldn't call it until I grabbed a wave or two. The sun hung low in the sky and the wind had picked up. I thought maybe it was best to get it over with.

I jump in the water and begin my "reset" ritual, which I learned from Kent Ewing, a spiritual guide and healer who's worked with surfers, including Greg Long before he won the 2009 Eddie. Floating there, I take deep breaths into my belly. I imagine breathing in all the energy around me. Energy from the water, from the fish swimming beneath me, from the trees on the shore.

A few minutes of this reconnects me to everything surrounding me, and I have a clear sense of purpose, and what I need to do next.

At this moment, what I need to do next is go to the bathroom. My wet suit is around my ankles when I hear Nicole's crackling voice on the walkie-talkie.

"You've got a macker coming, Garrett. I don't know how big it is, but it's big."

I'm done relieving myself and now I feel good and more excited than I've felt all day. I haul my wet suit back on, and grab the tow-rope. Cotty pulls me up just as the sets start rolling in.

"Wait for the third one, Garrett," says Nicole.

I do as I'm told. I wait.

Finally, I feel the third swell beneath me, lifting me up. I look out at the shore and I'm rising above the cliffs, above the lighthouse.

This wave has got to be at least sixty feet, tall as a six-story building. And I'm still going up. I close my eyes for a moment and when I feel as if I'm in the right spot I hold on for another half second, and then I let go.

The drop down the face is long. It feels endless. I rocket on down. The face is choppy, the wind is fierce. I can hear, as well as feel, the roar of moving water beneath me. I'm focusing on navigating the chops so I can pull into the barrel. I try to get deep, but then the wave crumbles as the lip crashes onto my shoulders. I breathe deep, stay present. I'm not feeling any rush, per se, just a nice wide-awake feeling.

I make it out and Cotty is waiting for me on the 'ski. I hop on the sled and, over the roar of the engine, yell to him to put me in deeper next time.

Nicole is on the walkie-talkie. "Time to go to the harbor," she says matter-of-factly. I know her well enough to know this tone. We're done for the day.

Only later, when we look at Jorge's footage (Thierry Donard had left the night before), do we realize this wave was a history-maker. Nicole, of course, had seen it immediately. The consensus would be that it was a rogue wave that had jacked up higher than the others. Still, it was the biggest wave we'd seen since the day we'd first set foot in Nazaré.

SEVENTY-EIGHT FEET

WITHIN A FEW DAYS a picture of me on what would become known as "the wave" made its way around the world. In it, the wave is front and center, a peaky deep-ocean blue monster left just about to break, white foam frothing on top. A thin white crescent-shaped line veers left, down and across the face. I'm the fleck of color at the end of the white line in the bottom right corner. In front of me and almost obscuring me is the bright white rooster-tailing crest of another wave.

While I was on the wave, and afterward, when Cotty swung over and picked me up on the 'ski, my main impression was that the drop was unusually long but at no point did I feel as if I'd just nailed the world's biggest wave. I was just enjoying the ride. Privately, I'd only wanted to get barreled that day. Deep down inside I knew that there were bigger waves, and this hadn't been one of them.

Two days later Kelly Slater tweeted about the ride, saying "I just saw a shot of Garrett Macnamara [sic] from Portugal on a stupidly big wave. He should post that thing ASAP. Looks like huge Jaws." A week or so after that a public relations firm in Nazaré sent out a release that said "Garrett Mcnamara Breaks World Record Riding A Wave Around Ninety Feet In Nazaré!!" Then the big media outlets hopped aboard. First, ESPN. Then CNN, NPR, *Sports Illustrated*, the *Daily Beast*, the *Huffington Post*, and *Good Morning America* all reported that I had surfed a ninety-foot wave, which would make it the biggest wave ever surfed in the world. The current record holder was Mike Parsons, who surfed a seventy-seven-foot wave at Cortes Bank in January 2008.

Of course no one knew how big it really was. Waves are tough to measure. They're always moving, and once they've broken they're gone and all you have are photographs and tape from a variety of angles, none of which is 100 percent reliable. Added to that, it's always been part of surf culture to refuse to know how big that wave is you just rode; if you are forced into estimating, you'd better downplay it.

But times change, even as we resist it. Now that surfers routinely towed in, all the once unrideable outer reef and even open ocean monsters are there to be ridden. It was no secret that the swells we were all chasing all over the world were the biggest we could find. Given that, the old habit of always underestimating the size of the wave you'd just managed to ride seemed, if not demented, then seriously outdated. If the wave you surfed was sixty feet, it should be acknowledged as sixty feet.

Bill Sharp, onetime editor of *Surfing* magazine, realized this and came up with the XXL awards (now sponsored by Billabong) as a way to point a big red flashing neon finger at big-wave surfing, to acknowledge and honor the accomplishments of surfers who are risking their lives to follow their passion, and also to capitalize on an ever-growing sport. The categories have evolved over the years: Biggest Paddle, Tube and Wave; Ride of the Year; Best Overall Performance for both men and women; and one I have won several times, the Golden Donut, for the most artistic wipeout.

Measuring is now taken very seriously by the XXL organizers. No more underestimating in the interest of false modesty. Every year a panel of surf photographers, filmmakers, journalists, and big-wave surfers and surf-world legends convene to examine photos and video footage of the nominated waves and rides. Their task is to measure the height of the wave from the trough to the crest. The biggest challenge is figuring out where the trough is—that's the bottom. Once everyone agrees on that, it's a matter of comparing the crest with the height of the surfer, usually in a crouch, taking into consideration how tall he is in his stance, no easy feat. There are hundreds of entries for Biggest Wave every year, and a lot of times the difference between winner and also-ran is a matter of inches, the decision sometimes unduly influenced by who sponsors the surfer, who he rubs shoulders with, and who might be his champion on the panel of judges. To say this is subjective is an understatement as big as the waves being judged.

It would be a few months before the XXL experts judged the 2011 waves, but in the meantime we sent footage of my ride in Nazaré to a few people whose opinion we trusted, including a former XXL judge (who pegged it at eighty-five to ninety feet), an oceanographer, and Kelly Slater and Greg Noll, who were and are fair and unbiased. Everyone said it was big, possibly record breaking. I said nothing, went about my business. Surfed Nazaré for the rest of November, mostly paddling out by myself, then returned to the North Shore for the rest of the season.

The surfers' code is that you surf your wave and let the world discuss it as you move on to the next one. That I was doing exactly that was lost on people. I never said a word about how big or small I thought the wave was. I didn't ask the good Kelly Slater to toss a tweet out there, nor did I know anything about any public relations firm. I didn't have a publicist. I had my love Nicole helping me. Still, it was generally assumed that I or someone I'd hired was breaking the code and claiming, bragging, about my ninety-foot wave.

Weirdly, I was also held accountable for the awkwardness of the mainstream media people who covered the story. CNN sportscasters don't generally report on surfing, and I think they can be forgiven for sounding dorky when they say "That was completely gnarly!," but many in the surf world found this to be heinous. By surfing my big, strange, off-the-beaten path wave I'd drawn the attention of kooks and outsiders. The surfing media made their feelings known about the whole thing by ignoring both the wave and my ride. I was upset by this not at all. My goal was simply to ride the biggest wave I could find, and also to show the world, not just the small surfing community, that Nazaré was (and still is) the only place on earth where an average person can experience the power and energy of a wave of this magnitude safely from shore.

Then, in May 2012, the jury came back and my ride won the XXL Award for Biggest Wave of the Year. The final measurement was seventy-eight feet, a mere foot taller than Mike Parsons's 2008 Cortes Bank ride.

Biggest Wave isn't the biggest in terms of payout. (I won $15,000, which I split with Cotty.) That distinction belongs to Ride of the Year, at $50,000; in 2012 Nathan Fletcher won for barely surviving a heavy close-out tube at Teahupo'o. But along with Biggest Paddle it's the most coveted and the most potentially career changing because they are recognized by the Guinness people as official world records.

The *Guinness Book of World Records* is one of the best-selling books in the world. People from all walks of life buy it and love it and swear by it. If you're a surfer with a world record, you're a surfer whose name and accomplishments will be recognized by people outside of surfing. That crossover appeal is the holy grail of corporate sponsors. You, along with perhaps two or three others, are now the face of surfing. To everyone who rents a board at Waikiki during their weeklong vacation or has to buy a pair of shorts for their kids, you are The Surfer. That I, who've never been the most popular guy on the block, should be granted this by God or the universe or whatever manages good fortune struck a lot of people as an example of how anything in life is possible.

I WAS honored and humbled that the panel didn't let politics cloud their ability to judge me fairly. After I made my comeback in 2002 and won the Jaws Tow-In World Cup, the eyes of the surfing world were on me in a way they'd never been before. When I took off on nearly vertical waves that no one else would touch, people assumed I had no fear. When they watched me suffer epic wipeouts then come up smiling, it was decided I had a screw loose. When I explored Childs Glacier, I got a bad rap as a crackpot and attention seeker. The truth is I'm afraid of a lot of things. Horses. Skydiving. The thought of rappelling down the side of a mountain. I just feel more at home in the ocean than on land, living among the world's big, barreling waves.

The politics of place must have also been tricky among the judges. Mike Parsons, the record holder before I came along, rode his winning wave at Cortes Bank. This felt right. Conventional surf world wisdom holds that Cortes Bank has the biggest rideable waves on earth. Part of it is location—the outermost point of the California Channel Islands chain with no land in sight, nothing but blue water, blue sky all around, pure wild ocean. A hundred miles due west of San

Diego, Cortes is a submerged seamount, part of the Channel Island chain. During the last ice age it was an actual island, a sandstone and basalt mesa with a few high spots, about eighteen miles long. The shallowest peak is called Bishop Rock and rises up between three and six feet beneath the surface, depending on the tide, and this is where the monsters break. It takes all night to get there in a powerboat, an adventure in itself, and everyone believed—not without good reason—that someday when someone tows in or paddles into a hundred-foot wave, it will be at Cortes Bank. This was before Nazaré was put on the map.

To acknowledge that the biggest wave in the world might be a shore break off a little Portuguese town no one has ever heard of flies in the face of what passes for reason in the surf world. That it was ridden by Garrett McNamara, daredevil–cowboy–action figure–future *Fear Factor* contestant–brother-of-etiquette-challenged Liam (I'm missing a few adjectives, but you get the picture), is to commend the integrity of the judges. I was and am grateful.

STILL, THERE was something else. Since I'd met Nicole I'd begun thinking more deeply about my life and my place in it and about my desire for worldly success. I'd spent my entire adult life thinking that if I just got a magazine cover, just placed in the money in that contest, just won that XXL award, just got invited to the Eddie (actually, it's still an honor to be invited, and every year I get amped like a little kid before Christmas in the weeks before they announce the invitees), I would feel successful and whole.

During the week we spent together in Las Vegas, Nicole started reading Deepak Chopra's *Seven Spiritual Laws of Success* to me. She would read a chapter every morning. I was crazy in love by then, completely entranced by this woman who was beautiful and warm and smart and deep. And full of surprises. No one, outside of maybe my kindergarten teacher at Malcolm X Elementary, had ever read aloud to me.

There was and is so much to absorb. About non-judgment, giving, karma, intention and desires, least effort, and the one that struck me immediately—dharma, our purpose in life.

My dharma in life was to surf. It was my abiding passion, the thing I was devoted to above everything else, the thing I excelled at. Aside from the love I have for my children and for Nicole, there was nothing else. But was that it? Securing new sponsors and winning prizes and being invited to surf in the Eddie?

I didn't think so. I thought about my upbringing, not just the poverty, but the lack of guidance, the lack of any adult taking any genuine interest in nurturing my brother and me. I ran wild and got into trouble and could have ended up in prison. But for some reason I didn't. I kept moving forward, kept surfing, kept trying to make a living surfing, my great passion. I failed time and time again, made bad decisions and did stupid things and hurt people and shot myself in the foot. And yet, I kept on.

And now I found myself here. *Guinness Book of World Records* holder for riding the biggest wave on earth, sought after by sponsors who would have never taken my phone call. And marrying my true love.

November 22, 2012, was a perfect day. Surfed all morning in glassy twenty-foot swells, then took a shower, put on a pair of white pants and a classic patchwork Nazaré shirt designed for me by Nicole, then married her on top of the lighthouse. My hard-luck life and now all this good fortune. I followed my heart, and this is where it had led.

INCIDENT AT CORTES BANK

WE RENTED A LITTLE house in Praia do Norte. It had a 180-degree view of the Atlantic from the living room. We turned it into the master bedroom so we could lie in bed in front of the fireplace and watch the waves. Celeste had become our Portuguese mother and her niece, Maria Ana, an attorney in town, joined our close circle of Nazarean friends. We were starting to think of the village as our second home. Every day I continued to monitor the swells from around the world, and in December, not long after the wedding, there was a promising forecast for Cortes Bank.

Cortes Bank doesn't break very often. In a good year there might be three chances to ride those eerie, open ocean waves. In December 2012 the forecast was promising, so Nicole and I flew from Portugal to California. Once we arrived, I called Greg Long and we set about chartering a boat. Even though Cortes has traditionally been a tow-in spot, our mission was to barehand it, and I couldn't have been more excited.

Paddling into big waves was deep in the middle of a comeback. I was amused by the turn of events. The old way of catching a wave was now the new way. Towing in, once a genius solution to both the problem of overcrowding on the inner Hawaiian reefs and a way to ride waves thought to be unrideable, was now out of style. It still solved the same problems—inner reefs were still crowded, and a wave with a seventy-foot face was still largely unrideable—but surfing technology had evolved since the early 1990s. With the advent of inflatable flotation wet suits and life vests and the WaveJet—a surfboard equipped with battery-powered jets that gives you a little more speed—in order to grab that much faster moving wave, tow-in-only waves were now being routinely paddled into by the best of the best. Even as I write this the Pe'ahi Challenge, the first ever big wave paddle-in contest, is being held at Jaws, formerly the tow-in capital of the world.

Within a day, word of a paddle-in assault on Cortes Bank had gotten around, and other friends wanted in. Greg Long and I decided that I should charter another boat. My unpopular attitude has always been the more the merrier. I hate crowded lineups as much as the next guy, but this swell at Cortes was likely to be historic, and I didn't want good friends to miss out. Kealii Mamala, Chappy Murphey, Kohl Christensen, Danilo Couto, Alex Grey, and Dave Wassel all quickly signed on; and also Liam's kid, Landon. At sixteen, he was already charging in the big waves.

Despite my reputation as a daredevil I am a freak about safety. Surfing Cortes carries with it more risk than surfing any other spot in the world. You're in the middle of the ocean and there's no calling an ambulance if something goes sideways. I hired Shawn Alladio, founder of K38 Water Safety and the best big-wave safety person in the business. She brought along her five most trusted medics. The day before we launched, we double-checked to make sure we had everything we'd need to ensure our safety—extra flotation gear, oxygen, defibrillator, backboards, trauma kits, and six 'skis for safety patrol and rescue, designed specifically for the job.

It was Christmastime in Southern California, clear and cold. We left Dana Point harbor at 3 a.m. Everyone was bundled up in jackets and knit caps. Keyed up a little. The forecast wasn't perfect. It would be windy out there—15 miles per hour was predicted—but the waves would be perfect for a big-wave paddle challenge, fifty feet, give or take.

The water was silky smooth to San Clemente Island. Past that, it was open ocean and the chop began. Five miles this side of Cortes Bank there was a bright flick of something against the early morning sky. I looked through the binoculars and saw waves cresting and breaking.

We stopped at the buoy at Bishop Rock. Brown California pelicans and seagulls wheeled around overhead. Despite the chop the visibility was good. I could see fish swimming among the long tangled ropes of bull kelp. Cortes Bank was also a big fishing and diving spot—yellowtail tuna, black and white sea bass, and huge schools of baitfish were all down there, as well as sea lions and the sharks they attracted. There were a few shipwrecks down there too.

The boat rocked and the buoy bonged and we staggered around the deck trying to pull on our wet suits. Greg Long's boat was stationed maybe fifty yards away. His photographers and videographers and safety crew were already in the water. Eventually, everyone made his way to the half-mile-long lineup, around fourteen surfers in all.

It was partly cloudy and cool. The waves a little mushy due to the wind. Nothing but ocean, 360 degrees of it, far as the eye could see. Sitting in the lineup at Cortes was just plain bizarre. Surfers typically use landmarks on the shore to position themselves—lifeguard towers, public restrooms, tall trees, cliffs, boulders, homes, snack shacks. Out there are only your very tiny-looking boat and the clanging buoy and miles of rolling blue seas straight to the horizon in every direction. That, and instinct.

ESPN HAS called Greg Long the best big-wave paddler of the twenty-first century, and I can't disagree. He's won every big-wave paddle award there is to win, including the Eddie, in 2009, in fifty-foot waves. He's won more Billabong XXL awards than anyone else. Born in San Clemente, California, where his father was a lifeguard, he was named for Greg Noll, another excellent citizen of the sport. Like all of the greats, he started surfing seriously when he was in grammar school. In his teens, he started surfing Todos Santos off the coast of Baja and Dungeons off Cape Town, South Africa, both gnarly, complicated waves that take no prisoners.

Greg Long is also a really good guy. He's smart and well-spoken and fair. Many say he's the most decent guy in surfing. If the lineup is like high school, with prom kings and jocks and soshes and nerds, and troublemakers and stoners who are one infraction away from getting expelled, then Greg Long is the popular student-body president and star football player. When he wins the awards that he keeps winning, year after year, the applause is always loud and heartfelt.

We are spread out across the break, hunkered down on our boards in our wet suits and black hoods. The waves are miles long here, since there's nothing to impede or steer their progress. The takeoff zone changes from set to set, sometimes by as much as fifty yards, and

I'm trying to gauge whether I'm in a good spot for the next set. The first wave rolls in but I'm not in position so I let it go. Greg Long is paddling past as Landon takes off.

"How old is he?" Greg asks, laughing. When I say sixteen he says, "That kid just became a legend."

We lose site of the pack and find a spot at the end of the lineup. A few minutes later there is a set on the horizon. I paddle as fast as I can toward the channel, thinking there is no way Greg can keep up.

Another set arrives. I let the first one go, but when the second wave rises up I paddle as fast as I can. There's no holding back in waves like these, no room for second thoughts. Once you've begun to move you're committed. It's second nature, and we're all trained this way. There's no "after you; no, after you" in big-wave surfing. These waves are so long several people can share them and do, all the time, but from my vantage point I am alone. In front of me I see only the steep, bumpy face and the rough cobalt-blue sea, no sound aside from the low roar of the wave pulling itself up to its full height.

I'm trying out my new WaveJet. It seems perfect for these waves. An average big wave moves at 25 miles per hour, but out here they move faster, more like 40 miles per hour. All morning long guys have been missing waves they'd paddled for because they simply aren't going fast enough. The wave is an open ocean right. I skitter over the chop to the bottom, start to make my turn when over my shoulder I glimpse the heavy lip curling and about to crash. There's no doubt that this isn't going to end well. I jump off my board, take a few deep breaths to prepare myself. I'm wearing two flotation devices—a Body Glove survival suit and a Patagonia vest. I deploy my vest and pop up after the expected heavy pounding.

After I catch my breath and get my bearings I see something that's not quite right—two jet-skis idling nose to nose, a rescue sled in between and someone in the water pulling Greg Long onto the sled. His eyes are closed and he looks a little purple. I figured he must have gotten worked on the wave after mine.

Once he was secured on the sled they drove him back to his support boat, leaving one of the jet-skis bobbing nearby. I drove it over to his boat to find him lying on the deck looking dazed. He'd just regained consciousness, and as he came to he turned his head and started vomiting blood and water. One of his safety people was tending to him, but I didn't think it would hurt to have more hands on deck. I drove over to our boat and picked up an EMT and our backboard, just in case. When we returned, Greg was conscious and alert, but clearly traumatized. He bore the signs of someone who'd nearly drowned. They decided to radio the Coast Guard, and three hours later he was airlifted to a hospital in San Diego.

Meanwhile I noticed that all the safety 'skis were bobbing beside the support boat—all safety personnel having responded to the emergency—and that no one was watching the half dozen surfers still out in the lineup. I took one of the 'skis and worked safety until the last surfer was done for the day.

It was after dark when I finally returned to my own charter. It was only then, when I looked at the footage, that I saw Greg and I had shared the same wave. He was behind me and I'd never seen him.

Later, after we were back on shore and Greg had been released from UCSD Medical Center, where they kept him overnight for observation, I learned that his own flotation vest had malfunctioned and he'd tried to climb his leash back to the surface. He'd been held down for three of the four waves in that set and finally blacked out from lack of oxygen. DK Walsh had pulled him from the water, where he had been floating facedown. Photographer Frank Quirarte and firefighter and paramedic Jon Walla had resuscitated him.

TWO DAYS later Greg issued an eloquent statement to the press explaining what happened and thanking everyone who saved him. He acknowledged the high level of risk involved in surfing big waves, and at Cortes Bank in particular. He never mentioned my name, but he didn't have to. The surfing press was already buzzing, accusing me of dropping in—the most heinous crime in surfing—and further raking me over the coals for using the WaveJet, an invention I'll always defend because it gives folks who might otherwise never have the opportunity a chance to experience the exhilaration and pure joy of riding a wave. Some surfers just need a little extra speed, but there are also people like Jesse Billauer, a California surfer who became a quadriplegic at seventeen when he broke his neck during a wipeout, who've been able to surf again unassisted using WaveJet technology. It's also been adopted with enthusiasm by lifeguards, since the WaveJet allows them to reach drowning swimmers faster.

Surfing purists, who would have us all surfing on planks of wood and wearing loincloths, despise pretty much all technological advances in the sport, and wanted my head. During interviews surf journalists, who are supposed to be impartial, prefaced questions with stuff like, "Garrett McNamara . . . essentially cut him off. And on top of that Garrett McNamara was riding a WaveJet. Those things repulse me. I am not a big fan of WaveJet at all. I don't think they belong in the lineup. That's just me. What's your take on it?"

The comment sections of every surf news report and blog post of the incident bristled with stories of what a monster I was, of how I'd dropped in on them in two-foot waves fifteen years ago at a place I'd never been to and practically killed them. If I'd dropped in on all the people who said I'd dropped in on them, I would have been banished from the sport long ago.

Even though Greg kept reminding the world that big-wave surfing, especially at a place like Cortes Bank, is a high-risk activity and what happened to him was not unexpected and that he'd trained for such a thing for years, someone needed to take the heat.

I issued my own statement telling my side of the story and apologizing for any part I may have played. It fell on deaf ears. Three weeks later, in early January 2013, Greg issued another statement saying that I wasn't to blame.

WHAT COULD I do? I was devastated that Greg, someone I thought of as a friend, had had to endure this. I was hurt that surfers whose opinions I respect thought I might have caused it. As for the legions of Internet haters, it gave me an opportunity—minute by minute!—to embrace the practice that "lions don't care what sheep think."

After I said my piece I kept quiet and didn't try to defend myself further. Nicole and I were still reading Chopra every morning. The fourth Spiritual Law of Success is the Law of Least Effort, part of which asks us to learn to accept things as they are. "Today I will accept people, situations, circumstances, and events as they occur."

It also calls for embracing an attitude of defenselessness. People waste most of their energy defending their point of view. By letting go of the compulsion to defend yourself, you free up enormous amounts of energy to do meaningful things and make the world a better place.

I accepted everything that was said about me and tried to view it as the opportunity for growth it most surely was.

BIG MAMA

IT WAS LATE JANUARY, only weeks after Cortes Bank, and we'd just made our way back to Hawaii. In 2012 Nicole and I secured some property on the North Shore near Waialua, a few miles and worlds away from Cement City. It was a little under two acres, a long thin parcel of land off Farrington Highway. The main house looks out over Moku-lēʻia, an off-the-beaten-path break I used to frequent when I was still strictly a Six Feet and Under boy. It was built in the early 1960s and looked as if no one had done so much as slapped a coat of paint on since that time, and there were three four-unit apartment buildings that needed refurbishing.

My mom still lived on the North Shore, in a condo near Turtle Bay, out past Sunset and Velzyland, at the other end of Kam Highway. Throughout her life she's been on a spiritual quest and is now born-again. She's found happiness with a Polish American, Bernard Rzeplinski. She plays Scrabble and bridge and has started golfing. She lunches with her friends from church. We laugh that she's a hippie gone yuppie, with a lot of Christianity sprinkled on top. She finally settled on a name for herself: Malia, the Hawaiian name for Mary.

Liam retired from surfing about ten years ago, having won more

Pipeline trials than any other surfer in history. Once in a while he still competes, just for fun. He's a North Shore legend now and something of a retail mogul, with three surf shops, two clothing boutiques, a shrimp truck, and a shave ice truck. His focus is on business and his three sons, my nephews. Makai is twenty-one and has become a top contest surfer. He was the standout surfer in the recent Volcom Pipe Pro and the crowd favorite. Landon plays ukulele and guitar, has just signed with Ford Models, and is still charging hard. Ledgen, the youngest, is good at everything. He adopts a sport, excels at it until he's the best on the team, then moves on to another one. When he was born I told Liam he had to leave the *d* off because you aren't born a legend, you have to become one. Guess he took my advice.

We had been home only three days after four long months away when the forecast for central Portugal showed a thirty-foot swell was heading toward Nazaré. A low-pressure system moving from New York southeast across the Atlantic. This spelled huge waves, sixty-five, seventy minimum. Possibly even the rogue hundred-footer I'd been waiting for. It wasn't quite the right direction we wanted, but it was the right height with a good enough interval. I couldn't help but hope this would be Big Mama.

My tow-in partner Kealii had coined the term. Big Mama was the big, perfect, hundred-foot wave, the wave of a lifetime, the wave that, once you rode her, if you never rode another one that would be okay, because you'd already experienced Big Mama. For me, she was the wave that was going to be massive enough and fast enough, a true moving mountain of water that gave me the rush I had once experienced the time I first rode big Sunset, or the first time I towed into Jaws.

The Nazaré forecast is always unpredictable and this one was typical: One day perfect, the next day lousy, then perfect again, quickly deteriorating to lousy with maybe a three-hour window that morning, with light winds offshore and waves in the seventy-plus range. We decided it was worth driving to Honolulu and making our way back across the world to Nazaré. The chance that Big Mama would show up was always worth it.

We arrived in Nazaré around midnight, in time to hear the swell starting to pick up. At dawn it was huge, and the tide was going out. I was on the rope. Kealii would tow me in; Kamaki Worthington, a firefighter friend from the North Shore, was on the safety 'ski; and Hugo Vau was on the backup safety. Game plan was to drive out into the channel and just sit and wait and only take the wave that has Big Mama potential, nothing less.

It was a gray day, fully winter. Low clouds, gray ocean. We bobbed in the channel for two hours.

Finally, a ridge starts to form. It goes up and up. Doesn't look as if it's moving forward on its way to breaking, but like it's rising up straight out of the ocean like some movie special effect. Up it goes, faster and faster. Kealii tows me onto it. We're trying to find the spot where it looks as if it's going to break, but it's anyone's guess.

Kealii has an expert's eye and puts me in the right spot, right in the middle, so I don't have to cope with all the bump and chop. He's driving full speed, turns out, and I let go of the rope. Must be going sixty miles an hour. But the wave keeps backing off. It just wants to go up. It doesn't want to break. It's like I'm snowboarding. Board chattering down the mountain, brain rattled, body rattled. My back foot comes out of the strap and I manage to jam it back in.

And still the wave won't break.

I'm finally forced to kick out when I reach the rocks at the base of the lighthouse and the next wave is right there. Kealii tries to drive between them to pick me up and misses. The second wave breaks. The white water is roaring toward me. I push my board toward the channel and swim under the wave. I'm breaststroking in the dark, roar in my ears, under I go. Somehow, by the grace of God, I come out the back and turn to see the wave spill straight onto the rocks.

Meanwhile, Kealii tries to outrun the wave. I surface to see him hit a big bump. He flies off the 'ski. He goes one way, 'ski goes the other. I'm in the impact zone, heading toward the rocks. Kamaki on the first safety 'ski grabs me. Hugo, on backup safety, grabs Kealii.

Kealii takes his turn and surfs a handful of heaving monster waves, riding them with effortless Hawaiian ease. Then Hugo's up and does the same. It occurs to me, watching them charge, that the best rush is when I can put my friends on waves they'll be telling their kids about.

When we make it back to shore Nicole is waiting for us. She had been standing on the cliff, watching. Her face is ashen.

"For the first time, I had to look away," she said.

I was disappointed. What I rode that day was a huge, freakish swell that never broke. It crumbled a little at the top, then flattened out and disappeared. They say Eskimos have fifty different words for snow. Maybe surfers need that many for waves. We totally need one for what I rode that day in Nazaré.

SOMETIMES I think back at myself with my little portfolio of surf-mag clippings, going from office to office in Tokyo trying to woo sponsors and marvel at how low tech it all was. The biggest media splash imaginable was landing a cover on *Surfer*.

The thing I rode that January day was documented by a photographer I didn't know. The picture was taken from behind and above the lighthouse. There are some phone lines in the foreground, the roof of the lighthouse with the light on the left and a few very tiny spectators on the right. In back of them, rearing up much higher than the lighthouse, is a huge gray wave/swell with a little foam on top, and me rocketing down the center.

The photographer zipped it out to *Surf Europe* and the XXL Awards, and in a matter of days headlines on the Internet were screaming about how I'd ridden a hundred-foot wave. I was just like, *What the hell are these guys doing?* The wave barely broke.

The picture is amazing. The angle makes it look bigger than it is and from a purely photographic perspective the Nazaré wave has an advantage that no other monster wave possesses—it can be compared to something other than the little surfer at the bottom of it. The viewer sees the lighthouse perched high on a cliff and thinks, *What is that, eighty feet up?* And the wave looks even taller. It requires no leap of the imagination. It's something everyone can relate to. The viewer thinks, *That could be me standing on the roof of that lighthouse.* Holy shit!

The picture went viral. The media kept pumping it up as the hundred-foot wave no matter how much I said that it was an intense swell to ride but I'm not sure it was even a wave, technically, and I have no idea how big it was anyway. Really, no one cared what I said.

Predictably, the surfing world lost its mind over my "claiming," even though anyone who cared to click around a bit for ten minutes would see I had nothing to do with it. Likewise, bitter, would-be surfers who sit in an office all day more or less dismissed Nazaré as having any kind of viable waves, much less a world-class giant. In fairness, some of the good guys stepped up and acknowledged that

I'd achieved something most surfers dream about—discovering and pioneering a new wave and making a career out of surfing. South African big-wave charger Grant "Twiggy" Baker, 2014's Big Wave World Tour champion and a regular at the XXL Big Wave Awards, admitted that what I'd accomplished was "every man's dream." But there was also the usual bad press. I was used to it by now. All that daily practice of acceptance. In April, Anderson Cooper did a segment on Nazaré and me for *60 Minutes*, and I was happy that the town, and the sport of surfing in general, reaped all that international attention.

Surfing as a sport also got a boost, too. I started getting e-mails from all over the world. People from the Middle East, Russia, and Timbuktu (literally) wrote to say how inspired they were, asking what it was like and saying they wanted to try it. I also started receiving invitations to give talks about my life, how I'd gone from scrappy semi-pro to washed-up at thirty-five to living my dream.

The ride itself may have been a letdown, but it taught me something about expectations. By having them, we limit possibilities. What's happened since I surfed the Wave That Was Not Big Mama has more than exceeded them.

I've stopped searching for her. I've surfed that perfect big wave so many times in my mind I don't need to do it in real life anymore. I've become unattached to the outcome.

Well, mostly.

I HAD been thinking for a long time about being more responsible about what I stood for. When I was getting my business education from Lowell Hussey, I didn't think about what I was putting out there. Any corporation that wanted to sponsor me I wanted to be sponsored by; I didn't care whether what they produced was harmful or not. I started looking at how impressionable my own kids were, how they looked up to this surfer or that singer and wanted to emulate them. I decided I didn't want to do that anymore.

With that in mind, in March I decided to pull the wave from consideration for the XXL Awards. In my statement I said it was because I was opposed to the event having an alcohol sponsor. I've been thinking a lot about what we really contribute to this world, and at the end of the day you've got to make choices. I don't want kids to think that they're going to be able to accomplish their goals in life by drinking alcohol. I didn't want to be associated with that.

I also said that I decided to pull it because I did not go out that day and surf for a world record or to win any XXL prize money. I was out there, I said, because I live to surf the big waves, and that was more than enough.

DHARMA

NO MATTER WHERE WE are in the world, Nicole and I still wake up in the morning and read a little from the *Seven Spiritual Laws* together, usually over some hot water with lemon. Sometimes we continue where we left off, rereading from beginning to end, and other days we just open it to any page. Then we talk about the day's reading. We write down what we want to work on personally for the day, whether it be listening or accepting or non-judgment. We also discuss what we want to focus on business-wise. We write down what we want to manifest.

THE YEAR Liam and I showed up on the North Shore in 1978, amid the cool local boys and fierce, competitive Aussies, there was a grinning, fun-loving, half-black, half-Hawaiian named Buttons Kaluhiokalani. His real name was Montgomery, but on the day he was born his grandmother decided his hair looked like black buttons against his scalp, and the name stuck.

Buttons grew up in Waikiki where his heroes were Gerry Lopez, Jock Sutherland, and Eddie Aikau. But he also paid attention to what Dogtown's Z-Boys were up to in Southern California and brought skateboard moves to the waves—the same ones Liam and I had practiced back in

Berkeley. His carving 360s and spinners, roundhouse cutbacks and aerials made surfing look like a ton of fun. He isn't called the father of modern surfing for nothing—every flashy, radical maneuver we take for granted in twenty-first-century surfing can be traced back to Buttons.

But that's not what people loved about him. With his big Afro, sun-bleached at the tips, crazy snaggletoothed smile, and off-the-charts charisma, he was like no one else. For Buttons, it was always about having a good time. There was no lighter, brighter spirit in all of the islands.

The highpoint of Buttons's career was winning the Malibu Pro in 1979. He placed in a few other contests, but he didn't have the fierce personality required for successful competing. He was a lover. Like so many surfers he struggled with drugs off and on, until finally getting clean once and for all in 2007.

One day I was headed out for a tow-in session at Log Cabins with Uncle Dane Kealoha, and Buttons was hanging out on the beach doing nothing much. I convinced him to hop aboard. He was forty-nine, had been out of the pro surfing scene for a while, but he was game. The waves were firing out there, glassy and huge, a perfect North Shore day. Buttons had never driven a 'ski, never towed in, and the waves were getting bigger and bigger.

"You got this, Buttons," we said.

"Are you sure? Are you sure?" Even as a grown man he was child-like and unashamed to ask for reassurance.

"Yes, we're sure. Just don't drop to the bottom. You got to ride the face."

"Are you sure? Are you sure, Garrett? I don't know. I'm scared, Garrett."

"No, it's good! It's going to be the best thing ever. You can win a double XXL. Just don't drop to the bottom."

He hopped on the 'ski, shoved his feet in the straps, grabbed the rope, and off he went. We put him on a wave in the perfect spot . . . and he dropped straight to the bottom. He was thoroughly pounded, then popped up with silver dollar eyes, whimpering with fear. I quickly scooped him up and we headed back to the channel.

Uncle Dane had to take off and it was just Buttons and me as the sun dropped in the sky. The sets started getting bigger. Instinct told me that some big waves were still on the way. It takes some convincing, but I finally talk Buttons into putting me on a wave. He doesn't want to disappoint me, and on the first wave of the next set he drops me at the perfect spot. But another tow team drops in right behind us, and I'm only halfway down the face when I collide with the other surfer and a yard sale ensues. While I'm held under the only thing I can think about is whether Buttons is going to be able to rescue me. I wouldn't have been surprised to surface only to see him sitting in the channel shaking with fear. But when I finally pop up he's right there, and he reaches down and grabs me and hauls me on the sled. I thank him and I'm so grateful for his competence I want him to have at least one good ride before we call it a day.

"Oh, I don't know, Garrett. I just don't know. I'm pretty scared," he says.

I beg and plead and wheedle and coax and finally, reluctantly, he agrees. He eases himself into the water, slides onto the board. When the next wave comes, a big one but nothing heart-stopping, I put him on the shoulder and he drops straight to the bottom, just like he did before, and gets pounded. When I swing over to pick him up, he says, "No more, Garrett, please, no more!" We call it a day, and from that moment on we are friends.

• • •

IN AUGUST 2013 Nicole and I returned to the North Shore from Nazaré and the first piece of news we heard was bad: Buttons was in Queen's Hospital in Honolulu. He'd been complaining of pain in his back for almost a year. It got so bad he finally summoned the courage to go to a doctor, who suspected he was there only for the painkillers and sent him home with ibuprofen. He spent every day on the beach at the surf school he'd opened on the North Shore, and every day the pain got worse. This went on for a year. One day he reached back and felt a lump the size of a mango. A new doctor diagnosed him with stage IV lung cancer.

When we got to the hospital his room was packed. Buttons had had several families during his life, producing eight children and nine grandchildren and all those children had friends who loved Buttons, and friends of friends who loved Buttons. Pretty much everyone on the entire island felt a connection to him, and were stunned by the news, stricken, and had come there to be in his presence. Every day more friends from around the world came to be with Buttons.

Buttons lay in the bed in a blue cotton hospital gown. His skinny tattooed arms poked out of the sleeves. His dark face was gaunt and lined. When we made our way through the crowd his big eyes, normally snapping with mischief, looked scared. "Garrett, Garrett," he said, "I don't want to die. I don't know what to do. Please help me."

He gave us permission to meet with his doctor, who said the prognosis wasn't good. Only six months to live, even with chemotherapy provided he was strong enough to tolerate it. He said there was nothing more he could do, but if Buttons was interested in alternative options that was certainly something we might try.

He was discharged and went home to the little house in Waialua he shared with his current wife, Hiriata, and their children, both under the age of five. We went to visit and the place was jumping. Empty pizza boxes scattered around, TV blaring, friends coming and going and weeping at Buttons's bedside, beside themselves. Everyone really did love Buttons and could not imagine losing him.

He called me over and I sat next to him on the couch. He took my hand and leaned over to whisper. "Garrett, Garrett, I don't want to see nobody. But what can I do. What can I do?"

Buttons asked if he could move into our house, and Hiriata agreed. She was all for it. She was sad and worried and pulling her hair out from trying to prevent his well-meaning cronies from slipping him cigarettes. The next week we moved Buttons into the master bedroom of our house in Moku-lēʻia. From there he could watch and listen to the waves. It was just the two of us, very quiet. Nicole made him green smoothies. She made him oatmeal. We drew up a blueprint for his survival, which included eating clean, light exercise and rest, allowing us to dispense his pain medication, and staying away from cigarettes. We said we were there for him in every way we possibly could be, but he also needed to commit to his own healing. He signed off on the plan without a beat of hesitation.

For the first few weeks he seemed to be feeling better. He was relieved to be alone, to be free of having to bear witness to the grief and distress of other people. He would take little walks on the beach and sit in the sand and watch the waves. He dutifully drank his green smoothies and ate his steamed vegetables. Every so often he would pull me aside and say, "Garrett, Garrett, you need to give Nicole a baby. She would make the best mother." I'd laugh and remind him I already had three beautiful children. He would giggle and say, "But you and Nicole, Garrett. You and Nicole."

Perhaps because he was feeling better he thought it would be safe to cheat a little on the program. One day I went to take out the garbage and saw that he'd been throwing away the veggies, only pretending to eat them. Another day, when it was time to give him his pain medication, he didn't want it. "I'm feeling great without it, brah, great without it. I don't think I need my pain pills anymore." That night, Nicole found a baggie of drugs in his shoe. A friend who'd showed up unannounced for a visit had slipped it to him while we weren't looking.

When we confronted him he cried and said he was sorry.

There was a well-respected doctor in Los Angeles who offered an alternative cancer treatment. It was expensive, of course, and not covered by insurance. I called my friend Rick Salomon to see if he could help. He had become good friends with Buttons in the winter of 2009 while he was in Hawai'i filming a reality TV show with me. He is a generous guy with a lot of resources thanks to his skill as a high stakes poker player, and without skipping a beat he offered to help in any way he could.

In September we brought Buttons to LA to begin treatment. Rick agreed to pay for it, and he also arranged for us to stay at a house in Paradise Cove, Malibu. Buttons continued to get stronger. He was still rail thin, but his eyes were brighter and he had more energy.

In October I was expected in Nazaré, and we asked Nicole's brother CJ if he would come and stay with Buttons. CJ agreed so we flew him to LA from his home in Florida. We're still not sure what happened, how things went south so quickly. CJ came to help out, and a few days later Hiraita came, followed by Buttons's friends from around the world, who started trickling in, some bringing healthy love and support, and others their version of love and support: junk food, booze, cigarettes, and drugs. A trickle became a flood, and soon Buttons was steeped in the chaotic, toxic environment he'd begged to be rescued from. CJ is a laid-back, gentle guy. He's not an enforcer.

He wasn't about to chase off the dear friends of a dying surf legend.

We suggested to Buttons that he go home to Hawai'i, go be with his children and everyone he loved. Shortly thereafter he contracted pneumonia and was hospitalized. The doctors quickly administered chemotherapy, but he passed that night. Looking back now on everything that transpired, I feel everyone involved was just doing their best, what they thought Buttons would want, trying to make him happy.

ON THAT very day, before we heard the sad news, our son was conceived. I strongly believe Buttons's soul flew over that day. And on August 9, after twenty-three hours of intense labor, my love, my best friend, my soul mate, my inspiration, and my biggest hero gave birth at home to Garrett Barrel Moore McNamara, 9 pounds, 14 ounces, 21 inches long. He was strong and healthy and a perfect cross of his mother and me, but I would not have been surprised if he'd come out giggling, a black baby with tiny button curls all over his head.

My daughter Ariana was eighteen and had grown into a lovely young woman. She had a fledgling business designing bikinis and also played the ukulele with lively charm. Titus was sixteen. Big-shouldered and quiet, he was kicking around the idea of becoming a firefighter. Tiari, at four, was fearless, and liked to get things stirred up. I could already see myself in her. Now that I'd been blessed with baby Barrel my beautiful *'ohana* was complete.

'Ohana is Hawaiian for "family."

WE TRAVELED to Fort Lauderdale for the birth, so that we could be with Nicole's parents. I had also been invited to give a talk at the Bienes

Center for the Arts at St. Thomas Aquinas High School. It would be an hour-long conversation with a young local surfer, Hunter Gambon. They would also show clips and there would be a question-and-answer period. This was a little out of my comfort zone, sitting in front of a paying audience (all proceeds donated to the local Surfrider Foundation chapter) and holding forth. But I treated it as I do a big swell rising up on the horizon. I don't think about it. I put on a nice plaid shirt with a collar and some clean jeans and made sure to show up on time.

Right off the bat Hunter asked how I got into surfing. When I said how our mom forced us to move to Hawaii everyone laughed. I told how we didn't have much, but our mom saw to it that we had a surfboard and how I cut it in thirds in my bedroom and stuck it back together with resin. I told how the waves were a place to escape, a place to express myself, a place to be free. I said that then, as now, every time I paddle out I thanked God for my life, and for the ocean—my playground, my office, my church.

When asked about fear I said that fear is a choice, something we manufacture in our minds. When we think about the past or the future, we become afraid. We're afraid because we remember when something bad happened before, and we're scared it's going to happen again. If we're in the moment and enjoying the moment and making the best of the moment, there is no fear.

They showed a clip of me getting worked over at Jaws, falling off my board a second after I took off and cartwheeling straight down the face, the equivalent of falling off a five-story building. I said that people thought I was crazy because I didn't fear my wipeouts, but that I trained for them and had safety in place so that I could be sure of a rescue.

I thought of wipeouts as the ride after the ride. When I was getting pounded I just let go and went with it. I've probably had some of the worst wipeouts in surfing, and I've enjoyed every one of them. I said how getting tumbled beneath the surf, thrown this way and that and having no control, made me feel alive.

I was asked how I'd been able to turn my passion into a career and told about how I'd had a so-so pro career, and how by the age of thirty-four my sponsors had dribbled away to nothing, so I opened the surf shop for security. I told about the blueprint, and how I wrote *keep surfing* at the top. The audience laughed at that, and I was surprised. I didn't know whether it was because the goal seemed so pie in the sky or because here I was, all these years later, surfing for a living.

I told how under *keep surfing* I wrote down *win the Eddie and Jaws Tow-In contests*, and then what I would need to do physically, emotionally, and spiritually to achieve my goals and how I then focused 110 percent. And lo and behold I won the Jaws Tow-In and was able to close the store and keep surfing. Everyone applauded. It was a streamlined, setback-free version of the truth, but it was the truth nevertheless.

I told how the key was figuring out what you're passionate about. Maybe you're not the surfer. Maybe you're the photographer. Maybe you're the designer with a clothing company. Maybe you're the medic and jet-ski driving expert specializing in rescue. Maybe you're the one who organizes and publicizes the contests. No matter what you do in life, everyone is born with a unique talent. It may not be a grand, world-shaking talent, but it's something that you do a little differently, a little better than everyone else. Figure out what you need to do to be able to do what you want, and also how you can be of service to others while doing it.

I said that I was living proof that if you make your blueprint and follow it that anything is possible. It's never too early and it's never too late.

Onstage I sat across from Hunter in nice, living room–type chairs, a little table with a black cloth draped over it between us. There were water bottles on the table. On the wall behind us there was a big screen where they showed clips and also projected the interview for the people sitting in the back. On either side of the screen, propped up like a pair of Hawaiian tikis, were my bright green surfboards, created for me by Mercedes-Benz.

Immediately after the world-record wave a lot of big global corporations had reached out, wanting to sponsor me. McDonald's wanted to create a signature GMac fish sandwich, and Wild Turkey wanted to feature me in an ad campaign. I turned them both down without a second thought. I was always thinking about kids these days, and careful about what I endorsed. Then one day in 2013 I received an e-mail from someone at Mercedes. He said they had an idea for a campaign. He said, we don't just want to sponsor you. We don't want to write you a check or give you a car. We want a chance to get in the water with you.

I thought someone was pranking me. I've been known to pull a lot of pranks myself, to the point where my Nazaré friends had started calling any kind of a practical joke "pulling a Garrett." I thought one of them was pulling a Garrett on me. But the call was legit. Soon I was flying to Germany, where I sat down with a team of technicians, engineers, and designers in Mercedes headquarters in Stuttgart. I described my magic surfboard to them, based on all my years of experience. They went to their drawing boards and designed a board especially for me, my style of riding, and the waves of Nazaré. Like a racehorse or a yacht it had a fancy name—the Silver Arrow of the Sea—and a built-in telemetry system that reads sensors in my wet suit to provide data about my performance. Across the back in bold black letters it said "Designed Especially for Garrett McNamara." It is the best tow board I've ever ridden, and hands down my most prized possession.

Since then they've continued to build me new boards, experimenting with different materials and designs. Together we designed one made with Amorim cork. Portugal is the world's top producer of cork and also boasts the largest cork forest in the world, and wouldn't you know it is pretty much the perfect material to withstand the impact of Nazaré's powerful wave. We are also experimenting with a material called Varial foam, a staple of the aerospace industry, that is also both incredibly strong and flexible.

I'm still at a loss for words.

About six months after my talk at the Bienes Center, Nicole and I went to the French bakery in town, Le Vinois, one of her family's favorite spots. A man approached me as we were standing in line to order, and stuck out his hand. He was of average height, middle-aged and unassuming. Unexpectedly, he said he wanted to shake my hand for everything I had done for his country. I recognized his accent as Portuguese. He didn't mention having been at my talk, but this sort of encounter always moves me, and I was very touched but then thought no more about it.

The next spring we flew back to Nazaré for business. It was offseason, and I was only moderately obsessed with keeping an eye on the swells. We were there for meetings to set up a summer surf camp for disadvantaged kids, to film a commercial, and do some interviews and visit some schools.

We also met with some city officials, the Portuguese minister of tourism, and professors from the University of Coimbra about turning the first floor of the lighthouse into an interactive museum of oceanographic science. The lighthouse roof was convenient for standing on and wave-spotting, but when we arrived in 2010 the building itself had been closed for many years. The locals were skeptical that it could be reopened and repurposed, but after a solid year of meetings with the city fathers, we had succeeded.

These days pictures of the world-record waves hang on the stone walls, and Zon's and my *North Canyon* project documentary is played on a continuous loop. Our meeting took place on the roof of the light-house. It's the off-season, cold and gray, but the place is busy with people climbing the stairs to stand and soak in the amazing view of the sea, and also poke their heads into the exhibit and have a look around. A young couple who'd obviously been traveling—tan, frayed shorts, little knapsacks—emerged from the exhibit and kept looking over at where we sat, pointing and whispering. I excused myself and walked over and introduced myself. They asked for an autograph, and wanted to know whether intermediate surfers could ever surf here. I said there was pretty much room for every level, for paddle-in and towing both; it just depended on the waves. True whether you were a beginner on a fun board or, well, me.

The village seemed lively on that day, a random Tuesday in late March. It made me think back to the first day we showed up five years before and there was no one at the lighthouse, no one on the beach, no one at Restaurante a Celeste. We would stroll in at noon and the place would be empty.

Now, the first swell hits in the fall and surfers start arriving, with them the media and also visitors from other parts of Portugal and beyond, there to see Mother Nature in action. The lighthouse is crowded most days with people mesmerized by the waves, and by the thundering white water you can feel in your chest and the power and energy of those crazy heavy swells that have been here all along.

Also, most days, there's a wait to get a table at Restaurante a Celeste. Sometimes we even have to stand in line and wait our turn.

ON THIS day, part of our hectic schedule included traveling to a city in the northern part of the country to meet with the director of innovation at Amorim Cork. He had contacted me and was interested in designing and developing a cork stinger for surfboards. It would be a nice addition to the company portfolio, he'd said, and also stimulate the local economy.

Nicole and I walked into his office, and there stood a man I couldn't place, but who looked familiar. I meet a lot of people these days and I couldn't remember how I knew him.

He grinned and shook my hand. "That night in Florida, after your talk, I went home and made a blueprint."

I remembered, then. He was the Portuguese man who had approached me at the French bakery in Fort Lauderdale. The one who'd thanked me for helping his country.

"I'd been living in Florida for ten years and was so so unhappy, very miserable, actually," he continued. "I wanted to be able to move back home to Portugal and work with a respectable company. After the blueprint, I put together my résumé and sent it out to every company in Portugal I could think of. I was surprised when numerous offers came back. I chose this place, and I was able to follow my dream of moving back to my country because of you."

I smiled, speechless. Nothing could have made me happier.

ACKNOWLEDGMENTS

The author with his wife, Nicole, and a local participant at a Surfers Healing camp in Puerto Rico, where they had met a year earlier, April 8, 2011.
(Nancy Hussy)

This book would not be what it is without the dedication of Karen Karbo. She took my vision and turned it into a reality. I'm forever grateful for the countless hours she put in and for her faith in my story. Also, thank you to Karen Rinaldi, Hannah Robinson, Victor Hendrickson, and the rest of the publishing team at HarperWave for believing in what I wanted to share with the world and for all the time and effort it took to make this book the best it could be.

Thank you to my friends who had a hand in helping throughout the long writing and editing process. To Khalil Rafati, who inspired me by having the courage to tell his own story in *I Forgot to Die*. He was also one of my dear friends who took the time to read the finished manuscript and offer his thoughts. To Alex Von Furstenberg for lending us his picturesque Malibu beach house, a calm spot where we could focus on adding the finishing touches to the story.

Thank you to Rick Salomon, one of the most generous and caring people I've met in my life, for believing in me even when I wasn't making the best choices and inspiring me every day through your sobriety and kindness.

Thank you to Mark Bell for always being in my corner and only a phone call away for the serious and not so serious moments of life. I aspire to accomplish even half of what you have done in business. And to Michael Vlock for literally changing the way I live my life. You have helped me focus on what is really important—my family and having fun. Somehow you believed in me too and I am eternally grateful for that.

Thank you to all my friends who inspire me in one way or another to be either a better father, husband, or businessman. To not take myself so seriously and enjoy my blessings. To the Schlesingers for adopting my family and treating us like your own. The Redfords for being there for me during one of the most desperate times of my life. Stuart Parr and Allison Sarofim for their friendship and believing in me and helping with my current healing process. Reggie Barns and Jocylene Tracy, Michael Whalen, the Dawsons, the Farrers, and all the friends and families near and far, all over the world, who have taken me in during my adventures—I'm forever grateful. My Chile family, my Peru family, my Tahiti family, my Indonesia family, my

Australia family, my California family, my Japan family, my Hawaiian Islands families, and many more.

I have been so blessed in my life with amazing people supporting me it makes me sick to think I have forgotten to mention anyone who deserves to be on these pages. I pray that if I have forgotten anyone, which surely I have, that they know how much they have impacted my life and that I love them.

Thank you to Izzy Paskowitz who has changed my life in more ways than one and has also enriched the lives of thousands of children and their families. He deserves a statue! It was because of Surfers Healing that I found an emotional outlet and place to share my passion and also where I met my wife. Without Izzy my life would be on a completely different path. He also inspired me by having the courage to tell his story through *Scratching the Horizon: A Surfing Life*.

Thank you to Deepak Chopra for writing *The Seven Spiritual Laws of Success*—it has had a profound impact on how I live my life daily. And to Kent Ewing for encouraging me to stay PCP and helping me sort the chatterbox in my head.

The town of Nazaré and the country of Portugal deserve an entire book of praise. Thank you to Lowell Hussey for helping me make the website that helped Dino Casimiro track me down, and to Dino for hitting SEND on his first email. He could have reached out to anyone and I thank the heavens above it was me. To the town of Nazaré for being a little hesitant but in the end welcoming me with open arms and making me part of the family. To the original team in Nazaré for having the heart to go after your dreams. To Mama Celeste for always believing in me and taking care of me like I was her own son. To everyone in Celeste's family—Andre Botelho, Ana,

Vovo Cila, Maria Ana, Gil, Ricardo, Catarina, Julio, and all the other amazing humans.

A big thanks has to go out to all the charities I work with. Volunteering is a funny thing to me, because although you are giving your time to others, you walk away feeling so good that it's like a selfish thing. I love all the work I do with the Red Cross, the Marconi Foundation, Heal the Bay, Surfrider, and most especially Surfer's Healing. It's where I feel I can make a real difference in a family's life by sharing my passion for the ocean and waves. I commend Izzy Paskowitz for his dedication to enriching the life of autistic children and their families.

A million thank-yous to my partner, Andrew Cotton, surfing for Queen and Country. He is the most humble man I have ever met, and without him coming into my life I wouldn't have ridden some of my most magical and memorable waves. He is also responsible for putting me in the perfect spot on the historic record wave which single-handedly changed my life forever. Also to Hugo Vau and Kealii Mamala for being loyal and keeping us safe, and to Jorge Leal for capturing all the moments so we could share it with the world. Also to all my other tow partners and water safety support throughout the years: I have always said and still do to this day that you are only as good as your team. Thanks for being there.

To the people of Nazaré—the body boarders, firemen, lifeguards, and police. The women with seven skirts. Paulo Salvador, Pedro Pisco, Paulo Caldeira, Guti Martin, and Sergio. To everyone in Nazaré and Portugal who have welcomed us and gave us a second home, *obrigado*!

I'm thankful for all the surfboard shapers who have supported me through my life. There are so many of you that have dedicated your time and energy to perfecting the shapes of the boards we rely on to enjoy the waves and do our job. It's a true art form and I am extremely grateful to all of you who have made a board for me. Roy Patterson believed in me in the beginning. Dick Brewer shaped a number of magical boards for me over the years and used to let me hang out in the shaping room. What most people don't know is he is the Kevin Bacon of shaping—directly or indirectly every shaper in surfing learned from Dick Brewer, but he is too humble to ever tell you that. And now Carl Schaper, who has devoted his craft to perfecting all my shapes. And SPO, who put their heart and soul into making me the most perfect tow board for Nazaré that I have ever ridden.

Gratitude goes to all the photographers throughout my career who have spent countless hours on land or in the water to capture "the shot." Without you guys we wouldn't have a profession. So many of you have helped me over the years it wouldn't be fair to try and list you all in fear of forgetting someone.

Deepest thanks goes to my mother and father for creating me and bringing me into this world and providing me with the experiences that have made me who I am today. To my mother for forcing us to move to Hawaii, where I found my lifelong passion. And for both my parents for supporting me in whatever I do. To my brother Liam for always standing by my side, and to my other brothers—Michael McNamara, Allan and Bill, Michael, BJ and Joel Welsh—for doing the same. To Liam and Brandee for creating my nephews, the amazing Makai, Landon, and Ledgen who are carrying on the McNamara surf legacy.

I never thought we would be where we are today, but thank you to Connie for sticking with me when it was nearly impossible and blessing my life with three incredible children—Ari, Titus, and Tiari. Thank you to my children for loving me even with my flaws and for creating their own path through life.

For Rose and Carlos Macias for accepting me into their family as one of their own and loving me unconditionally. I know I can be a real pain sometimes, so I appreciate you seeing me for who I really am and not giving up on me.

And if the phrase *Last but not least* ever had any real meaning it would be now. My wife, Nicole McNamara. I guess she saw a diamond in the rough when she met me and for that I will be indebted to the universe for the rest of my life for blessing me with an angel to stand by my side. She inspires me every day to be a better man for her, our children, and the rest of the world. She doesn't let very many people in, so those that get to truly know her are some of the luckiest people on earth. Thank you for keeping me sane and helping me to see what's important and staying true to myself and helping me to see when my ego is taking over. Thanks for helping me find my life purpose and figuring out how to serve the world with it. I love you more than you will ever know.

ABOUT THE AUTHOR

Garrett McNamara holds the Guinness record for surfing the world's largest wave, in addition to his numerous first-place wins in professional competitions around the world. He is the first foreigner ever to be awarded the prestigious Vasco de Gama Medal of Honor from the Portuguese Navy. McNamara splits his time between Hawai'i, Portugal, and the rest of the world, where he explores with his family.